Value Investing in Asia

Value Investing in Asia

The Definitive Guide to Investing in Asia

Stanley Lim Peir Shenq
Cheong Mun Hong

This edition first published 2018
© 2018 Stanley Lim Peir Shenq and Cheong Mun Hong

Registered office
John Wiley & Sons Ltd, The Atrium, Southern Gate, Chichester, West Sussex,
PO19 8SQ, United Kingdom

For details of our global editorial offices, for customer services and for
information about how to apply for permission to reuse the copyright material in
this book please see our website at www.wiley.com.

Wiley publishes in a variety of print and electronic formats and by print-on-
demand. Some material included with standard print versions of this book may
not be included in e-books or in print-on-demand. If this book refers to media
such as a CD or DVD that is not included in the version you purchased, you may
download this material at http://booksupport.wiley.com. For more information
about Wiley products, visit www.wiley.com.

Designations used by companies to distinguish their products are often claimed as
trademarks. All brand names and product names used in this book are trade names,
service marks, trademarks or registered trademarks of their respective owners. The
publisher is not associated with any product or vendor mentioned in this book.

Limit of Liability/Disclaimer of Warranty: While the publisher and author have
used their best efforts in preparing this book, they make no representations or
warranties with respect to the accuracy or completeness of the contents of this book
and specifically disclaim any implied warranties of merchantability or fitness for a
particular purpose. It is sold on the understanding that the publisher is not engaged
in rendering professional services and neither the publisher nor the author shall be
liable for damages arising herefrom. If professional advice or other expert assistance
is required, the services of a competent professional should be sought.

Library of Congress Cataloging-in-Publication Data is Available

ISBN 978-1-119-39118-0 (paperback)   ISBN 978-1-119-39120-3 (ePub)
ISBN 978-1-119-39121-0 (ePDF)   ISBN 978-1-119-39127-2 (Obk)

10 9 8 7 6 5 4 3 2 1

Cover Design: Wiley
Cover Image: © Lisa Kolbasa/Shutterstock

Set in 11/13pt NewBaskervilleStd by SPi Global, Chennai, India

Printed in Great Britain by TJ International Ltd, Padstow, Cornwall, UK

For Jo Ying, Howey and Hong Vee. Remember to let money be the tool that helps you work towards your happiness, rather than being the reason for your happiness.

– Stanley

For my wife, Sze Wing, who has always believed in me.

And for Sonia, may this book inspire you to have the courage, convictions, and perseverance to chase your dreams. Even if you want to be a princess with a pet unicorn.

– Mun Hong

DISCLAIMER

All views or opinions articulated in this book are expressed in the Authors' personal capacity and do not in any way represent those of the company, their employers and other related entities.

This book is based on the study and research of the Authors, and represents the written collection of the Authors' opinions and ideas. As such, the information in this book are for educational purposes and/or for study or research only. For all intents and purposes, the contents of this book are not intended to be, and does not constitute financial, investment or any other form of advice or recommendations to buy or sell any shares, securities or other instruments.

Information used in the publication of this book has been compiled from publicly available sources that are believed to be reliable. Hence, the Authors do not take responsibility for any factual inaccuracies made. Any expression of opinion (which may be subject to change without notice) is personal to the Authors, and the Authors make no guarantee of any sort regarding the accuracy or completeness of any information or analysis supplied.

It is also important to bear in mind that any investment involves the taking of substantial risks, including but not limited to the complete loss of capital. The Authors do not take responsibility whatsoever for any loss or damage of any kind incurred from the views or opinions articulated in this book.

Finally, it goes without saying that the Authors' views and opinions should never be regarded by the readers as a substitute for the exercise of their own judgement. As every investor has different investment objectives, goals, strategies, risk tolerances, time frames and financial situation, you are advised to perform your own independent checks, research or study before making any investment decisions.

Always remember, YOU are ultimately responsible for your own investments.

Note: The Authors have investment positions in some of the companies discussed in this book.

Contents

Foreword

Everyone wants to buy a dollar-worth of assets for 50 cents. That is at the very heart of value investing – to buy an asset at a price that could be valued at significantly more. But what exactly is value?

Are they always shares that are trading below the sum of their net assets? Or are they shares in stable companies that have been underappreciated by the market? There is another way of looking at value – they could be shares in fast-growing companies where the potential for growth has been underestimated for a variety of reasons.

The concept of separating price and value is handled with surgical precision by Lim Peir Shenq and Cheong Mun Hong. They draw on their vast stock market experience to take readers on a whistle-stop tour around six Asian bourses in search of value investments. They touch on the thorny topic of corporate governance and why it should matter when we invest.

Peir Shenq and Mun Hong pay special attention to the use of strategies. While there is no one-size-fits-all approach for value investing, the use of a consistent approach to identifying value cannot be stressed strongly enough. In other words, if you don't know what you are looking for, then how can you possibly know when you have found it?

The two writers cleverly categorise value under three main headings, namely, asset value, current earning power value and growth value. Through a step-by-step process, they provide a useful guide to help readers to understand the different ways to identify value and when a company could be considered to be undervalued.

There is also a useful discussion of screens and how they can be used with good effect to help separate out the wheat from the chaff. Peir Shenq and Mun Hong also provide some useful tips on how to reduce the number of shares that need to be filtered.

The 5-Finger Rule is a clever way that they have developed to remember the basics of investing, and not just value investing. The rule behind the Rule is that an investor should only consider investigating a business further if it fulfills at least half the criteria.

There is a very instructive chapter on how to read annual reports. Most investors can find the once-a-year tome from companies quite a chore to plough through. But Peir Shenq and Mun Hong show you how to get to the nub of any report quickly. What exactly should we look out for when we read the letter to shareholders? How honest and candid is the letter? Does it tell shareholders everything that has gone on at the company, warts and all?

The two writers pepper the book generously with real examples that readers can use as case studies for their own investments. This is not just a book about value investing. Instead, it is a manual for value investing with an Asian twist that investors with an eye on the fastest-growing region in the world will reach for whenever they have questions that need answers.

David Kuo
CEO, The Motley Fool Singapore Pte. Ltd.

Preface

The stock market is filled with individuals who know the price of everything, but the value of nothing.

– Philip A. Fisher

If we compare what generally happens in a stock market to the real world, it would be like being in the largest casino ever. Think Macau, the gaming capital of the world, only bigger. Players and speculators all over the place, goading one another to ever-higher bets. Frenzy surrounding the tables which players deem "hot". Everyone jostling for a seat at those tables. Greed and manipulation are the names of the game.

In Asia, many still view the stock market as a speculative pursuit, associating equity investments with gambling. Those "not in the game" might be confused with the market's sudden highs and lows, where "hot" companies are valued astronomically and "boring" ones are priced as though the business and its assets are worth nothing.

The casino operator, in this case the stock exchange, does not bet with or against any players. It is merely a place to hold these games, a platform for players to play. It earns not from the winners or losers of the game, but simply from the number of games inside its door. However, in this stock-market casino, there is also something more unique. Every game taking place is like a game of poker.

This is because, like poker, when we invest, we are not playing with the house (stock exchange), we are playing against the player on the other side of the table. As we know, there are two ways to play a game of poker, based on pure luck or based on skill and probabilities. For players who base their play on skill, there is a higher chance that they might walk out of this "casino" richer than before.

This book is a guide for that journey, the journey of how to enter the stock market based on skill and probabilities. It is about understanding the difference between gambling and investing, and how to go about investing. It is about how to keep our heads level during the game, and invest logically, instead of emotionally. *This* is the journey where we show you how to find value in our speculative world.

This is the key concept we hope to drive home about the stock market. Yes, in many ways, it is still a casino. Yes, you can, and many players do, play with nothing other than luck. But *you* can choose how you want to play the game. Instead of relying on luck, you can learn how to earn serendipity, how to create luck by stacking the odds in your favour.

Investing in the stock market, like poker, is a game of both skill and luck. If you take the time to learn the skills needed and keep your emotions in check, if you can "keep your head when all around you are losing theirs", there is a good chance that you will be able to walk out of the stock market wealthier than before.

This is not a "get rich quick" book. It is not a book about making millions overnight. This book is about understanding the skills needed to play the game intelligently and for the long term. This is a book about learning how to play the stock market game with skill and not luck, arming you with a framework for your investment journey and allowing you to tailor it to suit your needs.

Also, this book does not attempt to predict how markets will behave in the future. Instead of showing you how the "perfect" market should be, we want to show you how it really is, and how you can navigate through these waters. In this imperfect market, we feel that our investment process will help you make sense of, and benefit from the market.

The reason why we need such a process is simple. In this time and age, there is simply an overload of information and we need a process to help us to separate what's important from the noise. We believe that investors looking towards Asia are in need of a locally constructed framework to assess both the quantitative and qualitative sides of equity investments.

Investing is both an art and a science. We strongly believe that with both the "right" mindset and an appropriate investment process, investors willing to put in the effort might find the experience of investing in Asia to be both exciting and wildly rewarding. It certainly has been the case for us.

To demonstrate that this is not just nice-sounding theoretical stuff with no practical applications, we have included plenty of case studies, together with our personal experience. We hope that the lessons learned from these case studies will bring these experiences to life and translate into practical applications for you in your investment journey.

Moreover, we have produced additional bonus chapters for you. These are meant to prepare you for the next stage of your investing journey after you have completed this book. Feel free to view your bonus chapters at https://www.valueinvestasia.com/valueinvestingbook/.

No one can make you rich or successful in investing. All we can do is provide the tools for you to make intelligent decisions. Such is the purpose of this book.

Thank you, and let's begin our journey.

Acknowledgments

This book is only possible with the effort of so many people. First and foremost, we are extremely grateful to the team at John Wiley & Sons. We would like to thank Thomas Hyrkiel and his team for accepting our proposal; we can never thank you enough for believing in us. Next, our project editor, Jeremy Chia, who has spent countless hours helping us with the publishing process. If it were not for Jeremy, you would not be reading our book right now. We would also like to thank Gladys (Syd) Ganaden, who helped us, two hopeless designers, immensely in the coordination of the design of the book, as well as Tan Chin Hwee, who kick-started our Wiley journey by introducing us to Thomas and his team.

We became evangelists for value investing through books written by Benjamin Graham, David Dodd, Philip Fisher, Robert Hagstrom, Barton Biggs and Bruce Greenwald. Without their books, we would not be who we are as investors today. These are the men who planted the trees for us to sit under, and we hope to be able to spread their wisdom here in Asia.

We are also deeply appreciative that the following individuals were willing to share years of their investment wisdom for this book. Their perspectives broadened our understanding on the Asian investing climate and we hope you will benefit from their advice as much as we did from them: David Kuo, Tan Chong Koay, Wong Kok Hoi, Yeo Seng Chong, Wong Seak Eng, Kevin Tok and Eric Kong.

Over the years, we have formed a close-knit investment community here. There is a saying that hanging out with smarter people makes you smarter. This definitely holds true for us. We have learned so much from being in your company over the past few years. We have immensely benefited from your investment wisdom, and more importantly your friendship, and we hope that will carry on for years to come.

Also, not forgetting Willie Keng, co-founder of ValueInvest Asia.com and our investment group; we always remember the times when it was just the three of us.

Lastly, after years of experimenting, we also like to thank Mr Market for his mood swings over the years, without which we would not have been able to benefit.

From Stanley:

Firstly, I would like to thank David Kuo for being a mentor to me. Through working for him, I have learnt so much on how to invest better, write better and communicate better.

I am forever grateful to my parents; my dad for teaching me all he knows about business through all his life stories of being an entrepreneur since the age of eight. To my mum, who has been there to ensure I stay on the right track in life.

Lastly, to my wife, Wendy, who has been the pillar of my life for the past decade.

From Mun Hong:

To my wife, Sze Wing, thank you for always believing in me. Any day with you is my favorite day, and I look forward to many more years together. It is written that houses and wealth are inherited from parents, but a prudent wife is from the Lord. I could not ask for a better wife.

To my parents, I am forever grateful to you for bringing me up well. Especially my dad; if I could be as good a father as my dad was to me, that would be one of my greatest achievements.

In my professional career, I would like to thank Samuel for taking a chance on me, for taking me under his wing. Time and time again, he has selflessly imparted his wisdom, and continually opened doors for me.

About the Authors

Stanley Lim Peir Shenq, CFA, has spent the last decade in the investment industry. Over the course of his career, he has kick-started a few businesses, worked in the family office industry and most recently in the investment advisory industry. He has been a writer and analyst for The Motley Fool Singapore from 2013 to 2017. During his time at The Motley Fool, he was one of the pioneer staff in building up the business and has successfully launched three products with the company.

Throughout his career, he has written close to 2,000 articles online, on investment education and market analysis. Over the last decade, he has gained valuable practical experiences in investing across a wide range of asset classes, ranging from Asian equities and properties to start-ups and venture capital.

Stanley has also been interviewed by media outfits such as Channel News Asia and the Manual of Ideas. He is the co-founder of ValueInvestAsia.com.

Stanley is a CFA Charterholder.

Cheong Mun Hong, CFA, started his investment career as an investment analyst at a Singapore licensed Trust Company. Over the course of his work, he has dealt with investments involving public and privately held entities. Mun Hong sits on the boards of listed companies.

He studied mechanical engineering at Nanyang Technological University and graduated with a minor in Business. Mun Hong has been involved in equity investments for close to a decade. He is the co-founder of ValueInvestAsia.com.

Mun Hong is a CFA Charterholder.

CHAPTER 1

Value Investing in Asia

You're looking for a mispriced gamble. That's what investing is. And you have to know enough to know whether the gamble is mispriced. That's value investing.

— Charlie Munger

We wrote this book to share with you about the practical applications of a value investing approach here in Asia. With many books written on investing 101, introductory concepts of value investing are not the focus of our book. However, we still like to do a quick refresher before heading on to the fun stuff.

Value investing was first made famous by Benjamin Graham, with many considering him as the father of value investing. We believe that walking along this path of value investing will provide you with a disciplined approach in your financial adventures.

To start, we first must draw a clear line between what is an investment and what is a speculation. Even after 80 odd years, the explanation by Benjamin Graham and David Dodd in *Security Analysis* made the most sense to us. They stated: "An investment operation is one which, upon thorough analysis, promises safety of principal and an adequate return. Operations not meeting these requirements are speculative". Nicely put.

From where we stand, speculation is more like guesswork without evidence. With its negative long-term expected return, a good example of speculation is a lottery. Buying a lottery ticket and hoping to

1

win is speculation. If you really want to try your luck, no one is stopping you. However, we should not confuse the two.

On the other hand, an investment is something you buy now based on reasons that make sense, and with reasonable confidence that you will receive more money down the road. For us, value investing is simply a strategy of stacking the odds in your favour. Imagine being able to consistently buy a dollar's-worth of asset for 50 cents over and over again. Over the long term, this should work out much better than just buying the lottery ticket and hoping for the best.

With that said, here is what we think value investing is all about.

Finding Value

Great investors come from across a spectrum of investing styles – from legends like Warren Buffett, Walter Schloss and Irving Kahn to fund managers like David Einhorn, Guy Spier and Joel Greenblatt. Even in Asia we have famous investors like Target Asset Management's Teng Ngiek Lian, APS Asset Management's Wong Kok Hoi, Pheim Asset Management's Dr Tan Chong Koay and Value Partners Group's Cheah Cheng Hye and Yeh V-Nee. Value Partners Group Limited is the first independent asset management firm to be listed on the Hong Kong Stock Exchange – and one of Asia's largest.[1]

The differences in strategy and style among value investors are countless. Some go for large-cap stocks while others spend their whole careers in small-cap stocks. There are successful investors who invest domestically in just their home market, while many venture overseas as well.

Although the practical application of value investing differs among individuals, the common underlying theme is similar. At the end of the day, everyone tries to find discrepancies between the market price of the stock and their estimated value of the company, commonly known as intrinsic value.

Even with the diversity, there are some fundamental characteristics common among most value investors. They

- accept that mistakes do happen and learn from them
- do not feel the need to fit in with the market
- follow the margin-of-safety principle
- have conviction in their analysis and decisions that are based on logic and reasoning
- think and invest like a business owner.

In a nutshell, value exists when you think that the asset is worth more than its market price with the probability of this asset appreciating in value being more likely than not.

The Investor and the Market

Two of the most important concepts regarding value investing are best described in the book *The Intelligent Investor* by Benjamin Graham, specifically in Chapters 8 (how the investor should view market fluctuations) and 20 (margin of safety). These were the two chapters recommended by Warren Buffett so that "you will not get a poor result from your investments".

The Investor and Market Fluctuations (Chapter 8 of The Intelligent Investor)

Most of us hold the misconception that the market price of a stock is the intrinsic value of the company. However, these two terms are as different as day and night. Market price is easy to understand; it refers to the current market price of the asset. On the other hand, value is what that investment is worth to you. And this is when things start to get confusing, because value is a matter of opinion and can differ greatly between investors.

John Burr Williams, one of the pioneers on investment valuation and the author of *The Theory of Investment Value*, stated: "The market can only be an expression of opinion, not a statement of fact. Today's opinion will make today's price; tomorrow's opinion, tomorrow's price."

At any time, market price simply reflects the opinions of the most optimistic non-owner (bid) and the most pessimistic owner (ask). To put it simply, price fluctuations are nothing more than the consequence of supply and demand between the buyer and the seller, and market price is nothing more than the result of the marginal opinion. When asked about what the stock market would do next, John Pierpont Morgan (better known as J.P. Morgan) simply replied, "It will fluctuate."[2]

Yet why do so many investment professionals still relate price volatility to investment risk? If you think about it, all volatility symbolises is the changing opinions of the market. It is worth thinking about this logic while reading this book. To us, this logic is pretty illogical. Interestingly, this irrational volatility is also how most value investors can hunt for bargains within the stock market.

Mr Market (Chapter 8 of The Intelligent Investor)

To better appreciate how the market works, we like to introduce you to Mr Market, a metaphor coined by Benjamin Graham in *The Intelligent Investor*. Mr Market is a representation of how the market works. But who exactly is this Mr Market?

Mr Market is an imaginary, highly emotional investor driven by panic, euphoria, greed and apathy. Basically, Mr Market is an emotionally unstable person who approaches investing based on emotion rather than through analysis. Think of him as your business partner in the company you invested in. Every day he tells you what he thinks your interest in the business is worth and offers to buy your share or sell you more shares. Sometimes his offer appears reasonable while at other times he lets his enthusiasm or fears dictate his offer and to the point of being ridiculous. Does this remind you of anyone? Not so imaginary now, is he? This, guys, is how the market works.

Benjamin Graham famously said, "In the short run, the market is a voting machine, but in the long run, it is a weighing machine." In the long term, prices should reflect business value. However, short-term price movements tend to have little to do with the fundamentals of a business. Sometimes prices move on fundamental reasons and sometimes just for the fun of it. Why? Just because they can. Therefore, as investors, we should stick to the business over the long term instead of worrying about the emotions of the market in the short term.

However, due to our strong need to make sense of the world, we cannot help but try to make sense of every single price movement in the market. Notice the number of pundits that will take a shot at finding a reason for every single price movement. Seeing three pigeons on your roof just before the Hang Seng Index tanks by 10% does not mean that those three crafty-looking pigeons perching on your roof evaporated those billions!

This might have been why theories like the efficient market hypothesis grew to become the main school of thought in the finance world. Most of these theories within efficient market hypothesis work well in a perfect and hypothetical world. Working most of the time and working all the time are two different things. Unfortunately, our world is much more unpredictable than finding out what is inside a Kinder Surprise. In theory there is no difference between theory and practice; in practice, there clearly is.

On a personal note, our experiences during the Global Financial Crisis in 2008 taught us how hard it is not to join in the irrationality of the market during times of panic. Saying that market prices did not seem to reflect reality during that period was an understatement. Even a "Blue Chip" like one of Singapore's largest listed company, Singapore Telecommunications Limited ("SingTel"), saw over 40% of its share value wiped out in just two months. But did SingTel lose 40% of their customers in those two months? We do not think so. That said, although it is easy to spot the irrationality of the market, it is extremely difficult not to get sucked into the vortex of negativity.

Essentially, most of these modern market theories assume that we are all rational and can make the most efficient choice in every situation. This implies that we are both emotionless and have perfect information to make logical decisions. Doesn't this sound like something out of a fairy tale? That's what Snow White and her seven dwarfs thought as well.

In reality, our decision-making process typically involves making sense of the situation based on what we know, how we feel and our past experiences. That is why the price of the stock can differ from *our* estimated value of the company.

We should always remember that Mr Market is just here to provide us with options. It is 100% up to you to decide if it is to your advantage to act on them. As investors, the advantage we have is patience. No one can force us to act. All we should do is sit patiently and wait for the right hand before striking. We can take advantage of Mr Market's over-optimism and his panic desperations.

To round up our discussion on Mr Market, we will leave you with the wisdom of Howard Marks – "If you think markets are logical and investors are objective and unemotional, you're in for a lot of surprises. In tough times, investors often fail to apply discipline and discernment; psychology takes over from fundamentals; and 'all correlations go to one' as things that should be distinguished from each other aren't."[3]

Margin of Safety (Chapter 20 of The Intelligent Investor)

We like to start with a quote by a former United States Secretary of the Treasury, Timothy Geithner, in his book *Stress Tests: Reflections on Financial Crises*: "Even the best forecasts, I learned, were just educated guesses. They could tell a story about how the economy might evolve, but they couldn't predict the future."[4]

Even though Timothy Geithner referred to economic forecasts, we felt that this also applied to our expectations of a company, especially when it comes to valuation. When reading through equity reports, we are frequently amused that an exact value (sometimes even down to two decimal places!) can be pegged on a business, especially when the valuations are based on so many assumptions! Remember, forecasts tell us more about the forecaster than the company, thus it is important for us always to read the assumptions made for a valuation exercise.

Given the large number of assumptions we need to make during a valuation exercise, we believe that at best valuation can be narrowed down to a range. Herein lies the essence of value investing: the importance of having a margin of safety. A discussion of value investing is not complete without a margin of safety. With a margin of safety, you need not know the exact value of a company to conclude that it's undervalued. You do not need to understand every single detail to survive in the world of investment.

A margin of safety is a way for investors to control the risk of investing by having a safety gap between the market price of a company and our estimated intrinsic value. A good analogy is an engineer's safety factor calculation. When constructing a bridge to handle a load of 1,000 tonnes, an engineer doesn't build it just for 1,000 tonnes; this bridge might be built to hold 2,000 tonnes, 3,000 tonnes or more. Why? Because in the real world, unexpected things happen, so it's always better to be conservative.

Thus, having a margin of safety makes it unnecessary for us to need a crystal ball when analysing a company. Here is an example that shows why.

Let us assume that Singapore-listed CapitaLand Limited, the largest property developer in Southeast Asia, was priced at S$8 billion in the stock market, and you have estimated the company's value at somewhere between S$10 and 14 billion. At S$8 billion, you would have at least a 20% *margin of safety* even in your "worst case" scenario.

In the context of investing, this is like having a buffer between what you think the asset is worth and what the asset is priced at. Based on your data and analysis, if you think that this company is worth $2 and you get it at $1, you have a margin of safety of 50%. This means that if your estimates are off by 50% you might still be able to protect yourself from making a loss in your investment.

Unlike the "perfect economic man", who makes perfect and logical decisions every time, we are more than capable of making mistakes. Some might even say that we are well versed at it. Therefore, only by insisting on a margin of safety before we make an investment are we able to minimise the risk of making an expensive mistake by not overpaying. Remember, the best investment is one bought at a good price.

We hope that appreciating Mr Market and the concept of having a margin of safety will help you as much as they have helped us. A good start to having a successful value investing journey is to have the right mindset in place. However, this is just the beginning. Like everything else, we need to train ourselves before we can be good at something. Investing is no different. We definitely do not want to shoot ourselves in the foot by assuming that as long as we have the right idea, we can throw everything else aside. We cannot just will ourselves to get up and run a marathon without training for it. That will not end well.

Why Value Investing Works

Every boom and bust in the financial markets might be different, but what many don't notice is that history tends to repeat itself and investors never seem to learn. The more things change, the more they tend to stay the same. Ironically, this irrationally provides us with windows of opportunity. For most publicly traded companies, there will be times of under- and overvaluation, simply because shareholders do panic and act irrationally from time to time. When the right opportunity arises, we just have to exercise conviction in our judgements.

Thus, Rudyard Kipling's famous words, "If you can keep your head when all about you are losing theirs. . .", ring true for a level-minded value investor if they are to take advantage of what Mr Market has to offer. And this unchanging aspect of human emotions is what makes value investing work. The key attraction of value investing is its logical and commonsense approach. In the stock market, you will soon realise, common sense is not really that common.

Instead of trying to predict the future, we should spend our time trying to find value from the realm that is relatively more knowable – companies, industries and securities – rather than basing our investment decisions solely on, as Howard Marks puts it, "the less-knowable macro world of economies and broad market performance".

If you still have doubts on the utility of value investing, we recommend that you look at the short story "The Superinvestors of Graham-and-Doddsville" in *The Intelligent Investor*. This was from an edited transcript of a Columbia University talk in 1984 by Warren Buffett commemorating the 50th anniversary of *Security Analysis*. Buffett presents a group of investors who have, year in and year out, beaten the Standard & Poor's 500 stock index. Perhaps his story may lay your doubts to rest.

For the rest of us, let's get to work. Here are the three types of value you can find in the stock market.

Three Types of Value to Be Found

Before exploiting any opportunity, we must first know what we are looking for. We can start by understanding the different types of value to be found in the market. Otherwise, we may be as confused as Alice when she just arrived in Wonderland.

Before diving in to estimate the intrinsic values of companies, we need to be able to differentiate between the types of opportunities before us. As investors, we want to know where we are going, and we believe that there are three major areas where value can be found in the market.

Asset Value

First, value may be realised from companies trading at levels significantly below their asset value. Asset value can be the liquidation value of the company, the replacement value of the business or just the sum of its net assets. This generally applies to companies in capital-intensive industries with assets underappreciated by the market.

Typical companies with value under this segment could include utilities-related companies, property-related companies, Real Estate Investment Trusts or even conglomerates.

Current Earning Value

Value can be found in companies with strong and stable earnings. Some of these companies might be trading at a deep discount compared to the estimated intrinsic value. Bear in mind that we focus mainly on the current earnings when estimating intrinsic value for these companies. This means that we might assume zero to moderate growth in these companies. These possible undervalued gems turn up when our estimates of their value are much higher than their market price.

Typical companies with value under this segment could include companies in industries with a decently long history of profitability that are operated in conditions that are unlikely to be massively disrupted. Examples include consumer staples and healthcare.

Expected Growth

This type of value is based primarily on projecting the future. Generally, these investments are considered relatively riskier, given the uncertainty in the future. However, this segment can also present to you the highest potential in returns compared to the other two segments. This is because companies with undervalued assets or current earnings potential tend to have a limit on how much the value can be. However, a company with future growth potential can theoretically have unlimited growth potential in the future. After all, who would have thought that Apple Inc., with an initial public offering value of close to US$1 billion back in 1980,[5] would grow to a size of about US$600 billion by the end of 2016?[6]

To illustrate the diversity of values, consider these two companies. The first is Hong Kong-listed Orient Overseas (International) Limited ("OOIL"), an asset-heavy container shipping company in a cyclical industry currently in a down-cycle. The second is NASDAQ-listed Baidu Inc., a Chinese web service company with a huge growth potential. Both these companies can turn out to be great investments in their own rights. However, it is obvious that the method we use to estimate the intrinsic value for OOIL should be vastly different from the way we value Baidu Inc.

Under the appropriate circumstances, OOIL might appear undervalued relative to its asset value. On the other hand, the bulk of value from Baidu Inc. might potentially be derived from the future growth of the business.

Notes

1. Value Partners Group Limited. "Annual Report 2015".
2. Benjamin Graham. First Collins Business Essentials. "The Intelligent Investor". Edition 2006.

3. Howard Marks. Oaktree Capital Management, L.P. Memo to Oaktree Clients. "The Lessons of Oil". 18 December 2014.
4. Timothy Geithner. Random House Business Books. *Stress Test: Reflections on Financial Crises.* Published: 2014.
5. Apple Computer, Inc. Common Stock Prospectus. 12 December 1980.
6. Google Finance. Apple Inc. https://www.google.com/finance?cid=22144. Accessed: 27 April 2017.

2

Key Developments in Asia

History does not repeat itself, but it rhymes.

— Mark Twain

As the largest continent, with over four billion people and a very diverse demographic, it is no surprise that Asia presents many opportunities. In September 2014, the market capitalisation of roughly 24,000 companies listed in the Asia-Pacific region was around US$20 trillion, not too far from the Americas' US$30 trillion.[1] Conventional wisdom has it that a diversified portfolio requires about 30 holdings.[2] Asian investors have just as many choices and opportunities available to them as US investors do.

What Is in Asia?

With 50 countries,[3] comprising a diversity of cultures, economies and even languages, we find it impossible to view Asia as one homogenous entity. For this book, we will focus mainly on the markets within the Greater China and Southeast Asia region. Here are the key Asian exchanges on our radar.

Hong Kong Stock Exchange

Owned by Hong Kong Stock Exchange Group, HKEX is Asia's 2nd largest stock exchange (2014). The HKEX Group is also the owner of the London Metal Exchange, one of the world's largest industrial metal trading platforms. In 2014, there were 1,752 companies listed on HKEX, with total market capitalisation of over HK$25 trillion.[4] Blue-chip companies within the Hang Seng Index include CK Hutchison Holdings Limited, HSBC Holding PLC (Hong Kong), Swire Group's Swire Pacific Limited, China National Offshore Oil Corporation's Limited and the technology giant, Tencent Holdings Limited.

Due to their proximity with China, many HKEX-listed companies are incorporated in mainland China. These companies are commonly known as "H-Shares". If the company happens to be listed in one of the mainland exchanges, those would be referred to as the "A-Shares". Dual listing of both H-shares and A-shares of the same entity are by no means unusual. In fact, many companies, such as Bank of China Limited, Ping An Insurance (Group) Company of China Limited and PetroChina Company Limited, have both A-shares and H-shares offerings.

Shanghai and Shenzhen Stock Exchanges

The People's Republic of China is home to two major stock exchanges – the Shanghai Stock Exchange and the Shenzhen Stock Exchange. In late 2014, there were 979 companies listed on the Shanghai Stock Exchange, with total market capitalisation of close to RMB17 trillion.[5] The main index of this exchange is the market capitalisation-weighted Shanghai Stock Exchange Composite Index. The other exchange – Shenzhen Stock Exchange – consisted of 1,601 listed companies with a total market capitalisation of over RMB11 trillion in 2014.[6]

Unlike most profit-driven exchanges in the region, these two affiliated entities of the China Securities Regulatory Commission are considered "not-for-profit" organisations to ensure the development of the Chinese capital markets. These two exchanges were previously closed to foreign investors. However, with the 2014 "Shanghai–Hong Kong stock connect" initiative and plans for a Shenzhen–Hong Kong stock connect following that, it appears that the long-term plan is to open the Chinese market to the world.

Singapore Stock Exchange

Singapore Exchange Limited is a public-listed company in the exchange itself. As "The Switzerland of Asia", Singapore is often seen as the de facto financial hub of Southeast Asia, leading to SGX being considered as one of Southeast Asia's key exchanges. In 2014, SGX was home to more than 700 companies.[7]

The market cap-weighted Straits Times Index ("STI") tracking Singapore's top 30 listed companies is widely viewed as the go-to benchmark for the Singapore market. However, with many of these 30 companies having significant overseas business exposure, we feel that the STI is far from being just a proxy for Singapore's economy alone. Almost all 30 companies in the index have an international presence.

Many of the STI's constituent companies, such as Golden Agri-Resources Limited, Thai Beverage Public Company Limited and Hutchison Port Holdings Trust, derive the bulk of their revenue beyond Singapore. In 2014, the S$14 billion property powerhouse CapitaLand Limited had 58% of their assets beyond the shores of Singapore.[8] In fact, 38% of all SGX-listed companies had origins beyond the shores of Singapore.[9]

Bursa Malaysia

Bursa Malaysia Berhad came about from the split of the Stock Exchange of Malaysia into the Kuala Lumpur Stock Exchange and the Singapore Exchange way back in 1973. Like the Singapore Exchange, Bursa Malaysia is also a publicly listed company, listed in Malaysia. Bursa Malaysia had one of the largest numbers of public companies listed on its exchange compared to its Southeast Asian peers. However, with all the companies listed on the exchange having a total market capitalisation of about US$527 billion,[10] it is still smaller than the Singapore Exchange.

The exchange is represented by the Kuala Lumpur Composite Index, a market cap-weighted index of the largest 100 companies listed on Bursa Malaysia. Companies that call Bursa Malaysia home include Sime Darby Berhad (the conglomerate with a market capitalisation of over US$15 billion), Public Bank Berhad (one of Malaysia's largest domestic banks) and Tenaga Nasional Berhad (the largest power company in Malaysia).

Stock Exchange of Thailand

Even with 599 companies listed on the exchange (2014), Stock Exchange of Thailand was not one of the heavyweights in the region. The exchange includes companies with a total market capitalisation amounting to about US$450 billion.[11]

Some of the major companies listed on the Stock Exchange of Thailand include PTT Public Company – the major integrated oil and gas company and also one of the largest company by market capitalisation listed on SET, with a market capitalisation of over THB900 billion (2016).[12]

Another notable company on the SET is Siam Cement Public Company, a leading conglomerate in Thailand, with operations ranging from building materials to chemicals and packaging operations. The SET has some interesting companies listed on it, such as the Airports of Thailand Public Company. Not only does the company operate six international airports in Thailand,[13] they also have several other real estate-related operations.

With such a wide variety of companies to choose from, it pays for investors to be patient when it comes to the selection of an investment opportunity here in Asia. The next time someone tells you about the lack of investment opportunities in Asia, you know where to point them.

What Has Happened in Asia?

Now that we know the different stock markets in Asia, we can take the next step and look further towards finding a great investment within these markets. To first have an idea of the future of Asia, it's always good to start by studying its past. Although history doesn't repeat itself, it does rhyme. Hence it pays for us to focus and learn from the economic history of Asia.

Saying that Asia has grown in the past few decades is a gross understatement. Even if we just consider the situation from the start of the 21st century, there is much to talk about. Here are several key investment themes that have played out in Asia over the past decades.

The Rise of Chinese Consumers

Probably the greatest growth story of the last 30 years is China. China has risen from being one of the world's poorest nations to the world's second-largest economy.[14] Pre-1979, China was a relatively closed and isolated country. However, since Deng Xiaoping's "Open Door Policy" in 1978,[15] China's annual real domestic product grew by about 10% a year over the next three decades,[16] making it one of the fastest-growing economies in the world.

The mercurial rise of China was in no small part due to China transforming from an isolated nation to one that embraced globalisation. China pushed itself to work with the global communities such as joining the World Trade Organization and establishing trade relations with the United States in 2000. During this period, China rode on the advantage of Asia's low-cost production ability to meet the demand of the developed nations. This was reflected in the 700% increase in China's GDP per capita (US$) since the start of the 21st century (2000–2015).[17] Even the 2008 global financial crisis did little to slow this runaway growth train.

Yet what's fascinating is that even after the rapid growth in the past 30 years, China's real per capita GDP was still only roughly 20% of the United States in 2012.[18] This led to the common belief that it is no longer a question of *if* China will overtake the US as the world's largest economy but *when*. And as China develops from a production-based to a consumption-based economy, we are looking at one of the most-publicised investment themes – The Asian consumer story. With over a billion people moving up the economic ladder, it's not surprising that the China consumer story is one of the most popular investment themes. As people grow wealthier, their consumption could increase.

This was particularly evident from the huge push by three of the largest luxury goods companies to move into China:

- LVMH Moët Hennessy Louis Vuitton SE: Louis Vuitton, Bulgari, Moët & Chandon
- Compagnie Financière Richemont SA: Dunhill, Cartier, Montblanc
- Kering: Gucci, Saint Laurent Paris, Bottega Veneta

For FY2014, China/Hong Kong was Richemont's largest revenue contributor, with a contribution of €2.6 billion, or about 24% of their top line.[19] In FY2004, their Asia-Pacific segment only generated sales of €0.6 billion, with China/Hong Kong not even reported separately.[20]

LVMH's store expansion in Asia painted the same picture. In 2004, LVMH had 338 stores in Asia (excluding Japan).[21] In 2014, LVMH has expanded its store count to 870 in Asia (excluding Japan), contributing 29% towards the group's revenue.[22] In the last decade, LVMH's Asia (excluding Japan) store count expanded at the fastest rate of any of its other major geographical segments. With the wave of luxury European brands coming into China, PRADA S.p.A. went even further, with an initial public offering of the company on the Hong Kong Stock Exchange (HKSE) in 2011.[23] This showed the growing importance of China both as potential customers as well as potential investors for these companies. And this was not a one-off event, given that HKSE is also home to Trinity Limited (owner of Gieves & Hawkes) and YGM Trading Limited (owner of Aquascutum), both European brands with histories of royal warrants.

The China consumer story is not just about luxury goods; in fact, that is only the tip of the iceberg. The consumer sector is a broad sector, ranging from consumer discretionary (things we want) to staple items (things we need). Think along the lines of what you eat, drink, wear and use daily. Imagine the potential of the number of people migrating from rural to urban areas: they might want to eat more meat, buy better cars, drink more bottled drinks and use more disposable baby diapers. Maybe this was why Warren Buffett's Berkshire Hathaway Inc. paid good money for consumer staple companies like H.J. Heinz Company and its subsequent merger with Kraft Foods Group.

Along these lines, we might expect The Coca-Cola Company and PepsiCo, Inc. ("PepsiCo"), given their huge global footprint, to also be the dominant beverage players in China. Interestingly, local players like Hong Kong-listed Tingyi (Cayman Islands) Holding Corporation ("Tingyi Holdings") and Uni-President China Holdings Limited have a similar strong presence in the country. Tingyi Holdings even has a strategic alliance with PepsiCo in China and is the primary supplier of beverages to Shanghai Disneyland.[24] This was the first time in at least 25 years since PepsiCo last sold its beverage through Disneyland, implying the reach and influence of Tingyi Holdings.[25] *Note: PepsiCo had expectations of China being the world's largest beverage market by 2015.[26]*

Tingyi is not just a beverage giant; they also own the Master Kong brand, which has a whopping 46% market share (2014 volume) of China's instant noodles market,[27] more than twice its closest competitor, Uni-President China Holdings Limited.[28]

For sportswear, Nike Inc., with over US$30 billion in sales (2015),[29] had a target of sustainable double-digit revenue growth for the Greater China region.[30] Even within China, local sportswear players have been creating waves, with the listings of Li Ning Co Limited ("Li Ning") (2004), Anta Sports Products Limited (2007) and Xtep International Holdings Limited (2008), all major local sports brands. These companies are already building their global brand image, with sponsorships of NBA stars like Dwyane Wade[31] and Klay Thompson.[32]

When it comes to fast food, one of the most successful foreign food company in China is Yum! Brands, Inc. – operator of KFC,

Pizza Hut and Taco Bell. In the past, eating at restaurants might be reserved only for special occasions. But with the rise of the middle class and the urbanisation of China, visits to these restaurants became more of a common occurrence. In fact, sales in China contributed to over 50% of Yum!'s revenue between 2012 and 2014.[33] Given this positive demographic backdrop, one might expect good returns from investing in consumer companies. Or at least that was what was most expected. But was this really the case?

With over four times the population of the United States of America (2014) and a GDP per capita of only 20% of the United States of America, one would expect the growth in the China's consumer industry to be on fire. However, in recent years, the stock performances of many major China-based consumer-related companies served as cautionary tales for investors on the dangers of over-expectation. With China's demographic presenting such a compelling case, we are not opposed to their consumer story. Rather, what we are concerned with is investors overpaying for the ultra-optimistic future.

Even with a good growth story, fundamentals still do matter, and China's post-Beijing Olympics sportswear industry was an interesting case. Most of these sportswear brands rode on the Beijing Olympics wave to raise capital in the financial market. Up till 2008, business was booming, with some of these companies being given lofty valuations. However, investors should never make the mistake of assuming that growth of such magnitude will carry on forever. Finally, in 2011, after three years of weakening operational data, fundamentals eventually prevailed and 50% vaporisations of the market capitalisation of these sportswear companies were not an uncommon sight. In hindsight, this was a disaster waiting to happen.

Since 2008, most sportswear companies in China overestimated demand for its product. This was evident from their marked increase in inventories and trade receivables. Unfortunately for sportswear, inventory is not like wine, it does not get better with age. Many of them ended up with inventories, such as shoes, that deteriorate in quality over time.

Moreover, some of the companies operated on a wholesale business model.[34] They ended up stuffing inventory down to distributors and retailers, which were already filled. In good times, these distributors and retailers would not have much concern about clearing their stock. But once demand slowed, things got ugly. And when sportswear giant Adidas AG reported that they had too much product in the Chinese market,[35] it should have been an "uh-oh" moment for investors.

If consumers are not buying more, inventory can only flow back, causing major inventory and receivable write-downs throughout their entire value chain. Imagine yourself at a buffet where you are already extremely full. Then someone comes and feeds you more food. You can imagine the ugly scene that follows. This was what happened to the sportswear industry in China. Even a company like Li Ning, one of the more recognised sports brand in China, met with such a fate.[36]

The simple and hard truth is that even when you are confident about your views on a certain macro trend, if you do not look into the fundamentals of the individual company, these investments may not result in the rewards you expect. This is because market prices are a combination of both the current reality as well as the future expectations. If future expectations have already been priced into the share price of a company, investors may not even benefit when the future is as expected.

More importantly, it is often a dangerous sign when most investors are betting that the fast growth rate of a company can continue its upward trajectory perpetually. During a time when the growth rate starts to slow unexpectedly, investors may realise that their past optimistic expectations have become unrealistic. As a result, we tend to see a reversion of the share price after such a realisation from over-optimistic investors. In summary: *never ever overpay*.

The Commodity Supercycle

From the late 1990s until the 2008 financial crisis, most commodities have enjoyed a great run. This period has been better known as the commodity supercycle and many companies within Asia have benefited from this thematic event.

During this supercycle, commodity prices were largely driven up by the rising demand from emerging markets such as the famous BRIC countries (Brazil, Russia, India and China). Commodities range from coal, iron ore and platinum to things like pork belly (yes, people do trade that), coffee beans and rice, even oil, gold and silver. For this segment, we will be focusing on basic resources and not commoditised products like generic drugs or microchips.

The commodity supercycle saw many commodities increasing in price rapidly. For example, the prices of crude oil, copper and corn have all risen by over 1,000%, 480% and 240% respectively (late 1990–2008).[37] Even gold had a very respectable gain of 500% since 2000, peaking at close to US$1,800/ounce in 2011.[38]

If we look into the economic history over the past 200 years, two other notable commodity supercycles came about: from the economic growth in the USA during the late 1800s to early 1900s; and from the post-war developments in Europe and Japan in 1945–1975.[39] It seems like the story repeated itself in the early 2000s, fuelled by the rising demand from the urbanisation and industrialisation of the BRIC nations (Brazil, Russia, India and China).[40]

Since supercycles tend to be driven by highly material-intensive economic activity, then it should come as no surprise that China was a huge contributor to the latest supercycle. China is handling possibly one of the largest rural-to-urban migrations in human history. Just imagine the amount of infrastructure spending required to accommodate this change. Try to visualise the amount of aluminium and iron required to build up a city centre. Now multiply that by a hundred or even a thousand. This was when infrastructure-linked companies like Hong Kong-listed Anhui Conch Cement Company Limited – one of China's largest cement makers – saw revenue of about RMB1 billion (2000)[41] soar to RMB46 billion (2012).[42] Beyond China, other commodity players throughout Asia, like oil palm giant Malaysia-listed Sime Darby Berhad[43] and Singapore-listed Wilmar International Limited,[44] have also enjoyed strong revenue growth in the early decades of the 21st century.

Food has also been experiencing a strong increase in demand as Asia progressed. With the increase in income levels and population within Asia, agricultural products were also in strong demand. Globally, agriculture products are dominated by four companies, commonly known as the ABCD: Archer Daniels Midland Company, Bunge Limited, Cargill, Inc. and Louis Dreyfus Company. Within Asia, there are a few companies that hold their own against the ABCD. Olam International Limited ("Olam") and Wilmar International Limited ("Wilmar") are two such companies.

From a cashew nut trader in 1989, Olam has developed into a global leader in cashew, rice and cocoa. The latter was due to its recent US$1.2 billion acquisition of ADM's cocoa business, making Olam one of the top cocoa processors in the world.[45]

On the other hand, Wilmar is a very different company. Not only is Wilmar among the top oil palm plantation owners in the world by planted area, it is also the world's largest processor of palm oil, with a booming branded consumer products business in China, India and Indonesia. Wilmar also invested heavily into the oilseeds and sugar sector. Today, Wilmar is not only one of the largest oilseed crushers in China, it is also among the top 10 raw sugar producers in the world. The massive growth experienced by Wilmar can be seen from its book value. Its shareholders' equity soared from US$0.6 billion[46] to US$15 billion in just 10 years[47] (2006–2015). In 2010, Wilmar had a market capitalisation of over S$40 billion,[48] making it one of the largest companies in Singapore. Not bad for a company that came to the market only in 2006.

When we talk about commodities, how can we leave out oil and gas? Although many integrated oil and gas companies within Asia are nationalised entities like the Saudi Arabian Oil Company (Saudi Aramco) or Malaysia's Petroliam Nasional Berhad (better known as PETRONAS), some of the largest of them all are also listed firms. Dual-listed oil and gas giants such as PetroChina Company Limited, CNOOC Limited and China Petroleum & Chemical Corp (Sinopec Limited) are a few examples.

Apart from integrated oil and gas producers, there are some major service providers to the industry as well. For the Offshore and Marine industry, Singapore's duo of Keppel Corporation Limited ("Keppel") and Sembcorp Marine Limited are two of the top oil rig builders in the world. These companies also benefited from rising demand for commodities. In 2014, Keppel was a S$16 billion conglomerate generating revenue of over S$13 billion with S$8.6 billion from their key Offshore and Marine segment with operations from rig building to offshore engineering and construction.[49]

Following their lead are a whole slew of other specialised support providers, such as Ezra Holdings Limited, Ezion Holdings Limited and even the newly listed PACC Offshore Services Holdings Limited – part of Robert Kuok's empire. From just these few examples, it is clear that the commodity supercycle has kept many companies in Asia busy and very profitable in the early part of the 21st century.

The Growth of REITs

Due to its "tangible" nature, many in Asia still view property as a "safe" investment. Today, not only has this trend continued, it has also extended to the area of property-linked equities. In the last decade, the investment vehicle known as a Real Estate Investment Trust ("REIT") has taken Asia by storm.

REITs are vehicles with professionally managed real estate assets. REITs can own a wide range of property assets such as commercial buildings, retail malls, hotels, industrial buildings, data centres and even telecommunications towers. *As an exposure to RE + telecom*

REITs first started in the US market during the 1960s. In the late 1960s, European REIT legislation allowed the creation of European REITs. Australia followed suit in the 1970s, making it the first nation in the Asia Pacific region to form REITs.[50] In Asia, REITs only started taking off in early 2000. Today REIT markets in Japan, Hong Kong and Singapore are quite established. *Fun fact: The United States is still the largest REIT market, with assets from communication towers to billboards and even prisons!*

REITs have a few advantages for investors and property owners. For one, the REIT structure allows individual investors to gain exposure to huge properties which they would not have the resource to purchase individually. It also allows existing property owners to increase the liquidity of their otherwise illiquid assets. REITs are seen as a win-win situation between issuers that want to "unlock" property values and investors who want to be a minority landlord in a mega building. REITs allow investors to have a "rental stream" and capital appreciation without fully owning the underlying property or, in simple terms, REITs are seen as investments that give investors a stable income with potential upside that their prices will go up over time.

In 2011, Asia Pacific was the world's second-largest (21% of market capitalisation) REIT market, with Australia comprising 58%, followed by Japan (20%), Singapore (14%) and Hong Kong (8%).[51] The low interest rates environment during the past few years might have helped in pushing the demand for REITs in Asia. The average yield of a 5-year Singapore government bond was 1.4% in the last 10 years, lower than the 20-year average at 2.2%.[52] But why is cheap financing important for REITs?

A REIT is designed as an income-generating instrument, and to enjoy tax transparency a REIT is required to distribute at least 90% of its taxable income to unitholders.[53] Therefore, REITs have funding concerns when it comes to investing in new properties or performing "asset enhancement initiatives" – either way, you need cash.

Thus one key risk of REITs is the need to take on additional funding, either through equity or debt, for future development.

In 2014, Singapore-listed REITs, at S$68 billion, accounted for 6.8% of the market's total market capitalisation, the highest in the region.[54] Since the 2002 listing of CapitaLand Mall Trust (Singapore's first and largest REIT),[55] the number of listed REITs on the SGX Mainboard grew to 30.[56] This sector is such an important component in Singapore that over 20% of the Straits Times Index's constituents, such as Ascendas Real Estate Investment Trust, CapitaLand Limited, CapitaLand Mall Trust, CapitaLand Commercial Trust, City Development Limited, Keppel Corporation and Singapore Press Holdings Limited, either have investments in REITs or are involved in REIT operations.[57]

Other than the traditional four of commercial, hospitality, industrial and retail REITs, 2014 welcomed the first listing of a data centre REIT – Keppel DC REIT – onto SGX. With this listing oversubscribed,[58] could this be the start of more exotic REITs in Asia? However, before getting distracted, we shall return to the main issue at hand: Why are REITs important for investors?

Common benefits include:

- Tax benefits: Individual investors enjoy a tax-exempt distribution.
- Liquidity: Able to buy and sell mega properties easily.
- Portfolio diversification: Investors can now obtain real estate exposure without huge investment outlay.
- High distribution: This leads to high-yielding equity investments.

With their unique structure and in the absence of excessive leverage, REITs can be described as a form of convertible perpetual bond. As a bond substitute, REITs could provide you with both a constant stream of income and a capital appreciation "option". And with a rather decent performance showing in Asia in the past decade, REITs appeared to be doing well to fill up this void.

For a quick crash course on yields, we can calculate the dividend yield of an investment by the formula: "dividend per share divided by market price". For example, if a share is trading at $20 per share and is offering $1 per share in dividend, its dividend yield would be 5%

(dividend of $1 divided by the share price of $20). Moreover, due to share price movements, even if it is based on a constant dividend per share, the dividend yield fluctuates from time to time.

Going back to the previous example, if the share price of the company plunged to $10 right after your purchase, you will be enjoying a 10% yield. Sadly, that might not give you much comfort, especially when your share price was down 50%. On the other hand, if market price went up to $40 per share, your dividend yield would be down to just 2.5%; to keep things in perspective, your return on investment has now gone up 100%. Which would you prefer?

Instead of worrying about the dividend yield of a company, what we should always take note of is the sustainability of earnings and the cash flow to cover its dividends. Simply because an investment has a high yield does not mean that the yield is guaranteed. Dividend and distribution can be cut, and when they are, your yield can go to 0%. And 0% of anything is zero.

To enjoy the benefits of their structure, REITs have to pay out 90% of their taxable income. Inevitably, this has led to REITs having a much higher yield compared to the general market. This asset class might suit the portfolio of an income investor. It can also be an alternative to bond investors in regions where the retail bond market is still underdeveloped. From Figure 2.1,[59] we can clearly see how REITs (yield-wise) stack up against other traditional sources of income producing assets.

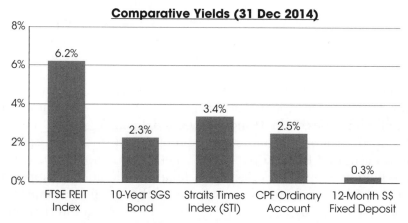

Figure 2.1   Singapore Comparative Yields

Yield-wise, REITs look to be heads above the other traditional sources of income producing assets. The only other asset class with comparable yields would be high-yield (junk) bonds. Compared to junk bonds, REITs are generally perceived as more conservative and accessible for most yield-seeking investors. Broadly speaking, investments in most Singapore-listed REITs in the past decade have been positive for investors.[60]

Although REITs are commonly thought of as income instruments, we noted that distributions contributed to about half the returns of 20 REITs over the period between 2002–2014.[61] Nonetheless, with a balance between capital gains and dividends, REITs could work out for investors striving to meet both their short-term liquidity needs as well as their long-term capital gains.

For those of you who are interested in knowing more about REITs, we highly recommend Bobby Jayaraman's *Building Wealth Through REITS* as a good starting point to learn about Singapore-listed REITs.[62]

Technological Charge!

China is already home to some of the largest technology companies in the world, whether in the hardware space, with companies like Huawei Technologies Co. Limited and Lenovo Group Limited, or software giants like Tencent Holdings Limited ("Tencent Holdings"), Baidu Inc. and Alibaba Group Holding Limited, which all have their roots in China. From the backwaters of the technology industry, China is now one of the fastest-growing technology centres in the world. In 2013, China's software industry reported a growth of 24.6% year on year for 2013, far exceeding the global average growth of 5.7%.[63]

Over the past three decades, Chinese hardware companies have gone international, and many have become truly international companies, with Hong Kong-listed Lenovo Group Limited ("Lenovo Group") as one such example. Back in 2004, Lenovo Group acquired IBM Corp's ("IBM") Personal Computing Division (the famous ThinkPad series) for a total consideration of approximately US$1.75 billion.[64] That was one of the first few examples of a Chinese company buying a global business from an international powerhouse. What's interesting was that out of the initial portion of US$1.25 billion transaction amount (the remainder of US$500 million was net balance sheet liabilities), 48% was done in Lenovo Group's common stock. At the end of this deal, IBM had an 18.9% stake in Lenovo Group.

This was not a one-off thing. In 2015, Lenovo Group made headline news when it went back to IBM to acquire their x86 server business for US$2.3 billion.[65] The deal propelled Lenovo Group's revenue to US$46 billion in 2015.[66] Today, Lenovo Group is not only the world's largest PC company, with 21.2% market share,[67] they have also become one of the top smartphone companies in China.[68] Within the same space, we also see fast-moving and innovative companies, such as Xiaomi Corp, becoming more dominant in the industry. Even so, after decades, most Chinese technology companies still appear to operate mainly in China. *Fun fact: China's Huawei Technologies is now the third-biggest smartphone maker after Apple Inc. and Samsung Electronics Co Limited (the world leader in the $400 billion market).*[69]

There are two possible major reasons for this situation. First, compared to developed nations, China appeared to be more resistant to foreign software companies attempting to expand within the country. And with what happened in the United States presidential election in 2016, national security might be viewed as an additional concern. A perfect case in point would be the restrictions placed on social media companies such as Facebook Inc. and Twitter in China. This close, restricted and regulated industry in China gives Chinese technology companies an advantage over their global peers when they are allowed to operate within the country. For example, Google Inc. struggled for many years in China before calling it quits in 2010.[70]

Of course, this is not a phenomenon unique to China. As a response to the heavy restrictions on companies outside China, many countries, especially the United States of America, are now also resistant to opening up to Chinese technology companies hoping to invade their shores.[71]

Second, due to China's unique culture and language, many companies that have successful operations in China might find it hard to export their businesses overseas. Moreover, with the local industry growing at such a fast pace, many software companies have not yet seen the need to venture outside the Middle Kingdom. However, as the local industry matures, we believe that more and more of its companies will start venturing outside of their motherland. In fact, companies like Tencent Holdings and Alibaba Group Holdings

Limited have been aggressively investing in companies and markets beyond China. Through Riot Games, Tencent Holdings owns the world's top eSports game, League of Legends,[72] which generates a whopping US$1.5 billion annually. As well as holding 100% interests, Tencent Holdings also acquires stakes in certain companies, with Activision Blizzard Inc. being one of them.[73] In 2016, Tencent Holdings, together with their partners, made their largest ever acquisition, with the US$8.6 billion purchase of 84.3% of the "Clash of Clans" maker, Supercell Oy.[74] We might one day see a truly globalised Chinese technology company in the near future.

These are some of the key areas of change we are seeing within Asia, especially around the East Asia and Pacific region: the rising demand of the Chinese consumer; the increasing demand for commodities due to huge infrastructure projects planned within Asia; the growing importance of Asia-based technology companies and the evolution of the financial markets here, leading to more asset classes such as REITs. These are all prime examples of how fast Asia is changing. Yet after decades of change and progress, Asia is still behind the developed world. Will Asia ever catch up? Or if you dare to dream, will Asia lead the charge forward in the future in all these areas? If so, what does it mean for investors like us? We do not know what the future holds for Asia, but we know that as investors we need to get prepared by learning about the region, or risk being left behind.

Notes

1. World Federation of Exchanges members. September 2014.
2. Meir Statman. How many Stocks Make a Diversified Portfolio? *Journal of Financial and Quantitative Analysis.* Vol. 22, No. 3. September 1967.
3. Countries-of the-World.com. https://www.countries-ofthe-world.com/countries-of-asia.html. Accessed: 4 April 2017.
4. World Federation of Exchanges members. September 2014.
5. Ibid.
6. Ibid.
7. Ibid.
8. CapitaLand Limited. Annual Report 2014.
9. Securities Trading Summary. Singapore Stock Exchange. April–June 2014.
10. World Federation of Exchanges members. September 2014.

11. Ibid.
12. Google Finance. "PTT Public Company Limited". https://www
    .google.com/finance?cid=1079066631482057. Accessed: 4 April 2017.
13. Airport of Thailand PLC. Annual Report 2015.
14. Xiaodong Zhu. "Understanding China's Growth: Past, Present, and
    Future". *Journal of Economic Perspectives*. Volume 26, Number 4. Fall
    2012. Pages 103–124.
15. Shang-Jin, Wei. Chapter Title: "The Open Door Policy and China's
    Rapid Growth: Evidence from City-Level Data". Volume Title:
    Growth Theories in Light of the East Asian Experience, NBER-EASE. Publi-
    cation Date: January 1995. Pages 73–10.
16. The World Bank. China Overview. Last Updated: 14 September 2016.
17. The World Bank. World Bank national accounts data, and OECD
    National Accounts data files. China GDP per Capita (current US$).
    Accessed: 14 December 2016.
18. Zhu. "Understanding China's Growth: Past, Present, and Future".
19. Compagnie Financière Richemont SA. Annual Report and
    Accounts 2014.
20. Compagnie Financière Richemont SA. Annual Report and
    Accounts 2004.
21. LVMH Moët Hennessy Louis Vuitton SE. Annual Report 2004.
22. LVMH Moët Hennessy Louis Vuitton SE. Annual Report 2014.
23. Prada S.p.A. Global Offering Prospectus. 13 June 2011.
24. PepsiCo, Inc. Press Release. "Shanghai Disney Resort Signs Strategic
    Alliance with PepsiCo and Tingyi Holdings". 27 February 2014.
25. Adam Jourdan. Reuters. "PepsiCo re-enters 'Magic Kingdom' with
    Shanghai Disney deal". 27 February 2016.
26. PepsiCo, Inc. Press Release. "PepsiCo Opens New Food Manufactur-
    ing Plant to Fuel Growth in China". 10 July 2012.
27. Presentation on 2014 Annual Results. Tingyi (Cayman Islands)
    Holding Corp. 23 March 2015.
28. 2015 Annual Results (IFRS) Presentation. Uni-President Enterprises
    Corp. Updated 11 April 2016.
29. Nike, Inc. 2015 Form 10-K.
30. Nike, Inc. Press Release. "Announces Target of $50 billion in
    Revenues by End of FY20". 14 October 2015.
31. Christopher Beam. "Dwyane Wade and Li Ning". ESPN. 18 April 2014.
32. Nick DePaula. Yahoo! Sports. "Kicks Fix: Inside Klay Thompson's
    shoe deal with Anta".
33. Yum! Brands. 2014 Annual Report.
34. Xin En Lee. CKGSB Knowledge. "Sportswear brand Li-Ning Strug-
    gles to Hold It Together". 4 November 2013.
35. Adidas Group. First Half 2010 Results. Q&A Session. 4 August 2010.

36. Patti Waldmeir. *Financial Times*. "Li Ning's rise and fall marks a cautionary tale". https://www.ft.com/content/0ece54f6-a03d-11e4-aa89-00144feab7de. 24 January 2015.
37. Nicholas J Johnson, Greg E Sharenow. PIMCO. PIMCO Insights. "Is the Commodity Supercycle Dead?" September 2013.
38. BullionVault Ltd. 20Y 1997–2016. https://www.bullionvault.com/gold-price-chart.do. Accessed: 4 April 2017.
39. Alan Heap. CitiGroup Smith Barney. "China – The Engine of a Commodities Super Cycle". 31 March, 2005.
40. Morgan Stanley Smith Barney. Alternative Investment. "Commodities Super-Cycle: Is It Coming to An End?". September 2013.
41. Anhui Conch Cement Company Limited. Annual Report 2000.
42. Anhui Conch Cement Company Limited. Annual Report 2012.
43. Sime Darby Berhad. Annual Reports 2007, 2011 & 2015.
44. Wilmar International Limited. Annual Reports 2007, 2011 & 2015.
45. Olam International Limited. Press Release. "Olam International Closes ADM Cocoa Acquisition to Create Globally Integrated Cocoa Business". 16 October 2015.
46. Wilmar International Limited. Annual Report 2006.
47. Wilmar International Limited. Annual Report 2015.
48. Google Finance. "Wilmar International Limited". https://www.google.com/finance?cid=457291003739554. Accessed: 4 April 2017.
49. Keppel Corporation Limited. "Report to Shareholders 2014".
50. CFA Institute. "Asia-Pacific REITs Building Trust through Better REIT Governance". February 2011.
51. Ibid.
52. Monetary Authority of Singapore. "SGX Prices and Yields – Benchmark Issues". 1988 to 2016 (Yearly).
53. Inland Revenue Authority of Singapore. IRAS e-Tax Guide. "Income Tax Treatment of Real Estate Investment Trusts (Fourth Edition)". 3 November 2015.
54. Tan Kok Huan, *The Business Times*. "The Reit market that defied the odds". http://www.businesstimes.com.sg/opinion/the-reit-market-that-defied-the-odds. 25 November 2014.
55. CapitaLand Mall Trust. Annual General Meeting Presentation. 12 April 2016.
56. Singapore Exchange Limited. Market Updates. "March Quarter Performance of Singapore's REITs". 30 May 2016.
57. Singapore Exchange Limited. "STI Constituents". Accessed: 23 December 2016.
58. *Today Online*. Business. "Keppel DC REIT's IPO heavily oversubscribed". http://www.todayonline.com/business/keppel-dc-reits-ipo-heavily-oversubscribed. 11 December 2014.

59. Cache Logistics Trust. Annual Report 2014.
60. Authors' research. Respective REIT Annual Reports 2002–2014.
61. Ibid.
62. Bobby Jayaraman. Marshall Cavendish International (Asia) Private Limited. *Building Wealth Through REITS*. First published: 2012, and reprinted 2013.
63. Ministry of Industry and Information Technology of the People's Republic of China. http://www.researchinchina.com/Htmls/Report/2014/6852.html. April 2014.
64. Lenovo Group Limited. News Release. "Lenovo to Acquire IBM Personal Computing Division". 7 December 2004.
65. Lenovo Group Limited. News Release. "Lenovo Plans to Acquire IBM's X86 Server Business". 23 January 2014.
66. Lenovo Group Limited. "2015/16 Annual Report".
67. Lenovo Group Limited. News Release. "Lenovo Statement on Quarterly PC Rankings CY2016 Q2 IDC & Gartner Rankings". 14 July 2016.
68. Lenovo Group Limited. News Release. "Lenovo Statement on China Smartphone Rankings". 10 August 2014.
69. Harro ten Wolde. Reuters. "Huawei Wants to Beat Apple in Smartphones in Two Years: Exec". http://www.reuters.com/article/us-huawei-tech-phones-idUSKBN12Y2TV. 3 November 2016.
70. Rebecca Fannin. Forbes. "Why Google Is Quitting China". https://www.forbes.com/2010/01/15/baidu-china-search-intelligent-technology-google.html. 15 January 2010.
71. Jim Wolf. Reuters. "U.S. lawmakers seek to block China Huawei, ZTE U.S. Inroads". http://www.reuters.com/article/us-usa-china-huawei-zte-idUSBRE8960NH20121008. 8 October 2012.
72. John Gaudiosi. *Fortune*. Tech. "This Chinese Tech Giant Owns More Than Riot Games". http://fortune.com/2015/12/22/tencent-completes-riot-games-acquisition/. 22 December 2015.
73. Reuters. Market News. "Brief – Tencent Holdings reports 5.023pct passive stake in Activision Blizzard". http://www.reuters.com/article/idUSFWN19F01H. 23 June 2016.
74. Juro Osawa and Sarah E. Needleman. *The Wall Street Journal*. Tech. "Tencent Seals Deal to Buy 'Clash of Clans" Developer Supercell for $8.6 Billion". https://www.wsj.com/articles/tencent-agrees-to-acquire-clash-of-clans-maker-supercell-1466493612. 21 June 2016.

CHAPTER 3

Uniquely Asia

Keep a cool head and maintain a low profile. Never take the lead – but aim to do something big.

— Deng Xiaoping

Asia, even after being one of the fastest-growing economies over the past decade, still possesses so much untapped potential. In just a few decades, many countries in Asia have experienced a rich history of economic growth and we believe that this trend may continue for many years to come.

Spanning from Japan to Turkey, Asia is not a single market but rather a giant melting pot of diverse cultures, economies, languages, regulations, religions, and even shopping habits! Since it is impractical to touch on every major market in Asia, we narrowed our scope down to two key regions: Greater China and Southeast Asia.

This area can further be divided into developed and developing economies, such as:

- developed: Hong Kong, Japan, Singapore, South Korea, Taiwan
- developing: China, Indonesia, Malaysia, Philippines, Thailand, Vietnam.

No two countries are the same, and this is even more true in Asia. Even within Asia itself, the ways of doing business may differ greatly. In an interview by *The Peak* with Dr Ng Chin Siau, CEO-Founder of Q&M Dental (Singapore) Limited, there was a short section documenting how business was done in China as compared to his company's base in Singapore.[1] To paraphrase, here are some of the examples given of how the way of conducting business differs between countries:

- In China, deals are struck at the dinner table; a round table is preferred as it allows everyone to face one another.
- The Chinese prefer face-to-face communication, not through email or telephone. Also, alcohol helps.
- If you are served bai-jiu (白酒), it means you are treated with the utmost respect. One should drink up, or learn to drink it.
- Once lawyers are involved, it may mean that the relationship is heading down the drain. Many deals are lost because of this.
- In China, there are no clear guidelines as there are in Singapore. In China, the cultural values are typically ranked this order: relationships, reason and, lastly, law. In Singapore, the reverse appears to be true.

We see this sharp difference in business culture across most Asian nations. Each country seems to have its own hidden rules on how business should be conducted. Therefore, to succeed in the business world, you need to know how to play by "the rules" in each country. Even with neighbouring countries like Singapore and Malaysia, which are literally just a bridge away, we can witness two very different business environments. Now imagine the difference between a company operating in China and another based in Indonesia. This is what makes Asia interesting.

In addition, we also notice that even multinational firms adjust their business strategies in Asia. For example, these companies might need to adjust their offerings to meet the unique needs of each Asian country. Some successful examples include Nestlé SA, which sells single-packed servings of instant coffee and soup stock cubes in Asia, and Unilever, which tapped into the Philippines market by selling starter packs of shampoo and conditioner costing just about US 10 cents each.[2]

There are also tonnes of examples of large corporations from the USA or Europe that failed to launch their business in Asia. Even tech mammoth Google Inc. faced challenges in China. These show that there is no "one size fit all" formula in Asia, and multinational companies that do not understand that might suffer here.

We would like to end this section with a story from Mr Daryl Guppy, a famous technical trader.[3] At a Chinese financial conference in Shenzhen, there was a renowned American financial trader giving a presentation to a Chinese audience. However, Mr Guppy wrote that the speaker completely misunderstood the thinking and aspirations of his audience. Listening to the comments from the few Europeans in the audience, they found his presentation inspiring, insightful and useful. On the other hand, the Chinese in the audience found his presentation irrelevant. The first task of a speaker is to create empathy and relevance. The American speaker tried to do this by highlighting the change in lifestyle for the audience from making money in the market, moving from the city to the countryside, an idyllic rural paradise. However, this was a Western dream. Although the audience and the speaker desired the same outcomes, their conception of those benefits was different.

Now imagine what would happen if you were to look at an Asian company through the same lens used for a company in the United States.

What Asia Has Going for It

Even in the face of global headwinds, developing Asia is still expected to contribute to 60% of the world's growth.[4] In this section we will introduce key macro-economic and demographical themes that Asia has going for it.

From being the "factory of the world", Asia has become the "millionaire factory of the world", with more millionaires here than in North America and Europe.[5] Not only are there more millionaires, Asia's millionaires' net worth of US$17.4 trillion was also more than North America's US$16.6 trillion. (Yep, a trillion is the one with 12 zeroes.) And we can expect more from Asia as traditionally production-centric countries switch gears towards consumption-driven industries.

Growing Workforce

Asia Pacific is home to about 60% of the world's population[6] or, to be more specific, 4.5 billion people. And many countries here are still in the phase with an increasing working population.[7]

An Asian Development Bank report in 2016 estimated that developing nations in Asia are still expected to grow at close to 6% over the next few years.[8] To place things in context, many developed nations in Europe and the USA are expected to grow at less than 2%.

Moreover, Asia also has lesser participation of women in the workforce. Studies showed that on average, Asian women are 70% less likely than men to be in the workforce. As the economy grows and education improves, the percentage of women participation should increase, as seen in many developed economies.[9] A higher participation of women in the workforce may further improve the economic situation of these countries. Even developed nations are trying hard to promote higher female labour contribution to their economy, such as Japan, as part of the economic plan proposed by its current Prime Minister.[10]

Other bright spots within Asia include the push for more integration within the Association of Southeast Asian Nations ("ASEAN").[11] The ASEAN economic community (AEC) is the mega-plan in the region to form a more-integrated economic partnership between the nations in Southeast Asia. If ASEAN can work more closely together, the region would be a major growing force in the global economy. Currently, the region is still growing around 4% to 5% a year and is expected to continue this level of growth for many more years.[12]

All these new developments are brightening Asia's prospect. As Asian countries grow, it is highly likely that their consumers' demand for goods and services will follow accordingly, leading us to our next point.

Increasing Consumption

Even with their many differences, the development in Asia does reflect some similarities with what has happened within the developed world. By looking at the industries that have flourished in developed countries, we may be able to find similar stories taking place in Asia.

A similarity we observed is the rise of the middle class, better known as the famous "Asian consumer story". As people move up the income ladder they might not be satisfied with eating chicken rice or prawn noodles every single day. Sometimes they might want to splurge a little: eat at restaurants, drink flavoured water, shop at places with more variety, and take better care of their bodies.

In hindsight, US investors may feel that investing in companies like Wal-Mart Stores Inc., The Coca-Cola Company, Procter & Gamble Co. and McDonald's Corporation seemed like a no-brainer, given their extraordinary returns over the past decades. Due to the relatively shorter history of Asian stock markets, not many companies have a market history that can be traced back over decades. And that works to our advantage. It means that the Asian "Coca-Cola" of today is still a relatively young and fast-growing company! If we can find the Asian equivalent of The Coca-Cola Company, Procter & Gamble Co. and McDonald's Corporation, then all we need to do is let time work its magic.

But where do we start from? One similarity among the four companies mentioned above is the fact that they sell products broadly described as "consumer staples". Consumer staples are things people use daily, like beverages, food, household products and tobacco; a low-priced "need" rather than a highly priced "want". Thus, regardless of where the economy is heading, these products will still be in demand. In this case, investors can buy these easy-to-understand businesses, as long as the price is right.

To illustrate our point, here are four Asian-based consumer staples companies. At this point we are highlighting them primarily for their operations, without any consideration of their valuations.

1. Hong Kong-listed Tingyi (Cayman Islands) Holding Corp ("Tingyi Holdings"): With the "Master Kong" brand as their flagship product, Tingyi Holdings was the instant noodle market leader in China, with market share of 45% (Q4 2015 Sales volume).[13] In addition, the group was also the market leader for ready-to-drink teas and egg rolls. In bottled water and the overall juice drink market, Tingyi Holdings was ranked number two in the market.

2. Hong Kong-listed Sun Art Retail Group Limited ("Sun Art Retail"): Sun Art Retail is in the PRC hypermarket business under Auchan and RT-Mart. In terms of retail sales, Sun Art Retail led Chinese hypermarkets with a market share of 14% (2014), even larger than Wal-Mart in China.[14]

3. Philippines-listed Jollibee Foods Corporation ("Jollibee Foods"): Jollibee Foods operates the largest fast-food chain in the Philippines.[15] With over 750 stores, Jollibee Foods has a larger share than all the other multinational brands combined. Some names in their portfolio are Jollibee, Chowking

and Greenwich. Interestingly, after acquiring a stake in the sole franchisee of the Burger King brand in the Philippines, Jollibee Foods is also the operator of the Burger King chain in the country.[16]

4. Hong Kong-listed Hengan International Group Co. Limited ("Hengan International"): Hengan International is China's largest manufacturer of household tissue paper, ladies' sanitary napkins and disposable baby diapers.[17]

If you have not noticed, these companies correspond with the operations of their four American counterparts mentioned above. However, being in the same business as the four American corporations does not conclusively mean that these companies will be great investments. Using this as a backdrop, though, may supply us with a blueprint of how things might develop in Asia in the years to come.

Keep in mind that we have only touched on consumer staples. Think of the potential if we were to consider discretionary purchases like cars, jewellery, luxury apparel and accessories and even entertainment and leisure!

Booming Infrastructure

Another of Asia's attractions is the state of its infrastructure, which is still in its infancy.

Asia is playing catch-up with the developed world, and that's good news for us. One area that many Asian countries are not afraid to spend on is infrastructure. Nearly 60% of the global infrastructure spending up to 2025 is expected to be spent here in Asia. Many countries within Asia are still in need of major basic infrastructure like water, power and transportation. Indonesia, the largest economy in ASEAN, fuelled by the heavy manufacturing sector, is expected to and is forecasted to spend US$165 billion on infrastructure in 2025. To support this development, public investment spending (government spending) is expected to grow by about 7% a year till 2025.[18] Likewise, most countries within ASEAN are expected to raise their infrastructure spending in the next decade.

To this end, China has pushed forward to form the Asia Infrastructure Investment Bank (AIIB) with 56 other founding shareholders.[19] The newly formed bank would be funding many infrastructure projects within its member countries. One such plan is the famous "one belt one road" initiative (一带一路), where China seeks to revive the Silk Road as its signature foreign policy initiative by connecting Asia to Europe in terms of infrastructures such as ports (Khorgos Gateway), roads, railways (China–Kyrgyzstan–Uzbekistan railway) and even pipelines (Central Asia–China gas pipeline). *Fun fact: The belt part actually refers to the physical road from China all the way through Europe to somewhere up north in Scandinavia. On the other hand, the road is actually the maritime Silk Road, shipping lanes from China to Venice.*[20]

Things are also heating up in the other parts of Asia beyond China. One area that has been much talked about is high-speed rail projects in the ASEAN space. Malaysia and Singapore have already signed a bilateral agreement for the high-speed rail project between their capitals, Kuala Lumpur and Singapore. This project is for a rail network of 350 km, not chump change.[21] Earlier in the same year, Indonesia also had plans for their very own high-speed rail network within Java. China is pushing for a Pan-Asia railway network that would connect Singapore to Kunming, China by rail, passing by all major cities along the way, from Myanmar to Vietnam.

All these investments in transport infrastructure do not just benefit material and construction firms. In the larger scale of things, infrastructure investments, if done well, have long-term economic benefits throughout the country. Two hours caught in the jam in downtown Jakarta could be better spent doing more productive tasks. Moreover, the lifeline for any businesses, especially when it comes to attracting foreign investments, is the state of the country's infrastructure.

It is not just the governments who are pushing for more infrastructure within the region. Companies such as the State Grid Corporation of China are also coming up with grand plans for a global integrated infrastructure future. State Grid Corp is the largest electrical company in the world, with revenue of more than US$300 billion in a year. The company has a bold plan to create a global power network that would connect the world's electrical grid together, and create a super grid enabling a market for countries to trade electricity frictionlessly. The plan would cost an expected US$50 trillion, and harnesses energy from Arctic winds and equatorial sunlight.[22]

Although all these plans could face huge political and social challenges before coming to fruition, nevertheless it gives us a glimpse of what the future might hold for Asia.

With the macro-economic and demographic themes favouring Asia thoroughly discussed, we will now head all the way to the ground level to see the other key factors in play when it comes to navigating Asia's investing waters. And we will start off with an oft-mentioned topic when it comes to publicly listed companies in these areas: shareholder structure.

Corporate Governance in Asia

Corporate governance is a guide to how a company should function. In countries like the USA, corporate governance might refer to guidelines on ethical behaviour, environmental concerns and shareholder welfare. The culture of having good corporate governance requirements in place is not exactly the same in Asia. And some investors foreign to Asia have learned this the hard way.

Of course, we do see improvements in this area. There are plenty of well-run companies in Asia that practise good corporate governance. However, as an investor in Asia, we believe that it is worth your time to know what exactly you are dealing with in order to prevent any unnecessary surprises. And the best way to kick-start this topic is through an understanding of ownership structures.

In Asia, it matters to know who is running the show, how, and why they do things in certain ways.

Shareholder Structure

Families still play huge roles in the corporate world in Asia. Many listed companies are majority-owned and managed by the founding families. With the decisions of a major shareholder able to influence a company, an understanding of the company's shareholding structure as part of our investment checklist is absolutely essential in these parts of the world.

Who Has Got Your Back?

At this point, we would like to steer away from quantitative concerns and towards the qualitative issue of knowing "who's got your back", an especially important point in Asia. In most developed markets, a 5% stake in a large-cap company could possibly place you as a majority shareholder. But here in Asia, it's an entirely different ball game.

It is not uncommon to find a controlling shareholder among large publicly listed entities in Asia. In cases of national interest, the government could be that major shareholder. Concerns with regard to the nation's demand for energy, food, healthcare and transport definitely fall under the government's jurisdiction.

Other than government institutions, Asia has also been home to many powerful families whose influence could potentially influence the future of not only the companies itself, but also the respective industries. Joe Studwell's *Asian Godfathers* had a comprehensive collection of some of Southeast Asia's most influential families.[23]

- Several of these godfathers called Singapore home, such as the Lee family, with interests in Oversea-Chinese Banking Corporation Limited, the Wee Family of United Overseas Bank Limited and the Kwek family of City Development Limited and Hong Leong Group.
- In Indonesia, the Salim Family controlled a wide industry of businesses through their main holding vehicle First Pacific Company Limited. The Riady family also stood out, with the control of Lippo Group, which counts OUE Limited and First Real Estate Investment Trust among its assets.
- Next, for Hong Kong, Li Ka-shing, Hong Kong's superman, has influences through his control of CK Hutchison Holdings Limited. Stanley Ho can also be considered as one of the power players in Asia, with his influence as a casino magnate.
- It is also notable that many families operate conglomerates with interests in many different industries. One prominent example is the Kuok Family, led by billionaire Robert Kuok. The group operates in the commodities, shipping, properties, logistics and even hospitality industries through its stakes in Wilmar International Limited, PPB Berhad, Kerry Group and Shangri-la Asia Limited.

Investors interested in Asia need to be aware of this characteristic of many companies here. This is because investing in a company with a large shareholder who is the key manager of the company means that minority investors are subject to the goodwill of the manager. We need to understand that we are not entering into a typical 50/50 share type of a business relationship. As minority shareholders, we are more like silent partners.

Again, we would point out that we do not feel that a company with a large majority shareholder is necessary negative – not at all. Our intention is to highlight the importance of being aware of whom you are associating with. An influential shareholder is a double-edged sword. If we manage to find the good ones with a good value proposition, all we need to do is to hang on for the ride – of course, at a reasonable price!

Given enough time, we believe that all this might change. Looking at developed markets such as Western Europe and the United States of America, they also started out with many family-owned entities in the past. As businesses matured and diversified, these family-owned entities became more investment-focused, gradually passing operational control over to professional managers, in turn developing a more-diversified shareholder base.

In Asia, Singapore-listed Oversea-Chinese Banking Corporation ("OCBC") comes to mind. In terms of asset size, OCBC (2015) was the second-largest financial services group in Southeast Asia. Established in 1919,[24] the group has a long history and its key founding family, through the Lee Foundation, is still one of its largest shareholders today. Over the years, the approach of the Lee Foundation has led to it becoming a professionally managed company, with the family predominantly functioning as an investor. In 2016, about 72.2% of the company was held in the hands of the public.[25]

Morten Bennedsen and Joseph Fan's *The Family Business Map* highlighted family firms as the dominant type of business in most Asian countries. A study covering 27 countries found that families controlled slightly over 50% of publicly traded firms, with an average market cap of over $500 million. In the US, family ownerships were present in one-third of the 500 largest firms. In Europe, it was almost half. And, as expected, Asia took the lead, with estimates indicating that over two-thirds of large business groups in India, Indonesia, Hong Kong, Malaysia, Singapore and Thailand are family-controlled.[26]

Let's look at one of Malaysia's largest conglomerates – Genting Berhad ("Genting"), with a market cap of over RM29.0 billion (USD7.0 billion) in 2016. Despite the large size of the company, Genting is still effectively led by the Lim family. Led by Tan Sri Lim Kok Thay, the Lim family, with an interest of at least 39.76% in Genting, had considerable influence over the Genting group of companies, such as Genting Plantations Berhad, Genting Malaysia Berhad and Genting Singapore PLC.[27] For instance, let's look at Genting's 52.89%-owned Singapore-listed subsidiary – Genting Singapore PLC.[28] Even though the Lim family might only have an effective interest of about 21% in Genting Singapore, they could be deemed interested in a higher percentage of the company's shares due to this structure. This means that the Genting group of companies are no easy pickings for activist investors.

With the holding company structure, the ultimate shareholder could have more influence, bringing new meaning to the term "top-down management". Therefore, it pays for us to appreciate who's really running the show.

And Links Aren't Just Linear

Just like life, relationships between companies are not that straight-forward. Company structures in Asia can be brought to a whole new level. *Kabushiki mochiai* (mutual aid shareholdings), more commonly known as cross-shareholdings, became famous in Japan after World War II till the 1990s.[29] Beginning as a structure intended to provide business stability, over time it may have led to exclusionary, anti-competitive business practices, possibly contributing to Japan's "lost decade(s)".

Cross-shareholding is a situation where a publicly traded com-pany owns shares in another publicly traded company. In short, listed companies own each other. A key concern for investors regarding this relationship is the inter-dependency of the publicly listed companies involved and the effect this has on valuing these companies. Imagine two listed entities where A owns 50% of B and B owns 50% of A (Figure 3.1). With such a significant position, the valuation of both companies is inter-dependent. If you were to solely rely on market valuation for your valuation, this could go on all day.

By itself, we don't think that such a structure is negative. For a real-life example, let's look at Singapore-listed Jardine Matheson Holdings Limited and Jardine Strategic Holdings Limited, both part of the Jardine Group. Controlled by the Keswick family, the group has leading businesses in the fields of engineering, construc-tion, mining and even agribusiness. To provide some background, after incurring heavy debts post-defence of Hongkong Land

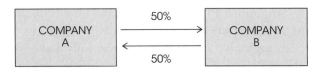

Figure 3.1   Cross shareholdings

Holdings Limited, the Jardine Group established this shareholding structure (Figure 3.2) in the 1980s to thwart potential hostile takeovers.[30,31]

Even with their cross-shareholdings structure, the Jardine Group have been good stewards of capital and fair to minority shareholders over the long term. In addition to their shareholding arrangement, the group is also notable for not playing by norms when it comes to their board structure. Yet those issues have not stopped investors from enjoying strong returns over the last decade. Over the past 10 years, all its main groups have produced an average total return of at least 15% a year.[32] In our books, this is definitely a positive example.

Now for an extreme case, we present to you one of the largest global conglomerates – Samsung Group. The group appears to have perfected this form of ownership, with one of the most complex company structures we have ever seen.[33]

From Figure 3.3, the de facto holding company – Samsung Everland Inc. (currently Cheil Industries Inc.) – owned 19.3% of Samsung Life Insurance Co Limited, which held 7.6% of Samsung Electronics Co Limited. In turn, Samsung Electronics held 37.5% of Samsung Card Co Limited, which held a 5% stake back in Samsung Everland Inc. And this was just a small portion of the structure. The shareholdings literally went a full circle. A 2013 Korea Fair Trade Commission reported that although the Lee Family's combined stake was only 1.53% in the Group, they controlled about 49.7% of the Group's 74 companies through the web of cross-shareholding![34]

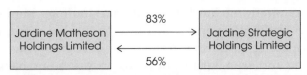

Figure 3.2   Jardine Matheson Holdings Limited & Jardine Strategic Holdings Limited Shareholding

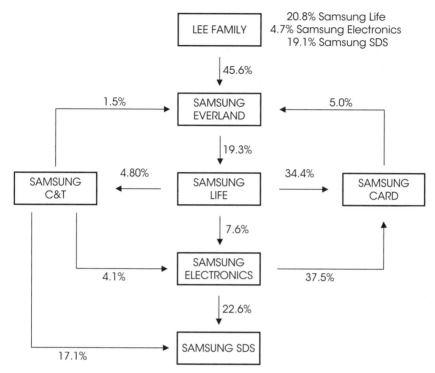

Figure 3.3   Samsung Group Structure from the *Wall Street Journal*

Succession

In Asia, control is key. This issue was further aggravated by a cultural reluctance to tackle the topic of succession planning, with mention of it seen as taboo. The younger generation might be seen as disrespectful, or even overly ambitious, if succession issues came up during conversations.

Although some successful Asian businesses are no longer in the management of the first-generation family members, the patriarch typically continues to have a certain degree of influence. Unfortunately (or fortunately), companies can survive for centuries but their founders cannot. With some well-known billionaires like Stanley Ho approaching the century mark, succession is a key concern, especially as his family feud was one of the most public we have observed in recent years.

Due to his complex family structure, his is a fascinating case. Most people would have their hands full with just one wife, but not Stanley Ho. With four families, three surviving wives and 16 surviving children, Stanley Ho had a lot on his plate.[35] With his family feud publicly played out for all to see, it is a clear illustration that succession was definitely not an easy process.

In the research paper "Succession: The Roles of Specialized Assets and Transfer Costs", a study was conducted over 217 succession cases from Hong Kong, Taiwan and Singapore, and found that succession tended to coincide with tremendous destruction of value. Over a period from 1987 to 2005, this study reported an average negative 56% net-of-market buy-and-hold (market-adjusted) stock return in the five-year period, and negative 16% when compounded three years before the succession year.[36] With a number of Asian tycoons approaching their golden years, this could be an interesting investment angle to look at. The Chinese proverb 富不过三代, meaning "wealth does not pass three generations", comes to mind.

Yet not all companies are unprepared for successions. Succession transition in blue-chip companies like Singapore-listed Oversea-Chinese Banking Corporation Limited ("OCBC") and Hong Kong-listed Li & Fung Limited ("L&F"), showed us that it is not impossible for a publicly listed Asian firm to move past one generation of managers.

The key aspects of their success relative to some of their peers were their greater acceptance of change, losing complete management control and willingness in engaging external management. Via their extensive global network, L&F is recognised as the world's leader in supply chain management, with a top line of US$19 billion.[37] The company is currently managed by the fourth generation, with Spencer Fung having taken over the reins of this juggernaut in 2014.[38] If we step back, we can see that L&F is more than just one company; from Figure 3.4, we can see that the entire group consists of much more.[39]

L&F hasn't been shy with engaging external talent. In May 2011, Bruce Rockowitz took over from William Fung as L&F's CEO. Rockowitz had been an executive director of the group since 2001 and president since 2004. Rockowitz joined the group after a company he co-founded was acquired by L&F.[40] And after the fourth-generation family member, Spencer Fung, took over as CEO of L&F in July 2014, Rockowitz was appointed as CEO of the newly listed

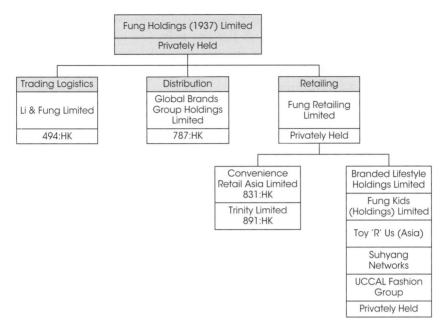

Figure 3.4   Fung Group Structure

Global Brands Group Holdings Limited. In an NUS Business School interview, William Fung reinforced the importance of engaging professional management by highlighting that unless ownership and management are separated, it would be tough to transit into a professional management era.[41]

However, with 65% of Asian firms still choosing a family member for succession, this is far from the norm in Asia.[42] The key hurdle isn't cultural, but rather an issue of trust. In just the past 100 years, the political situation within most Asian countries can at best be described as volatile. In Thailand alone, since the Siamese revolution of 1932, there has been a total of 11 other successful coups, including the latest in 2014, an astonishing one coup every seven years![43]

Basically, the volatile circumstances in Asia might have led to an environment that rewarded discretion and tight control. This strategy might have paid huge dividends in the past, but a fresh approach could lead to greater abundance if Asia needs to move forward.

We are not implying that a controlling shareholder is necessarily a negative. It all depends on the shareholder. If the controlling shareholder has a stellar record, we are all for it. If we are able to invest into such a company with the "right" business and at the right price, all we have to do is stay for the ride. On the other hand, if we as minority shareholders are not treated fairly, given the tens of thousands of listed entities here in Asia, there might be better opportunities for us out there.

Ultimately, we believe that action speaks louder than words. Instead of focusing on how well a company writes its corporate governance statement or how many independent directors sit on the Board, we find that the integrity, results and track record of the management is a much better way to assess the nature of a company. With that said, transparency and disclosure do make our job easier.

Disclosure and Transparency

If you had to describe publicly listed companies in Asia with two words, "disclosure" and "transparency" might not be the first two words that come to mind.

In 2014, *The Economist* published an article exploring the issue of where politically connected businessmen or women were most likely to prosper.[44] It was mentioned that successful businessmen had got rich through connections, mainly operating in rent-heavy industries. Rent-heavy sectors are industries involved in licensing or requiring heavy state involvement. These sectors would then be vulnerable to monopolistic practices. Typical examples of such industries include casinos, agricultural, mining, infrastructure, defence, and energy operations.

From the list, seven of the top 10 countries came from Asia, with four from Southeast Asia, implying that many businesses in the region still thrive due to good connections. No wonder people tend to have an impression that quality disclosure and transparency are not the strong suits of companies in Asia.

With this as a backdrop, we might wonder how such a preconception came about. One of the possible reasons could be due to the Asian markets' relatively closed structure. This inevitably led market participants to favour internal markets over external markets for resource allocation. The low transparency and high ownership concentration reflect the desire to protect information related to rent-seeking activities and could have also contributed to the perception of lower disclosure practices, thus creating a loop.

But, hey, it is just human nature to only want to do business with people you trust, through word of mouth or as some call it "*guanxi*". Think about it: if there were two proposals of the same quality and the only difference was that you had worked with one of the guys before, most of us tend to stick with the person that we have dealt with before; it is just human nature. There's absolutely nothing wrong with that. Of course, it goes without saying that this guy did not screw things up the last time; connections alone cannot help if the guy cannot get the job done.

All said, we just have to keep in mind the difference in culture and way of doing business in Asia; investors need to be aware of how to detect these issues by themselves when investing in Asia.

And things are not as bad as they seem. There are publicly listed companies in Asia, with a pretty good standard of disclosure and transparency. When we talk about disclosure and transparency, of course we do not expect companies to reveal their trade secret – if Yum! Brands don't go around disclosing the 11 herbs and spices used in Kentucky Fried Chicken, it does not mean that they aren't transparent enough. Ironically, if they do disclose it, then it might be a problem for shareholders. But how do we know what is enough?

When it comes to a company's annual reports and shareholder presentations, a good gauge of decent disclosure and transparency is that after going through a couple of the company's annual report and presentations, you should be able to understand at least:

- How did the company make money, or why did the company lose money?
- How did the entire industry perform?
- Who are the company's competitors and how did the company stack up to them?
- Did the company walk the talk?
- What does the company own, and what does the company owe?

To show that we are not kidding you, we have three companies with publications (annual report and presentations) that check most of these boxes.

Company 1 – CapitaLand Mall Trust

In general, we have found that REITs have rather high standards of transparency and disclosure – yes, even in Asia. And which better REIT to look at than CapitaLand Mall Trust ("CMT"), the first REIT listed on the Singapore Exchange?

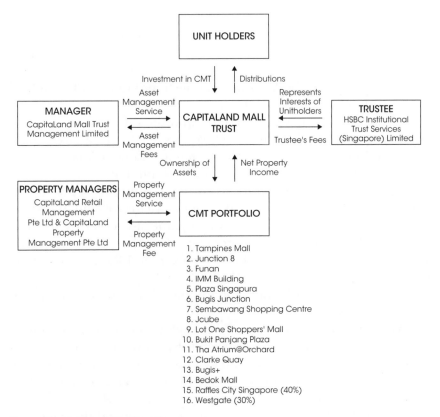

Figure 3.5   CapitaLand Mall Trust Structure

With simple to understand assets and operations, a REIT is the perfect example to kick off our analysis. This is because virtually all the information needed to understand REITs is publicly available. In layman's terms, a REIT is a company (structured as a trust) which owns and operates highly visible properties (a building does not just vanish overnight) and earns money from rental income.

With just this overview alone (Figure 3.5),[45] we can get a decent picture of how CMT functions.

- CMT has 16 properties in its portfolio.
- These 16 properties are managed by property managers that collect property management fees in return. Think of them as people you pay to get you the best deal without directly dealing with the tenants.

- At the REIT level, the managers (normally linked to the sponsor) are the Board of Directors. Like any other company, they set the strategic direction of the REIT and manage the assets and liabilities for the benefit of unitholders.
- With the basis of a REIT being a trust deed between the Trustee and REIT manager, a trustee is required. In brief, a trustee is there to protect the unitholders.
- Finally, in the case of REITs, unitholders are the equivalent of shareholders.

With a basic understanding of how a REIT works, let's see how well CMT fared when it came to the quality of their publicly available documents.

Asset Type   Not all REITs are created equal; each has its pros and cons. Think of a REIT's property as the underlying operating business of any other company out there. For example, Raffles Medical Group Limited, a healthcare service company due to the nature of its operations, is a totally different company to Sembcorp Marine Limited, a marine and offshore engineering solutions company.

Although there are many types of REITs out there, these three stand out:

- commercial – Tower Real Estate Investment Trust
- retail – SPH Real Estate Investment Trust
- industrial – Cache Logistics Trust.

They could even be like The Link Real Estate Investment Trust, with a mixture of retail, offices, fresh markets and even car parks in their portfolio. In CMT's case, with 16 shopping malls in Singapore, it is clear that CMT is a retail REIT.[46]

Together with the breakdown of their trust structure, we know exactly what industry they operate in (urban and suburban shopping malls), what they own (from % interest to strata lots) and where their properties are (even if we don't go down personally, Google maps are really clear these days). Additionally, CMT also had a write-up of their 14.55% stake in CapitaLand Retail China Trust – a China shopping mall REIT with ten shopping malls in China.

In CMT's annual report, the following were disclosed:

- top 10 tenants (tenant name, sector and percentage gross rental income)
- breakdown of tenant mix by sector (F&B, fashion, supermarket, etc.)
- breakdown of gross revenue and net property income by mall
- occupancy rate by mall
- tenant sales
- occupancy cost
- shopper traffic
- summary of lease renewal and lease by mall
- portfolio lease expiry for the year by mall.

CMT even went down to the level of the respective malls, with a detailed breakdown of their location, size, acquisition year, purchase price, tenant mix and even the number of car parks! With the quality of information at hand, we can get a pretty good idea of CMT without even speaking to anyone.

Furthermore, CMT's Annual Report also has a treat, with an "Independent Retail Market Overview" report prepared by a professional consulting firm and a section titled "Singapore REIT Sector" detailing not only the local, but also the regional outlook and state of the REIT industry.

Operational Track Record   When we talk about track record, other than profitability (a given), we also must see if the REIT walks the talk when it comes to project execution.

What we mean by this is: if they say that they are going ahead with an acquisition, asset enhancement initiative ("AEI") or even a disposal, we have to look back on how well they followed through. In FY2015,[47] CMT accomplished the following:

- IMM Building: Phase Two AEI completed
- Clarke Quay: completed reconfiguring
- Plaza Singapura: ongoing rejuvenation works
- Tampines Mall: completed education hub.

So how do we judge if the company was on schedule? Simple. Just refer to CMT's presentation in the earlier year – FY2014 under their "Looking Forward" section.[48] To their credit, CMT walked the talk.

Yield   For most investors looking at REITs, the dividend yield is their point of focus. To calculate dividend yield, you need two numbers – dividend per share and market price. Other than just reporting the dividend yield as a single number – 5.8% based on CMT's closing price on 31 December 2015,[49] just in case we want to work it out ourselves, CMT took it a step further by displaying its monthly closing unit price.

Investors looking for income-producing assets will also want to find out how CMT stacked up against other local instruments like government bonds, fixed deposits and even the Straits Times Index. And CMT did not disappoint (Figure 3.6).[50]

Although dividend yields are a key consideration for REITs, they are not the be all and end all. *Note:* Your *dividend yield is pegged to your purchase price and not the market price; the one pegged to market price is the current dividend yield.*

Another operational yield-related metric is property yield – net property income (NPI) divided by the property value. To simplify things, property yield shows how much a REIT gets from its property. For example, a REIT with an NPI of S$400 million and S$8 billion in property has a property yield of 5%. You should be able to get what you need from their Annual Report.

Company 2 – Samsonite International S.A.

Now if you travel frequently, here is a company you should be familiar with – Samsonite International S.A. (Samsonite). Samsonite is the world's largest travel luggage company, with brands like Samsonite®, American Tourister® and more recently Tumi®. In their Chief

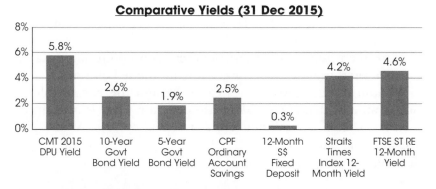

Figure 3.6   CapitaLand Mall Trust Comparative Yields

Executive Officer's words, their plan for Samsonite is to transform the company from being "a great travel luggage company which also does some bags", to being "the leading global lifestyle company".[51] And their US$1.8 billion acquisition of Tumi Holdings, Inc., announced in 2016, was a step in that direction.[52]

Detailed explanation of business   A good yardstick to understand a company is to find out how it makes money:

- What does it sell?
- Where does it sell?
- Who does it sell to?

Right off the bat, Samsonite's Management Discussion and Analysis (MD&A) answers most of these questions. Bear in mind that, regulatory-wise, the company might be going above and beyond what is required of them. Just in case you missed it in Note 4 of the company's Notes to the Consolidated Financial Statements, the MD&A includes a pretty detailed summary, together with the revenue breakdown of both the respective product lines as well as sales from their respective geographical regions. When we are talking about the geographical region, Samsonite don't just stop at Asia, but go all the way down to the country level, and even to the products that led to key impacts over the year.

Beyond the top line, the MD&A also includes a discussion of their expenses, not only showing the changes in their key income statement items (cost of sales, distribution expenses, marketing expenses, general and administrative expenses, etc.) but, more importantly, the reasons behind them. And why is this important?

Stating that a company's net profit is up by 10%, 20% or 30% is always nice. But is it helpful? Does it help us to assess the company? Without understanding the "why" behind the change, these are nothing more than numbers. Otherwise, there is no point knowing the price of everything without appreciating the value behind it.

Without understanding the reason behind the rise or fall, we won't be able to adequately evaluate the company. Here is an example.

In 2015, Company A's net profit increased by 50%. At face, that looks amazing. However, if you look into the notes and find out the following:

- Company A sold one of its only two operating business; and
- Company A's other operating business is not doing too well

then you might think again. If you were expecting Company A to repeat this sort of growth next year – well, the odds are that you will be disappointed. Remember, always start with "Why?"

Industry Analysis   If a company delivered an operating margin of 10%, is that good? Well, it depends on the business they do and how well are they doing in relation to their peers.

At first glance, you might consider a company with an arbitrary operating margin of 50% as a company with exceptional fundamentals. But what if its peers have higher margins, and are doing it with much lower leverage? How would you view this company now?

Hence, we have to consider how a company does compared to those in the same industry. This in itself is more than enough reason for us to read the annual reports of the company's competitors. First, to know what the company is up against. And second, more importantly, to know whether the company is a snake oil salesman. No company is an island. Of course, there are exceptions for those once-in-a-lifetime companies, but that's a story for another day. *Side note: Any company with an operating margin of over 50% is worth at least a look at.*

To this end, in their 2015 annual report, not only did Samsonite under their "Director's Report" include a section on their competition, they also had a rather detailed write-up on the global luggage industry. In this section, not only was the global environment discussed, but Samsonite took it a step further by going through each of their major markets both by product (travel bag, casual bag and business bag) and by their major geographic market (Asia, North America, Europe and Latin America).

For investors like us, this is some quality information right there.

Useful Information and Financial Metrics   With all that is said, numbers do matter. With the annual report, companies do have to follow a set reporting procedure when it comes to the financial statements and the corresponding notes. Working off this as the starting point, we should have a decent overall view of the company in terms of its financial health and performance. We should be able to tell how much revenue the company made, the net profit level, how much cash they have as well as how much they owed.

Beyond that, it is up to the company to help us along the way. In Samsonite's case, other than the usual year-on-year comparison of financial metrics such as revenue, operating profit and adjusted earnings per share, the company included three useful operational ratios – Average inventory turnover days, Turnover days of trade and other receivables and Turnover days of trade and other payables.[53] Although we are able to calculate all of these from the notes to the financial statements, this does save us some time. *Side note: Take note of the line items used, i.e. trade receivables or trade receivables and other receivables.*

Furthermore, Samsonite also reported an operational metric specific to retail operations: same store sales growth. This metric educates us as to how the company's existing operated retail stores (among those that were operational in the previous year) have performed over the year. And in a similar fashion, this was done for each major geographical segment.

Company 3 – AirAsia Berhad

Low-cost carriers have been growing dramatically for the past decade in Southeast Asia. One of the companies that have led this growth is Malaysia-listed AirAsia Berhad ("AirAsia"). Reading the annual reports of AirAsia would give you great insights on what it takes to win in the airline industry.

Useful industry-performance metrics   Apart from providing details on its past performances and how the company plans to continue growing, and other conventional financial metrics, AirAsia went a step further by providing investors with a comprehensive set of operational data commonly used within the industry.[54]

For instance, AirAsia constantly reports its cost per available seat kilometre, a key metric that the industry uses to compare the operational cost of airlines. AirAsia has been one of the lowest-cost providers in the industry for many years.

Other useful data points include AirAsia's:

- guests carried
- load factor
- total fleet
- number of destinations
- social media performance
- key milestones
- and even the market shares for its main markets (Malaysia, Thailand, Indonesia, Philippines and India) in the form of easy-to-understand infographics.

This was certainly a great touch by management to allow investors to understand the company better. We find this degree of transparency and openness a strong positive.

Experiment with a new medium to connect with investors AirAsia is one of the few companies which we have encountered that have tried to connect with investors using new technology. For example, AirAsia has an investor relations mobile app which allows investors to stay in touch with the company and its progress. Investors can easily find the latest information or events about the company instead of searching through records within the stock exchange, which are usually packed with information from thousands of other companies.

These are some of the features of companies going out of their way to educate investors about their business.

Now that we have touched on the positive cases, let's move on to the other end of the spectrum.

Now for Some Not-So-Positive Stuff. . .

On the not-so-positive end of the spectrum are companies with more-questionable practices. Given the weaker disclosure of Asian firms, many companies can hide questionable practices from investors and regulators. Maybe as a function of such weaker disclosure and transparency in the market, certain questionable activities are unavoidable. Thus, for investors looking at Asia, it is very important to learn how to detect and, more importantly, avoid the red flags.

Examples of such cases include the S-Chips fiasco and the small-cap saga, which both happened in Singapore. S-Chips is a common term for Singapore-listed companies with operations mainly in China. Well-known cases within S-Chips include:

- FerroChina Limited (delisted): Had a market capitalisation of more than S$2 billion at its peak in 2007 but defaulted on its loans and was forced to delist in 2010.[55]
- Oriental Century Limited (delisted):[56] CEO quits after allegedly inflating company's cash holdings and secretly channelling away the funds.[57]
- Eratat Lifestyle Limited (suspended): Even with a huge cash pile and low debt, they defaulted on their interest payments.[58]

Of course, not all S-Chip companies are shady. But with these high-profile cases, many of the remaining S-Chips ended up trading at persistently low valuations, with investors wary of companies with words like "China" and "Sino" in their company name.

Here is one case study on how you can learn to detect questionable behaviours within a company.

Case Study: Eratat Lifestyle Limited

Investing in a company with low valuation has its risk. One such risk is being caught investing in a value trap. Typically, a value trap is a company that appears "cheap" from quantitative screens. Some of these quantitative screens involved looking at the valuation of the company through its price-to-book (P/B) or price-to-earnings ratio (P/E).

However, things are not always straightforward. Investors need to understand that if a company is persistently trading "cheaply", there might be reasons for it. Generally, some common reasons are that:

1. The company is no longer growing or is in a sunset industry.
2. The company is seeing its business decline and has no concrete plans to turn around its operation.
3. Its management is extremely secretive in its operation and not open to the concerns of shareholders.

Here is a story of how we detected rather questionable behaviour in one such S-Chip company. Listed in 2008, Eratat Lifestyle Limited ("Eratat Lifestyle") started out as a sports apparel retailer in the People's Republic of China ("China") before its IPO. Interestingly, immediately post-IPO, the company decided to become a retailer for menswear.[59] This by itself should be a red flag to take note of. A sudden change in core operations is always something to watch for, as it is an extremely unusual move for a company if its traditional business was doing well. For example, can you imagine if one day Nike announces that it is closing down all its sportswear business and transforming itself into a menswear company?

In 2012, Eratat Lifestyle looked to have an extremely strong balance sheet, with a cash balance of RMB357 million with total liabilities of RMB74 million.[60] Furthermore, the company was also a consistent dividend payer. Placing things in perspective, Eratat Lifestyle's Net Cash position (Cash minus Liabilities) as at Q3 2013 was about S$80 million, but its market capitalisation stood around the S$50 million range.[61] What did this mean?

Theoretically, if someone bought the company for S$50 million, he would not only get back his investment from the company's cash holding of

Case Study *(Continued)*

S$80 million, he would also get the business for free. In layman's terms, you are getting "paid" to invest in the company! However, we need to ask ourselves, why was there such a huge discount to this company? It seems too good to be true; basically, what's the catch?

This was by no means an overnight downhill spiral. Things got out of hand way earlier. Fortunately for us, Eratat Lifestyle had more than one red flag. Looking at their financial statement in their Annual Report 2012, a few of these red flags were hanging out in plain sight. For starters, its trade receivables were over 50% of its revenue. For apparel companies to have trade receivable days outstanding of over six months is quite unusual, and thus raised a red flag for us. This meant that on average, the company took over half a year just to get paid from customers. Another sign was their surprisingly low inventory levels for an apparel company. These two factors alone highlighted to us that this company was more questionable than it seemed.

Next, a major alarm bell rang. In July 2013, Eratat Lifestyle completed the issuance of RMB134 million-worth of non-convertible bonds in July 2013. The bond's interest payment was 12.5% and was issued at 25% below par.[62] Even before accounting for the warrants, its creditor, a subsidiary of the Hong Kong-listed Sun Hung Kai & Co. Limited was getting an effective return of close to 30% on the bond (annual interest of 16.75% plus 11% annualised if the bond was redeemed at par). This was a very expensive loan for a company with a seemingly stellar balance sheet and a profitable business. The cherry on top of this epic sundae was the fact that Eratat Lifestyle reported a huge cash pile of RMB545 million[63] when this exercise was proposed. That was what we would call a *screaming red flag*.

And, true enough, things did not end well. In January 2014, Eratat Lifestyle defaulted on just its first few bond interest payments.[64] Even after a month, the Board was still unable to verify the state of the company's cash balance. The company has been suspended since then. After receiving Securities Investors Association of Singapore's Investors' Choice Award for Corporate Governance, Eratat Lifestyle was suspended just two months later.[65] The irony.

Unfortunately, the story of Eratat Lifestyle is not unique in the market. That is why investors need to learn to protect themselves by digging deeper into the business of the company, instead of relying solely on just quantitative screens when making investment decisions. If we were to leave you with a quote at the end of this segment, it would be to "Never take things at face value, and always ask why."

"Smart" Money Gets Hit Too

If you think that only small retail investors get hit with such issues, think again. Here's one of the UK's best-known fund managers – Anthony Bolton, the manager of Fidelity Special Situations fund from 1979 to 2007. £1,000 in his fund over the entire 28 years snowballed to around £147,000.[66] Yet Bolton is still human, and not immune to investments going awry.

Bolton was a contrarian, specialising in small and medium-sized companies. Following a trip to China, he came out of retirement in 2010 to launch the Fidelity China Special Situations investment trust. Performance-wise, it would be safe to assume that he did not have the best of times during his four years heading the fund. Bolton's subsequent decision to stop managing the fund highlighted the fact that even the most seasoned of investors can fall prey to ambiguous financial practices.

One of his high-profile experiences included an investment into China Integrated Energy, Inc. which lost 90% of its market value in 2011 following accusations of fraud and the resignation of its auditors.[67] In summary, his understanding of corporate governance appeared to differ from the local environment. And this caused a mismatch in expectations.

Furthermore, fund managers weren't the only ones affected. Even large businesses, in a bid to expand their mining machinery market in China, suffered this fate. A recent case was Caterpillar Inc.'s 2012 acquisition of ERA Mining Machinery Limited, the holding company for Zhengzhou Siwei Mechanical & Electrical Equipment Manufacturing Co Limited. Less than a year after the deal, Caterpillar announced the discovery of a "deliberate, multi-year coordinated accounting misconduct" related to the acquired firm. This led to a US$580 million write-down, 86% of their purchase price.[68] You could say that they got bulldozed.

It's not that Asian companies are less trustworthy *per se*. Remember Hewlett-Packard's US$8.8 billion write-downs of Autonomy in 2012? This was almost 80% of their acquisition cost of $11.1 billion just a year earlier.[69] Bad things can happen everywhere, it's just that it pays to pay more attention in certain places. Hence, it pays for any investor, big or small, to have a certain level of scepticism when investing in Asia.

Putting it bluntly, it's naïve for investors to simply implement the Western value system when investing in Asia. We certainly are not condoning fraudulent behaviour of any sort. With studies done that positively correlate corporate transparency to market returns, we ourselves welcome a fair and transparent reporting framework in Asia. But at the end of the day, like any market, the stock market operates under a *caveat emptor* environment. Thus, we always, always have to do our due diligence.

At the end of the day even with all that happened, Anthony Bolton was still positive on China's prospects, with mention of great investment opportunities there.[70] Considering his experience, that says something about Asia.

Government – The Elephant in the Room

Other than issues of corporate governance, another challenge faced by investors in Asia is political risk. In many Asian countries, the government might have a sizeable effect on how things pan out. In many cases, they are still the largest investors in their respective countries. Asia is also home to some of the largest sovereign wealth funds, here are a few of them:

- Singapore: With a net portfolio value of S$242 billion (2016), Temasek Holdings (Private) Limited, commonly characterised as a sovereign wealth fund, is also one of the largest investors in the stock market. It has substantial stakes in many Singapore-listed blue-chip companies, such as Singapore Airlines Limited, Singapore Telecommunications Limited and Keppel Corporation Limited.[71]
- Malaysia: Khazanah Nasional Berhad, the strategic investment fund of the Government of Malaysia, had a realisable asset value of RM150 billion (2015). The fund is also one of the largest investors in Malaysia, owning a major stake in some of the largest corporations in Malaysia. Its portfolio includes equity ownership in listed industry giants IHH Healthcare Berhad, Tenaga Nasional Berhad and CIMB Group Holdings Berhad.[72]
- Thailand: Likewise, Thailand Ministry of Finance is also an investor in publicly held companies. Its portfolio included a

substantial stake in PTT Public Company Limited – Thailand's major integrated oil and gas company[73] – as well as a controlling stake in Airports of Thailand Public Company.[74]

- China: Unlike most countries, where investment is done predominantly through a national wealth fund, China has many investment funds created by its state governments. The state funds have grown so much that many of the top publicly listed entities have some of the state government as their majority shareholders. Most of China's largest corporations are commonly known as State-owned Enterprise (SOE).

There are both pros and cons of the government being the major shareholder in companies you invest in. The key point to take home is to understand that at times, the government might prioritise national concerns over shareholder returns.

In cases when either the company operates in a regulated industry or where the government is the main shareholder, we must be aware that there might be occasions in the short term when the primary objective may not always be 100% profit-driven.

Case Study: SMRT Corporation Limited

As Singapore's first Mass Rapid Transit system provider, SMRT Corporation Limited ("SMRT") is one of the two main public transport operators in Singapore. It was also predominantly owned by Singapore's sovereign investment fund, with Temasek Holdings as its largest shareholder.[75] Over the years, SMRT also diversified into taxi and bus operations. Apart from its transportation services, SMRT generated additional revenue through renting out commercial shop space and advertising spaces within train stations and bus depots.

From 2004 to 2011, SMRT has been a consistent performer, with a return on equity averaging around 20%.[76] One reason could have been that SMRT operated in a duopoly-like environment. In Singapore, its only competitor was ComfortDelGro Corporation Limited. Together they provide a high-demand service with no other reasonable and affordable alternatives.

Transportation is a relatively simple and straightforward business to understand. After all, it is about moving people or goods from point A to B. However, operating in a highly regulated environment can cut both ways. On the bright side, there are high barriers to entry. On the flip side, its fare adjustments for its bus and train services are subjected to approval by

Case Study *(Continued)*

the Public Transport Council, which works closely with the Land Transport Authority of Singapore.

Let us rewind a few years to Singapore's 16th general election in 2011. The ruling party, the People's Action Party (PAP), had the poorest showing since independence. Not only did their vote share fall from 66.6% to 60.1%, it was also the first time that the PAP lost a Group Representation Constituency (GRC).[77,78] In instances when national interest might take precedence, government-linked entities like SMRT might be faced with a "catch-22". On one hand, they have to spend for capital improvement projects, while on the other, they could not unilaterally raise public transportation fares to offset these increases. And that appeared to be what happened to public transportation fares from late 2011 to early 2014.[79]

Faced with increasing operating costs but unable to raise its prices, SMRT was in a sticky situation. Since FY2011, its operating profit fell 57% from S$196 million to S$84 million in FY2014. From their segment breakdown, it was evident that their non-fare-based operations were subsidising their fare-based operations. Over this period, SMRT's fare-based operating profit fell from a profit of S$110 million all the way to a loss of S$25 million. And this was after accounting for the 18% increase in ridership from 604 million (2011) to 711 million (2014).[80] This might have been why SMRT had to explore non-core operations involving the rental of commercial and advertising spaces; more recently, SMRT even diversified into the property management business – Kallang Wave mall.

Eventually, things did turn for the better. However, SMRT's core fare-based operations were still dependent on government policy. In 2014, the Land Transport Authority announced a new public bus framework commencing in 2016, effectively changing Singapore's public bus service landscape.[81]

Before the proposed change, SMRT owned all the assets such as buses and depots. With the new model, the government proposed a privatisation model along the lines of the public bus service models present in London and Australia.[82] With the change, the government would own all bus infrastructure such as depots, as well as operating assets – buses. With this new model, the operators (SMRT) have to tender for routes to manage over a certain period. The operators would then get paid directly by the government for running the services, while 100% of fare revenue goes to the government.[83]

This transformed SMRT's bus business model completely. Its asset-heavy operation was changed into an asset-light operation with the direction of the government. With this, SMRT no longer needed to bear the heavy costs of upgrading the transportation infrastructure. From this, it was quite clear that

Case Study *(Continued)*

SMRT's "fate" is greatly dependent on the government policy. So was the value of the company.

The share price performance of SMRT was greatly influenced by the government policies. After SMRT started to experience declining revenue, its share price fell from a peak of S$2.31 (2010) to its lowest point of S$1.01. Only after signs of government intervention in 2014 did SMRT rebound back to the S$1.50 range. In November 2016, shareholders accepted the scheme of arrangement by Temasek Holdings to privatise and delist the company. Finally, in November 2016, after trying to balance public and private interests over SMRT's 16-year listing period, the major shareholder could have rationalised that it was probably time to delist SMRT to allow the rail operator to focus their attention on serving the public, without the distractions of being a listed company.[84]

The lesson here is that government policy in Asia can have a strong influence on the value of a company. Again, nothing too unusual about this; just remember that, when approaching government-linked entities, we just need to appreciate the local political situation as well as the issues at play.

Don't Bet Your House on Legal Prosecution

Another area for investors to look out for is the state of prosecution in the financial markets. And judging from what happened in the past, the level of prosecution might not be as strong as one might expect in Southeast Asia and China.

For starters, let's take a short look at some of the stock exchanges. The main markets of Malaysia[85] and Thailand[86] both have an independent stock exchange commission regulating their respective capital market. Whereas Indonesia and Singapore, on the other hand, allowed their respective exchanges to operate as self-regulatory organisations.[87] In reality, both systems have their own advantages and disadvantages; there is no single bulletproof system able to satisfy everyone.

In the case of self-regulatory organisations, it is even harder for the exchange to balance its role as both the market operator and regulator. As these exchanges operate as a for-profit entity, there might be tough situations which the exchanges need to handle very carefully in order to protect shareholder value and at the same time fulfill its duty as a regulator.

Case Study: Fountain View Development Berhad

In 2005, Dato' Chin Chan Leong ("Dato' Chin"), a former executive director of Fountain View Development Berhad ("Fountain View"), and his remisier, Hiew Yoke Lan ("Hiew"), were charged by the Securities Commission Malaysia, the regulator, for the manipulation of the company's stock between November 2003 and January 2004.[88]

During that 3-month period, the company's share price rose 200% from RM1.99 to RM6.05 per share, increasing the market cap of the company by about RM2 billion.[89]

In the absence of any business fundamental improvements, Fountain View's market capitalisation nearly tripled within three months! Even with considerable evidence, the case still dragged on for a protracted period of five years. It was only in 2010 that Dato' Chin eventually pleaded guilty to share manipulation.[90] Even then, it took another two years before Dato' Chin and Hiew were sentenced. Eventually, Fountain View was delisted from the exchange for failing to meet regulatory requirements.

How long does it take to prosecute?

Investors need to be aware that stock prices of some companies (predominantly small-capitalised and illiquid stocks) might be the potential go-to targets of such shady dealings. Unfortunately, prosecutions involving market manipulators do not arise that often and a typical prosecution of the parties involved might take years to complete. This is simply because in the absence of outright fraudulent activities, market manipulation is a rather tough nut to crack.

Furthermore, the eventual punishment meted out might not even be strong enough to act as a deterrent for future offenders. A classic example was the case involving a previously Bursa Malaysia-listed company, Fountain View Development Bhd.

The verdict?

Dato' Chin was fined only RM1.3 million and sentenced to a jail term of 13 months. Hiew had an even lighter sentence of RM1 million in fines and 10 months in jail. For manipulating the share of a company involving RM2 billion in market value, the combined fine of RM2.3 million was just 0.1% of the notional "illicit" gain,[91] akin to a slap on the wrist.

Often, the job of investing does not end at understanding and estimating the value of a company. In Asia, detecting dubious market activities is also a key part of an investor's job. *Side note: Even beyond Asia, this is a risk we do need to be aware of when investing.*

Activism and Shorting

Activism is a strategy whereby the investor proactively engages with management to unlock value. An activist investor normally starts by identifying a company with "trapped value". There are numerous reasons that could result in a company trading at a discount to its fair value, ranging from management being inefficient capital allocators, to conglomerates trading at a conglomerate discount, or even the straightforward case of mismanaged operations.

This is where the activist steps into the picture. By obtaining a sizeable stake in the company, this investor could get a seat at the proverbial table, allowing him access to the board and management to unlock this "trapped value". Sometimes, this might lead to hostile events such as removal of management or fighting for board seats in the company. This process could take months or years.

There are many famous and successful activist investors in the United States. Carl Icahn, Daniel Loeb and Bill Ackman are billionaire investors who made their wealth through activist investing in publicly listed corporations. But when we look at the Asian market, there is clearly a lack of such personalities. Why is this so?

A main reason for this phenomenon might be the shareholding structure, the high percentage of family-owned listed entities in Asia. Activist investors have a higher probability of success with diverse shareholding structures, especially those without a controlling shareholder. If there is already a controlling presence, it might be extremely difficult for any independent activist investor to push forward changes, regardless of their merits.

And we think that this applies to the low popularity of shorting in Asia as well. Up till now, we have only been discussing the long side. On the other side of the investing coin we have short selling, or the sale of shares not owned by you. How this works is that, after borrowing the shares from a broker, you sell them, hoping for a price decline. That way you can buy the shares back at a lower price to return to your lender, with the difference being your profit. For a short position, the dynamics of the game are totally reversed. Basically, for a short seller, your potential downside is unlimited while the upside is capped by your purchase price.

Be it legacy or cultural reasons, many Asian listed companies are still controlled by the founding family. This creates a problem for activist investment because it is not that easy to win a proxy fight against the major shareholders or in cases where the families are the management. In more mature markets like the United States, a 5% stake might get you a seat at the table. In Asia, by contrast, an ownership of 5% secures you a place on the top 20 shareholder list in the Annual Reports and might get you noticed. But to successfully outvote the majority shareholder is a whole different ball game. Practically speaking, you might not be in the best position if you are up against someone with a 51% stake in a company.

However, this doesn't mean to say that you can't make your voice heard. In Asia, hostile takeovers or high-profile boardroom tussles don't appear in the papers every day. Yet there might be another way to get your voice heard as an activist investor in Asia. The in-your-face style of doing things might not be that well received here; we prefer taking the high road, working together with the company instead of taking them head-on.

Primarily written for institutional owners who are asset owners and asset managers, we found that a piece titled "The Singapore Stewardship Principles for Responsible Investors" by Stewardship Principles Working Group provides an interesting way of being an activist.[92] This piece was succinctly summarised with the following seven points:

1. Take a stand on stewardship – Responsible investors establish and articulate their policies on their stewardship.
2. Know your investment: Responsible investors communicate regularly and effectively with their investee companies.
3. Stay active and informed: Responsible investors actively monitor their investee companies.
4. Upload transparency in managing conflicts of interest: Responsible investors make known their approach to managing conflicts of interest
5. Vote responsibly: Responsible investors establish clear policies on voting and exercise their voting rights in a responsible fashion.
6. Set a good example: Responsible investors document and provide relevant updates on their stewardship activities.
7. Work together: Responsible investors are willing to engage with one another where appropriate.

For us, the last point of working together is the key. Standing up and ranting at an Annual General Meeting, criticising the management and board of directors, gets you nowhere; it might even make things worse! There are much more subtle ways to engage with the company from written or verbal correspondence to closed-door meetings. Related to activism, but much less radical, this approach is much-preferred in Asia. On the flip side, do note that change tends to take time and it might come very slowly.

To end this chapter, we will be running through some learning points from a high-profile case involving Singapore-listed Olam International Limited.

Case Study: Olam International Limited & Muddy Waters LLC – Case Study

This case study taught us that:

- Short selling is not easy.
- The market is not as efficient as you think.
- Some companies are too complex for most investors to value.
- We need to appreciate the background of major shareholders.

Olam International is an agri-business supply-chain manager supplying food and industrial raw materials to customers worldwide. In November 2012, Carson Block, founder of the famous research firm Muddy Waters, presented Olam as a short candidate during a London conference.[93] This sent Olam's stock price tumbling. Block became one of the world's most-followed short sellers after his 2011 exposé of Sino-Forest, a massive billion-dollar case, where management was accused of fraud.

In the case of Olam international, Block alleged that the company has very loose accounting interpretations and over-indebtedness. What followed wasn't pretty. Allegations flew back and forth between Muddy Waters and Olam's management. Block even tried to place Olam in the same league as Enron Corp. Although Muddy Waters may have emerged victorious against Sino-Forest, it soon realised that Olam was a totally different beast.

The crux of the matter lay in the shareholding structure. Sino-Forest's largest shareholder was Paulson & Co.'s, a hedge fund that owned ~14%. In Olam's case, the bulk of their shareholders are "ultra-long-term investors" unlikely to sell the company solely due to some opinion from a research firm. In 2012, Olam's top shareholder was the Kewalram Chanrai Group, a large conglomerate. More importantly, their second-largest shareholder at 16% was none other than Temasek. Simply put, Muddy Waters was indirectly challenging a sovereign wealth fund.

Case Study *(Continued)*

Muddy Waters released a 133-page report highlighting possible value destroying expansions, internal control issues and accounting interpretations.[94] Olam then countered those allegations with its own 45-page report.[95] Allegations of defamation and share manipulation ran high. To stem the negative sentiments of the public at that time, Olam announced a rights issue of up to US$1.2 billion in December 2012. By effectively underwriting the entire issue, Temasek Holdings used this opportunity to deliver a strong vote of confidence to Olam. When the dust settled, Temasek emerged as Olam's largest shareholder, making it even harder for short-sellers to profit from their trade.

In March 2014, Temasek's indirect subsidiary announced its intention to make a cash offer for Olam shares, convertible bonds and outstanding warrants.[96] In short, this was a buy-out offer. Together, Temasek, Olam's founding family and executive committee members had majority control of the company, effectively pushing out short-sellers. In May 2014, Temasek became Olam's largest shareholder, with a 58.53% stake in the company.[97]

Was it profitable for the short-sellers?

If you bought Olam at S$1.36 in Dec 2012 and sold out at Temasek's offer of S$2.23 in Mar 2014, long-only investors would have quite a decent return over less than two years. This also meant that short-sellers would have suffered over the same period. *Fun fact: Olam was one of STI's top performers in 2014.*

This case showed us:

1. The importance of appreciating the major shareholders.
2. Timing the market requires a magic crystal ball.
3. Complex business like Olam International can attract many points of view. But even with strong opinions and thorough analysis, it does not mean it will lead to great investment return.

How efficient was the market?

During the period around the announcement of their FY2012 results, Olam fluctuated around S$2.00 per share. Once Muddy Waters initiated their negative report, Olam's price tumbled by nearly 20% within a month. The share price of the company only recovered when Temasek came out with its voluntary cash offer, negative sentiments went right out of the window, pushing the share price above S$2.00 per share.

Notice that the share price might not be totally due to the operation performance of Olam International during that time. It was affected more by sentiments created by the negative report from Muddy Waters or the vote of confidence from Temasek Holdings.

This showed that at times in the short term, market prices did not appear to move with fundamentals and investors might need to be aware of general market sentiment with regard to their investment from time to time.

We always believe that the business value always dictates the stock price and never the other way around. Given Olam's position, it seemed unlikely that 20% of its business value vanished within a month and subsequently, without any significant operational change, it recovered within a month as well. This appeared to be another blow to the insightfulness of the herd. Since market prices are simply determined by the supply and demand of opinions, the only explanation would have to be that market participants have become more pessimistic (when the short report came out) and then more optimistic (when Temasek came in) about Olam.

Notes

1. Germaine Cheong. *The Peak.* "The Peak Interview: Dr Ng Chin Siau, CEO-Founder of Q&M Dental, On the Power of Human Relations". http://thepeakmagazine.com.sg/interviews/the-peak-interview-dr-ng-chin-siau-on-the-power-of-human-relations-q-and-m-dental-group/. 24 February 2016.
2. DBS Bank Limited. DBS Group Research. "Imagining Asia 2020". October 2011.
3. Daryl Guppy. *China Business Bites.* Major Street Publishing Pty Ltd. Print edition published: 2013.
4. Asian Development Bank. "Asian Development Outlook 2016 Asia's Potential Growth". 2016.
5. Tami Luhby. CNN Money. "Asian millionaires now the wealthiest in the world". http://money.cnn.com/2016/06/23/news/economy/asian-millionaires-wealth/. 23 June 2016.
6. United Nations. Economic and Social Commission for Asia and the Pacific. "Population Dynamics Challenges and Opportunities". http://www.unescap.org/our-work/social-development/population-dynamics/about. Accessed: 28 December 2016.
7. United Nations. Economic and Social Commission for Asia and the Pacific. "Population trends in Asia and the Pacific". November 2013.

8. Asian Development Bank. "Asian Development Outlook 2016 Asia's Potential Growth". 2016.

9. Asian Development Bank. "Women in the Workforce: an Unmet Potential in Asia and the Pacific". 2015.

10. Elena Holodny. *Business Insider Singapore.* "This might be the 'silver lining' for Japan". http://www.businessinsider.sg/japanese-women-entering-workforce-2016-4/?r=US&IR=T#HoTu0IrTxm2OpZq9.97. 9 April 2016.

11. The Organisation for Economic Co-operation and Development. OECD Development Centre. "Economic Outlook for Southeast Asia, China and India 2016 Enhancing Regional Ties". 2015.

12. Asian Development Bank. "Asian Development Outlook 2016 Asia's Potential Growth". 2016.

13. Tingyi (Cayman Islands) Holding Corp. Presentation on 2015 Annual Results. 22 March 2016.

14. Bloomberg News. "Dairy Farm to Pay $925 Million for China's Yonghui Stake". https://www.bloomberg.com/news/articles/2014-08-11/dairy-farm-buys-china-yonghui-superstores-stake-for-925-million. 12 August 2014.

15. Jollibee Foods Corporation. About Us. http://www.jollibee.com.ph/about-us/. Accessed: 28 December 2016.

16. Doris C. Dumlao. *Philippine Daily Inquirer.* "Jollibee buys Burger King Franchise in the Philippines". http://business.inquirer.net/22247/jollibee-buys-burger-king-franchise-in-the-philippines. 30 September 2011.

17. Hengan International Limited. "Hengan Brochure". November 2012.

18. PricewaterhouseCoopers LLP. "A Summary of South East Asian Infrastructure Spending: Outlook to 2025". 2014.

19. Cary Huang. *South China Morning Post.* "57 nations approved as founder members of China-led AIIB". http://www.scmp.com/news/china/diplomacy-defence/article/1766970/57-nations-approved-founder-members-china-led-aiib. Published: 15 April 2015.

20. Joe Ngai, Kevin Sneader and Cecilia Ma Zecha. The McKinsey Podcast Transcript. "China's One Belt, One Road: Will it reshape global trade?". http://www.mckinsey.com/global-themes/china/chinas-one-belt-one-road-will-it-reshape-global-trade. July 2016.

21. Lim Jia Qi. Channel NewsAsia. "Singapore, Malaysia sign bilateral agreement for High-Speed Rail project". http://www.channelnewsasia.com/news/singapore/singapore-malaysia-sign-bilateral-agreement-for-high-speed-rail/3363164.html. 13 December 2016.

22. Brian Spegele. *The Wall Street Journal.* Business. "China's State Grid Envisions Global Wind-and-Sun Power Network". https://www.wsj.com/articles/chinas-state-grid-envisions-global-wind-and-sun-power-network-1459348941. 30 March 2016.

23. Joe Studwell. Profile Books Limited. *Asian Godfathers: Money and Power in Hong Kong and Southeast Asia*. Published: 2008.

24. Oversea-Chinese Banking Corporation Limited. Heritage – Singapore. https://www.ocbc.com/group/who-we-are/heritage-singapore.html. Accessed: 31 December 2016.

25. Oversea-Chinese Banking Corporation Limited. "Annual Report 2015".

26. Morten Bennedsen and Joseph P.H. Fan. Palgrave Macmillan. *The Family Business Map*. Published: 2014.

27. Genting Berhad. "Annual Report 2015".

28. Genting Singapore PLC. "Annual Report 2015".

29. Mark Scher. Discussion Paper of the United Nations Department of Economic and Social Affairs. DESA Discussion Paper Series. "Bank-firm Cross-shareholding in Japan: What is it, why does it matter, is it winding down?". February 2001.

30. Jardine Matheson Holdings Limited. "Annual Report 2015".

31. Jardine Strategic Holdings Limited. "Annual Report 2015".

32. Jennifer Hughes and Ben Bland. *Financial Times*. "Jardine still marches to its own beat". https://www.ft.com/content/225d1bd4-a8da-11e3-bf0c-00144feab7de. 12 March 2014.

33. Aaron Back. *The Wall Street Journal*. "Samsung Restructuring Could Offer Opportunities". https://www.wsj.com/articles/samsung-restructuring-could-offer-opportunities-1402849806. 17 June 2014.

34. Ibid.

35. Staff Reporter. *South China Morning Post*. "Stanley Ho calls truce in family feud over fortune". http://www.scmp.com/article/740531/stanley-ho-calls-truce-family-feud-over-fortune. 11 March 2011.

36. Joseph P.H. Fan, Ming Jian, and Yin-Hua Yeh. "Family Firm Succession: The Roles of Specialized Assets and Transfer Costs". February 2008.

37. Li & Fung Limited. "Annual report 2015".

38. Li & Fung Limited. Group Chief Executive Officer. "Spencer Fung Bio". http://www.lifung.com/wp-content/uploads/2014/06/Spencer-Fun-Bio-March_30-20151.pdf. Accessed: 30 March 2015.

39. Data from Fung Group. Who We Are. "Group Structure". http://www.funggroup.com/eng/about/structure.php. Accessed: December 2016.

40. Isabella Zhong. Barron's Interview. "Advantage Mr Rockowitz". http://www.barrons.com/articles/advantage-mr-rockowitz-1439266535. 11 August 2015.

41. National University of Singapore. NUS Business School. Think Business Video. "Globalising an Asian family business: William Fung". http://thinkbusiness.nus.edu/videos/page/4/. 22 January 2013.

42. Fan, Jian, and Yeh. "Family Firm Succession".
43. Adam Taylor and Anup Kaphle. *The Washington Post*. WorldViews. "Thailand's army just announced a coup. Here are 11 other Thai coups since 1932". https://www.washingtonpost.com/news/worldviews/wp/2014/05/20/thailands-army-says-this-definitely-isnt-a-coup-heres-11-times-it-definitely-was/?utm_term=.ee4ebb7d1fa7. 22 May 2014.
44. *The Economist*. "Our crony-capitalism index Planet Plutocrat". http://www.economist.com/news/international/21599041-countries-where-politically-connected-businessmen-are-most-likely-prosper-planet. 15 March 2014.
45. CapitaLand Mall Trust. About Us. "Trust Structure". http://www.cmt.com.sg/trust-structure.html. Accessed: 8 January 2017.
46. CapitaLand Mall Trust. "Annual Report 2015".
47. CapitaLand Mall Trust. Presentations. "Full Year 2015 Financial Results". 22 January 2016.
48. CapitaLand Mall Trust. Presentations. "Full Year 2014 Financial Results". 23 January 2015.
49. CapitaLand Mall Trust. "Annual Report 2015".
50. Ibid.
51. Samsonite International S.A. "Annual Report 2015".
52. Samsonite International S.A. "Interim Report 2016".
53. Samsonite International S.A. "Annual Report 2015".
54. Airasia Berhad. "Annual Report 2015".
55. Jonathan Burgos. Bloomberg. "Singapore Exchange Sees End to Hiatus for China IPOs". https://www.bloomberg.com/news/articles/2014-09-21/singapore-exchange-sees-end-to-two-year-hiatus-for-china-ipos. 22 September 2014.
56. Oriental Century Limited. SGX Announcements. "Delisting of the Company's Shares". 23 May 2011.
57. Harry Suhartono (Reporting); Neil Chatterjee & Anshuman Daga (Editing). Reuters. "China's Oriental Century says CEO inflated '08 book". http://www.reuters.com/article/singapore-oriental-idUSSIN50269020090312. 12 March 2009.
58. Eratat Lifestyle Limited. SGX Announcements. "(A) default on Bond Interest Payment; (B) Suspension of Trading Pending Verification of Group's Cash Balance; and (C) Suspension of CEO and Appointment of Interim CEO". 29 January 2014.
59. Eratat Lifestyle Limited. "Annual Report 2010".
60. Eratat Lifestyle Limited. "Annual Report 2012".
61. Eratat Lifestyle Limited. SGX Announcements. "Unaudited Results for the Nine Months Financial Period Ended 30 September 2013". 12 November 2014.

62. Eratat Lifestyle Limited. SGX Announcements. "Proposed Issue of No-Convertible Bonds and Warrants". 20 June 2013.

63. Eratat Lifestyle Limited. SGX Announcements. "Unaudited Results for the Three Months Financial Period Ended 31 March 2013". 29 April 2013.

64. Eratat Lifestyle Limited. SGX Announcements. "(A) default on Bond Interest Payment".

65. Eratat Lifestyle Limited. SGX Announcements. "Eratat Receives SIAS Investors' Choice Award for Corporate Governance". 20 June 2013.

66. Anthony Bolton. *The Telegraph.* "Anthony Bolton: What I learnt in three decades of investing". http://www.telegraph.co.uk/finance/personalfinance/investing/10726245/Anthony-Bolton-What-I-learnt-in-three-decades-of-investing.html. 28 March 2014.

67. Simon Goodley. *The Guardian.* Investing. "Spooks, suspicion and slumps, the harsh reality of investing in China". https://www.theguardian.com/business/2011/nov/14/fidelity-china-fund-slumps. 14 November 2011.

68. Clare Baldwin and John Ruwitch. Reuters. World News. "Special Report: How Caterpillar got bulldozed in China". http://www.reuters.com/article/us-caterpillar-china-special-report-idUSBREA0M03720140123. 23 January 2014.

69. Ben Worthen. *The Wall Street Journal.* Tech. "H-P Says It Was Duped, Takes $8.8 Billion Charge". https://www.wsj.com/articles/SB10001424127887324352004578130712448913412. Updated: 20 November 2012.

70. Samsonite International S.A. "Annual Report 2015".

71. Temasek Holdings. "Temasek Review 2016".

72. Khazanah Nasional Berhad. "The Khazanah Report 2015".

73. PTT Public Company Limited. Investor Relations. "Major Shareholders". Accessed: 4 January 2017.

74. Airports of Thailand PLC. Investor Relation. Shareholder Information. "Shareholding". Accessed: 4 January 2017.

75. SMRT Corporation Limited. "Annual Report 2016".

76. Stanley Lim Peir Shenq, CFA. The Motley Fool Singapore. "Are the Worst Days of SMRT Corporation Ltd Finally Behind It Now?". https://www.fool.sg/2015/03/26/are-the-worst-days-of-smrt-corporation-ltd-finally-behind-it-now/. 26 March 2015.

77. Stephanie Ho. National Library Board Singapore. Politics and Government. Singapore Infopedia. "History of general elections in Singapore". http://eresources.nlb.gov.sg/infopedia/articles/SIP_549_2004-12-28.html. Updated: 1 September 2014.

78. Chew Hui Min. *Straits Times.* Politics. "GE2015: A look back at the last 5 general elections from 1991 to 2011". http://www.straitstimes .com/politics/ge2015-a-look-back-at-the-last-5-general-elections-from-1991-to-2011. 28 August 2015.

79. Public Transport Council. Facts and Figures. "Chronology of Fare Adjustments". Accessed: 5 January 2017.

80. SMRT Corporation Limited. "Annual Report 2014".

81. Land Transport Authority. Press Room. News Release. "Transition to a Government Contracting Model for the public Bus Industry". 21 May 2014.

82. Stanley Lim Peir Shenq. The Motley Fool Singapore. "New Business Model For Public Bus Services: How Are SMRT Corporation and SBS Transit Affected?". https://www.fool.sg/2014/05/22/new-business-model-for-public-bus-services-how-are-smrt-corporation-and-sbs-transit-affected/. 22 May 2014.

83. Ministry of Transport. Transport Matters. Public Transport. "Why Bus Contracting". https://www.mot.gov.sg/Transport-Matters/Public-Transport/Why-bus-contracting-/. Accessed: 5 January 2017.

84. Christopher Tan. *The Straits Times.* Opinion. "Fresh start for delisted SMRT". http://www.straitstimes.com/opinion/fresh-start-for-delisted-smrt. 1 November 2016.

85. Securities Commission Malaysia. https://www.sc.com.my/. Accessed: 5 April 2017.

86. The Securities and Exchange Commission, Thailand. https://www .sc.com.my/. Accessed: 5 April 2017.

87. Singapore Exchange Limited. Regulation. "How We Regulate". http://www.sgx.com/wps/portal/sgxweb/home/regulation/ howwereg. Accessed: 5 January 2017.

88. M. Mageswari. *The Star.* "Datuk and remisier charged over Fountain View shares". <http://www.thestar.com.my/news/ nation/2005/06/28/datuk-and-remisier-charged-over-fountain-view-shares/>. 28 June 2005.

89. Securities Commission Malaysia. Media Release. "Court of Appeal imposes 12 months jail sentence for market manipulation". https:// www.sc.com.my/post_archive/court-of-appeal-imposes-12-months-jail-sentence-for-market-manipulation/. 27 June 2012.

90. Securities Commission Malaysia. Media Release. "Fountain View market manipulation case: SC secures deterrent sentence". https:// www.sc.com.my/post_archive/fountain-view-market-manipulation-case-sc-secures-deterrent-sentence/. 5 February 2010.

91. Ibid.

92. Stewardship Asia Centre 2016 on behalf of the Singapore Steward-ship Principles Working Group. "Singapore Stewardship Principles for Responsible Investors". November 2016.
93. Sam Jones. *Financial Times.* "Short seller with Olam in his sights". https://www.ft.com/content/7944dae4-330c-11e2-aabc-00144feabdc0. 20 November 2012.
94. Muddy Waters Research. "Initiating Coverage on Olam International – Strong Sell". http://www.muddywatersresearch.com/research/. 26 November 2012.
95. Olam International Ltd. News. SGX filings. "Olam Dismisses Muddy Waters Findings". 28 November 2012.
96. Olam International Ltd. News. SGX filings. "Voluntary Conditional Cash Offer for the Company". 14 March 2012.
97. Singapore Exchange Limited. Company Announcement. Olam International Limited. "Disclosure of Interest/Change in Interest of Substantial Shareholder(s)/Unitholders(s)::Disclosure of Interest/ Changes in Interest of Substantial Shareholder". 26 May 2014.

4

The Future of Investing in Asia

Today is cruel. Tomorrow is crueller. But the day after tomorrow is beautiful.

— Jack Ma

We went through some of the risks associated with investing in Asia in the previous chapters. Yet despite some of these pitfalls present in Asia, we believe that there is still huge potential hidden within Asia. In fact, in many industries and countries, things are just getting started. In this chapter, we will be detailing some of the many investment opportunities present within Asia.

One way to spot possible opportunities is through the top-down approach. For this approach, we cast our sights across the overall macro-economic environment to identify certain industries or markets that might be of interest to us. We can then focus our attention on companies within these selected groups when we search for possible investments.

Once again, we would like to reinforce the point that all investment opportunities do come with their unique potential and risks. So, as you are reading through this chapter, think about these themes, both in term of potential risks and rewards.

ASEAN, Pushing Ahead

The Association of Southeast Asia Nations, better known as ASEAN, is home to more than 600 million people.[1] ASEAN is one of the fastest-growing regions in the world,[2] with its combined GDP expected to grow more than 5% for the next decade.[3]

When investing in Southeast Asia, markets like Singapore, Malaysia, Thailand, Indonesia and the Philippines come to mind. After all, these are the largest economies, with relatively mature equity markets within the region. From 2009 to 2014, most of the region's indices have done well.[4] In particular, the Philippines's PSE Composite Index stood out, with a return of over 300% during the six-year period from 2008 to 2014.[5]

With a young, educated population and a growing middle class, the Philippines holds strong potential for the future. This has led to foreign fund managers taking an increased interest in the Philippines. This interest in the Philippines resulted in a strong run-up in its stock market, sending valuation to about 18 to 20 times its earnings, a rather high figure for an emerging market index.[6] To a lesser extent, the same phenomenon can also be seen in the stock markets of both Indonesia and Thailand.

The rising demand for the ASEAN market is not without reasons. From 2007 to 2015, the ASEAN region has seen its real growth rate average 5.2% per year.[7] This level of growth has been even more impressive given that most developed nations have been struggling to grow at all after the 2009 global financial crisis.

It is not just the more-developed countries within ASEAN that are gaining interest from investors; there is also growing interest in frontier markets in this region. One such market is Myanmar. After decades of military rule, Myanmar did not have a reputation of being the most foreign investor-friendly country. Many investors and commentators have deemed Myanmar to be the final frontier, given its relatively low starting point in terms of its economy, the state of both their physical and financial infrastructure, and the potential for growth in the future. Peter Popham – famed writer and Myanmar expert, mentioned in his book *The Lady and the General*, that 60% of Myanmar's economy might be taking place over the black market,[8] indicating both how far behind this country is, and how huge the potential it has.

Since 2011, the country has been slowly opening up and transitioning towards a more democratic style of leadership. Previous

President Thein Sein has carried out a number of key reforms and the country might be ready to move forward from its troubled past. Following the landslide victory of the iconic Aung San Suu Kyi's party – the National League for Democracy – in the country's landmark 2015 general election, there has been a strong sense of hopefulness for the future in the country.

One of the key financial events was the launch of the country's own stock exchange, Yangon Stock Exchange, in 2015.[9] In 2016, there were only three companies listed on the exchange.[10] However, as their infrastructure improves, with better roads, increasing urbanisation, improving connectivity and a stronger financial market, Myanmar's future does look promising.

Given that there were only three companies listed on the Yangon Stock Exchange, there might not be many viable investing options for investors looking for a direct equity investment. However, we can approach this from another angle. An alternative is to invest in a foreign-listed company with exposure to Myanmar.

One such company is Singapore-listed Yoma Strategic Holdings Limited, a conglomerate in Myanmar. The company has multiple businesses in Myanmar, ranging from real estate, automotive and equipment, and food and beverage to operations in the tourism industry.[11] With the country, most of its businesses could stand to benefit as the economy improves.

Another approach to gain access to these emerging economies is to invest into well-established companies with investments in these countries. For example, if you are interested in the Vietnam market, instead of investing directly into companies listed in Vietnam, there are many foreign-listed companies with exposure to the country. One example is Singapore-listed Fraser and Neave, Limited ("F&N"). This is because following F&N's additional 5.4% stake in Vietnam's leading milk producer – Vietnam Dairy Products JSC, more commonly known as Vinamilk[12] – in December 2016, F&N stood as one of Vinamilk's largest shareholders,[13] with an interest of 16.35%.

As we warned earlier in Chapter 2 in the context of the rise of the Chinese consumer, investors should always keep their optimism in check. This is because expectations of the economy may not always translate into results in the stock market, especially when you are overpaying for future earnings. We will discuss further in later chapters how to balance our expectations when it comes to valuation concerns during our investment process.

The Wall Street of Asia

When it comes down to financial improvements in Asia, look no further than how far China has come in the last few decades, with banks that could rival their peers in Western nations. Even Jamie Dimon, Chairman of JP Morgan Chase & Co. ("JP Morgan"), highlighted in a 2016 interview that Industrial and Commercial Bank of China ("ICBC") was already earning nearly twice as much as JP Morgan.[14] He also highlighted that China's banks are probably growing faster compared to US banks and could one day be much bigger than them.

At the moment, China's financial industry has four mega-banks:

1. Industrial and Commercial Bank of China Limited ("ICBC")
2. China Construction Bank Corporation ("CCB")
3. Bank of China Limited ("BOC")
4. Agricultural Bank of China Limited ("ABC").

However, China's financial market is still viewed as highly regulated and somewhat underdeveloped. One reason is that almost all banks in China are viewed as state-owned enterprises where the government has a large influence over their directions. Even though the country has embarked on financial reforms with the objective of opening up its financial system, it is still a distance from being deemed a "free market".

The stock markets in China still experience wild fluctuation every now and then due to regulatory intervention. As recently as January 2015, the China Securities Regulatory Commission suspended three big brokerages from opening new margin trading accounts for three months after suspecting them of financing high-risk margin trading.[15] The market started freefalling after that. On 28 July 2015, the Shanghai Index fell about 8.5%, the largest percentage fall since February 2007. On the same day, more than 1,700 stocks listed on the exchange went down by their daily limit of 10%.[16] Such swift and strong curbs are not common in markets in the US and Europe. However, such actions are not uncommon for the Chinese financial regulators. Such interventions might not be all negative for investors though. There are some who believe that timely interventions could possibly mitigate financial meltdowns of epic proportions such as the 2008 Global Financial Crisis.

Table 4.1: Market Size

Sector (USD trillion)	Bank Credit	Stock	Fixed Income	Insurance	Asset Management Companies
Size (China)	10.7	3.7	3.4	1.2	0.4
Size (US)	7.6	18.7	38.0	4.8	36.0
% GDP (China)	128%	44%	41%	14%	5%
% GDP (US)	48%	118%	240%	32%	230%

The developing financial market in China also holds huge opportunities. The present tight credit regulations mean that there is a huge potential for the financial sector to expand greatly as regulators open up the financial system. The country is already experimenting with multiple initiatives such as the free-trade zone in Shanghai, the "Shanghai–Hong Kong Stock Connect" and the opening of Chinese Yuan clearing centres in major markets globally. The Chinese government is also paving the way for the Chinese Yuan to become a reserve currency.[17] Imagine the potential of a liberalised Chinese financial system.

China's debt market is another area of possible growth. From Table 4.1[18] we can see that bank credit still made up the bulk of financing for China's economy. It is worth mentioning that most of the credit still flows to large corporations, in particular to the state-owned enterprises.[19] However, as the industry liberalises, we might be able to see a more efficient financial system, allowing smaller companies to raise funds more easily, resulting in a more vibrant economy.

Nevertheless, there is still risk in the financial sector in the short term. Tight regulations have led to many companies resorting to "creative" fundraising methods, commonly known as "shadow banking".[20] Currently, the authorities are not reining in on them forcefully as they have not been proven to be a major disruption to the whole economy. However, if the situation gets out of hand, we might see significant short-term disruptions to the financial system.

From "Guanxi" to Transparency

关系 ("*Guanxi*") is the Chinese word for "relationships". It is also an important unwritten rule for doing business in the Middle Kingdom since ancient times. You could say that it is a deeper level of networking beyond just business. But, how did *guanxi* come about?

Guanxi may have developed as a product of the environment. In ancient China, it was well-nigh impossible to govern such a large territory through a centralised system, and weak enforcement of law and regulation was the norm. Because of that, it became crucial to develop another means of ensuring trust in both business and personal dealings between people. This resulted in a network effect known as *guanxi*. We see *guanxi* as a neutral word. *Guanxi* is not the same as corruption in business. It is merely the belief that trust between business partners should be valued. If exercised appropriately, it is not inherently a bad thing, as many western commentators believe.

However, there are signs that things might be changing. With Xi Jinping's elevation to the General Secretary of the Communist Party in 2012, things appear to be changing – for the better. Upon taking office, Xi Jinping famously proclaimed that the Central Commission for Discipline Inspection would be "striking tigers and flies at the same time", to crack down on corruption in China.[21] The government demonstrated that this crackdown was not an empty threat when Zhou Yongkang, a former member of the Politburo Standing Committee, the highest decision-making body in China, was sentenced to life in jail. This was unprecedented, as it broke an unwritten rule against prosecuting members of its inner circle. Zhou Yongkang was the most senior official to receive such a penalty since the Cultural Revolution.[22]

In term of the business world, the Chinese government crackdown on corruption has not only affected the usual discretionary goods retailers such as Hong Kong-listed Hengdeli Holdings Limited – the world's largest retailer of internationally renowned brand watches, and Hong Kong-listed Chow Tai Fook Jewellery Group Limited – the largest Hong Kong-listed jeweller (by market capitalisation). Even mooncake retailers were badly hit. As it turns out, giving mooncakes as gifts was a rather significant form of corporate gifting in China![23]

For an economy to prosper in a sustainable manner, corruption cannot be tolerated. Even with the crackdown affecting China's consumer sector and the gaming sector in Macau, we feel that these are necessary steps that would result in a stronger and more resilient Chinese economy in the long run.

The Future of Healthcare

As a country urbanises and its population grows more affluent, the demand for better healthcare tends to increase in tandem. More importantly, with better education, the population is more informed of the need for quality healthcare services, thus creating a strong tailwind for the healthcare industry.

Many of us are aware of the challenges related to aging population in Japan. With its population currently at median age of 47 years, it's definitely a demographical concern.[24] *Fun fact: The median age of China's population stands at 37 years.*[25] If we were looking at themes, an aging population with an increasing life expectancy most likely require more healthcare services.

As an industry, the healthcare industry is often seen as defensive with high barriers to entry. This is partly due to the fact that there is a long lead time and a high cost of training doctors. Moreover, medical services are not easily imported or exported. As such, this industry is considered relatively defensive compared to commodity-like industries such as steel and oil. In general, defensive industries such as healthcare tend to have more stable revenue. One reason for this is that the demand for healthcare services is highly correlated with the increasing standard of living of a country. Healthcare companies within Asia definitely have interesting investment potential for investors.

With stronger demand for medical services, demand for pharmaceutical products might also grow in tandem. With pharmaceutical giants like Novartis AG, Pfizer Inc. and Gilead Sciences, Inc. located mainly in the United States and Europe, it might be the national interest of a country like China to develop its domestic pharmaceutical industry, to be able to compete with their multinational peers in the near future.

Between 2004 and 2011, China's personal healthcare spending more than doubled, growing to an annual $102 a person as consumers become wealthier and government policies raised awareness of health issues.[26] With the number of private hospitals doubling since 2008 to more than 10,800 in 2013, the development of the healthcare sector in China does not appear to be slowing down any time soon.[27] According to a Research and Markets report, hospitals in China saw their revenue shoot up 163.3% from 2010 to 2016, to RMB2.7 trillion.[28]

The potential of the market and the relaxation of foreign investment into hospitals in China has led to many foreign health-care groups starting to invest in the country. In 2014, China started to allow wholly foreign-owned hospitals to operate in seven cities and provinces; previously, foreign stakes in hospitals were not allowed to exceed 70%.[29] Malaysia-listed IHH Healthcare Berhad ("IHH Healthcare"), one of the largest global healthcare groups, operates multiple clinics and medical centres in China. In 2015, IHH Healthcare entered into a lease agreement with Perennial Real Estate Holdings Limited to operate a 350-bed hospital in Chengdu, their first foray into tertiary healthcare in the Western side of China.[30] Even Singapore-listed Raffles Medical Group Limited has a joint venture to build up a 400-bed international hospital in Shanghai.[31]

In Singapore alone, the Singapore Exchange has seen multiple new healthcare companies listing from around Southeast Asia. Recent examples include Singapore O&G Limited (2015),[32] Talkmed Group Limited (2014),[33] ISEC Healthcare Limited (2014),[34] International Healthway Corporation Limited (2013),[35] Cordlife Group Limited (2012),[36] Q & M Dental Group (Singapore) Limited (2009)[37] and Singapore Medical Group Limited (2009),[38] which have gone public in the past few years.

The Asian Consumer Story Lives On

Today, Asia is not just about the China consumer story. We have the Asian consumer story that's gaining ground as well. Why?

Consumers are the heartbeat of any economy. No matter what goods and services you sell, you still need a consumer at the end of the line buying the final products. And with the rising middle class growing in Asia, consumer spending looks set to be rising too.

Broadly speaking, if we live in a relatively safe environment with our basic amenities met, most of us would want a higher standard of living. We want more convenience, we want to eat better, have more fun, take better care of ourselves and sometimes, splurge a little on that luxury bag we have been looking at for quite a while.

In 2015, the Hong Kong-listed Fosun International Limited acquired Club Med, and acquired stakes in Cirque du Soleil and Thomas Cook.[40] All these investments point towards higher expected spending in the discretionary category. *Fun fact: China is currently the largest automobile market in the world.*[41]

Even after what we said about Asia not being just about the China consumer story, we cannot deny that China has a huge impact on the region. Even with China already being the second-largest economy in the world, the Middle Kingdom is still expected to grow at a rate of around 6.5% between 2016 and 2020.[42] Comparing that to the 1–2% growth expectation of the developed world, it is not hard to see China becoming the most important consumer market for many companies in the future.

So how can investors invest in these trends? One simple way for investors to look for investment opportunities in this sector is just to look at your normal day-to-day activities. It's quite intuitive to understand how our spending benefits companies like Singapore-listed Old Chang Kee Limited (curry puffs), Hong Kong-listed Vitasoy International Holdings Limited (soymilk), Hong Kong-listed Belle International Holdings Limited (ladies footwear) and Hong Kong-listed Samsonite International S.A. (travel luggage). These companies provide products that we can eat, drink, wear and use.

Alternatively, we can research trusts like Singapore-listed Capita-Land Mall Trust ("CMT"), Singapore's first and largest Real Estate Investment Trust ("REIT"), with over 15 retail properties. In Layman's terms, CMT is simply a landlord, with their income coming from the rental collected from their tenants. Even though CMT does not sell either their products or services to us directly, they still do depend on us consumers. Why?

CMT's revenue depends on their customers like Singapore-listed Breadtalk Group Limited and Singapore-listed ABR Holding Limited, which operate famous restaurants like Din Tai Fung and Swensen's in Singapore respectively.

Region-wise, although China with a population of over 1.37 billion[43] is clearly a force to be reckoned with, the rest of Asia, especially Southeast Asia, with the region having a population of close to 600 million is also very much relevant. Some of the largest countries in the region in terms of population are:

- Indonesia: 258 million[44]
- Philippines: 103 million[45]
- Vietnam: 95 million[46]
- Malaysia: 31 million.[47]

Looking at just the modern grocery retail market, the penetration of modern retail as a percentage of the first four countries' grocery retail market size was less than 50% of the entire grocery retail market, meaning that most people within the countries still get their grocery from places like wet markets, wholesalers and roadside stores instead of supermarkets, hypermarkets and convenience stores. In the case of Indonesia and Vietnam, modern grocery retail was less than 25%. With increasing urbanisation, the potential of these markets is just as significant for investors like us. As a comparison, Singapore-listed Dairy Farm International Holdings Limited, one of the largest retailers in Asia, sees China as a US$793 billion grocery retail market, while the combined current grocery retail market of the above four countries was only US$62 billion at the end of 2015.[48]

Even at this point, we think that most Asian consumer brands are just starting out. As the leading brands consolidate, Asia's own Coca-Colas, Nestlés and Nikes will emerge. These Asian brands may be able to compete globally with their western counterparts in the long run. One area where Asian brands are already on the global stage includes electronic appliances giants like Samsung Electronics Co., Limited, LG Corporation, Lenovo Group Limited and Sony Corporation. The automotive sector also comes to mind, with players like Tokyo-listed Toyota Motor Corporation, Nissan Motor Corporation Limited and Korea-listed Hyundai Motor Company.

Notes

1. ASEANstats, ASEAN Secretariat. Association of Southeast Asian Nations. Resources. Selected Key Indicators. August 2016.
2. Vinayak HV, Fraser Thompson, and Oliver Tonby. McKinsey & Company. Public Sector. "Understanding ASEAN: Seven things you need to know". http://www.mckinsey.com/industries/public-sector/our-insights/understanding-asean-seven-things-you-need-to-know>. May 2014.
3. OECD Development Centre. "Economic Outlook for Southeast Asia, China and India 2016". 2015.
4. Historical Chart for Kuala Lumpur Composite Index (KLCI), Straits Times Index (STI), Thailand SET Index (SET) and Jakarta Composite Index (JCI); https://finance.yahoo.com/quote/%5EKLSE?p=^KLSE; https://finance.yahoo.com/quote/%5ESTI/?p=^STI; https://finance.yahoo.com/quote/%5EJKSE?p=%5EJKSE; https://www.bloomberg.com/quote/SET:IND. June 2016.

5. Chao Deng. *The Wall Street Journal.* Markets Main. "Philippine Stocks Add to a Hot Streak". https://www.wsj.com/articles/philippine-stocks-add-to-a-hot-streak-1422385362. 27 January 2015.
6. Doris C. Dumlao. *Philippine Daily Inquirer.* "Philippine stock market expects 7th straight year of growth". http://business.inquirer .net/184278/philippine-stock-market-expects-7th-straight-year-of-growth. 31 December 2014.
7. ASEAN Secretariat and UN Population Division. "ASEAN Economic Community at a Glance". First published: November 2015; 3rd Reprint: August 2016.
8. Peter Popham. Penguin Books Limited. *The Lady and the Generals.* Published: 10 March 2016.
9. May Wong. Channel NewsAsia. "Yangon Stock Exchange in Myanmar officially starts trading". http://www.channelnewsasia.com/news/ business/yangon-stock-exchange-in/2636394.html. 25 March 2016.
10. Yangon Stock Exchange. Listed Company. Company List. https:// ysx-mm.com/en/listing/company/. Accessed: 14 January 2017.
11. Yoma Strategic Holdings Limited. "Annual Report 2016".
12. Vietnam Dairy Products Joint Stock Company. "Annual Report 2016".
13. Fraser and Neave, Limited. "Annual Report 2016".
14. John Micklethwait. Bloomberg Markets. "Jamie Dimon on Finance: 'Who Owns the Future?'". https://www.bloomberg.com/ features/2016-jamie-dimon-interview/. 1 March 2016.
15. Bloomberg News. "China Suspends 3 Big Brokers from Adding Margin Accounts". https://www.bloomberg.com/news/articles/ 2015-01-16/china-suspends-3-big-brokers-from-adding-margin-accounts. 16 January 2015.
16. Josh Noble. *Financial Times.* "China markets rout resumes with 8.5% Shanghai sell-off". https://www.ft.com/content/2a17ec12-342c-11e5-b05b-b01debd57852. 28 July 2015.
17. Sarah McDonald. Bloomberg. Bloomberg Markets. "Why China's Yuan Is Set to Join IMF's Elite Club: QuickTake Q&A". https://www .bloomberg.com/news/articles/2016-09-27/why-china-s-yuan-is-set-to-join-imf-s-elite-club-quicktake-q-a. 27 September 2016.
18. Douglas J. Elliott and Kai Yan. John L. Thornton China Center Monograph Series. Number 6. "The Chinese Financial System". July 2013.
19. Stephen Letts. ABC News. "Chinese banks sitting on $1.7 trillion debt time bomb". http://www.abc.net.au/news/2016-05-24/chinese-banks-1.7-trillion-debt-time-bomb/7439844. Updated: 24 May 2016.
20. Christopher Balding. BloombergView. "The Shadow Looming Over China". https://www.bloomberg.com/view/articles/2016-06-06/ china-s-shadow-banks-now-pose-a-systemic-risk. 9 June 2016.

21. *South China Morning Post.* "Tigers and Flies: How two years of graft probes have shaken China's political elite". http://multimedia.scmp .com/china-corruption/. 3 November 2014.

22. Verna Yu. *South China Morning Post.* "China's disgraced security tsar Chou Yongkang jailed for life over graft". http://www.scmp.com/ news/china/policies-politics/article/1820432/chinas-disgraced-security-tsar-zhou-yongkang-jailed. 12 June 2015.

23. Adam Jourdan and Nick Macfie. Reuters. World News. "China warns again of dark side of the mooncakes". http://www.reuters.com/ article/us-china-corruption-idUSKBN0H00AF20140905. 5 September 2014.

24. Central Intelligence Agency. Library. The World Factbook. "Japan". https://www.cia.gov/library/publications/the-world-factbook/ geos/ja.html. Accessed: 14 January 2017.

25. Central Intelligence Agency. Library. The World Factbook. "China". https://www.cia.gov/library/publications/the-world-factbook/ geos/ch.html. Accessed: 14 January 2017.

26. Rachel Chang. Bloomberg. "Here's What China's Middle Classes Really Earn – and Spend". https://www.bloomberg.com/news/ articles/2016-03-09/here-s-what-china-s-middle-class-really-earn-and-spend. 10 March 2016.

27. Dexter Roberts. Bloomberg. "China's Fast-Growing Medical Industry Opens to Foreign Hospitals". https://www.bloomberg.com/news/ articles/2014-08-28/china-welcomes-foreign-hospitals. 29 August 2014.

28. Research and Markets. PR Newswire. "China Hospital Industry Report 2016-2020 – Research and Markets". http://www.about-pharma.com/blog/2017/03/13/china-hospital-industry-report-2016-2020-research-and-markets/. 13 March 2017.

29. Roberts. "China's Fast-Growing Medical Industry Opens to Foreign Hospitals".https://www.bloomberg.com/news/articles/2014-08-28/ china-welcomes-foreign-hospitals. 29 August 2014.

30. IHH Healthcare Berhad. "Annual Report 2015".

31. Raffles Medical Group Limited. "Annual Report 2015".

32. Singapore O&G Limited. "Annual Report 2015".

33. Talkmed Group Limited. SGX Announcement. "Miscellaneous:: Talkmed Group Limited – Admission of 657,143,000 Ordinary Shares to the Official List of SGX-Catalist". 29 January 2014.

34. ISEC Healthcare Limited. SGX Announcement. "Trading of Ordinary Shares in the Capital of the Company". 23 October 2014.

35. International Healthway Corporation Limited. "Annual Report 2013".

36. Cordlife Group Limited. "Annual Report 2012".

37. Q & M Dental Group (Singapore) Limited. Investor Relation. "Corporate Profile". http://www.qandm.com.sg/ir.aspx. Accessed: 27 April 2017.

38. Singapore Medical Group Limited. "About Us". http://singapore medical.id/about-us/. Accessed: 27 April 2017.

39. Fullerton Healthcare Corporation Limited. "Preliminary Prospectus". 28 September 2016.

40. Fosun International Limited. "Annual Report 2015".

41. Bloomberg News. Bloomberg Technology. "Alibaba Wants a Slice of the World's Largest Car Market". https://www.bloomberg.com/news/articles/2016-07-06/jack-ma-s-answer-to-apple-google-cars-begins-with-china-s-saic. 6 July 2016.

42. The World Bank. "China Overview". http://www.worldbank.org/en/country/china/overview. Updated: 14 September 2016.

43. Ibid.

44. Central Intelligence Agency. Library. The World Factbook. "Indonesia". https://www.cia.gov/library/publications/the-world-factbook/geos/id.html. Accessed: 15 January 2017.

45. Central Intelligence Agency. Library. The World Factbook. "Philippines". https://www.cia.gov/library/publications/the-world-factbook/geos/rp.html. Accessed: 15 January 2017.

46. Central Intelligence Agency. Library. The World Factbook. "Vietnam". https://www.cia.gov/library/publications/the-world-factbook/geos/vm.html. Accessed: 15 January 2017.

47. Central Intelligence Agency. Library. The World Factbook. "Malaysia". https://www.cia.gov/library/publications/the-world-factbook/geos/my.html. Accessed: 15 January 2017.

48. Dairy Farm International Holdings Limited. "2014 Full Year Results Presentation". 6 March 2015.

CHAPTER

Using the Right Process

Trust the process. Your life won't change in a day, week or month. Be patient. It takes time.

— Anonymous

When it comes to investing, it's simple to say that successful investing is all about finding the right companies (call us Captain Obvious). Yet in reality, the challenge lies in being able to consistently identify great investments and at the same time avoid huge losses. Hence, having the right process is crucial for long-term investors.

Well-known investors in Asia include:

- CHEAH Cheng Hye – Value Partners Group Limited[1]
- TENG Ngiek Lian – Target Asset Management Private Limited[2]
- WONG Kok Hoi – APS Asset Management Private Limited[3]
- Hugh YOUNG – Aberdeen Asset Management Asia Limited[4]
- TAN Chong Koay – Pheim Asset Management (Asia) Private Limited[5]
- YEO Seng Chong – Yeoman Capital Management Private Limited.[6]

If you do a search on famous investors such as those in this list, you will come to realise that each of them invests with varying strategies, and very often in very different companies too. Nevertheless, all of them are successful in their own right. Why? We believe it is because they stick by a structured investment process that consistently works for them.

Hence a well thought-out investment process is important to ensure our long-term investing success. A sound investment process gives us an advantage of minimising unforced errors. With the compounding nature that comes with investing for the long haul, more money saved leads to exponential returns.

In the next few chapters, we will explore our processes with you, from screening for opportunities all the way to finding out whether the valuation of a company is attractive enough to put our money where our mouth is.

For the first step, we must understand that to find value, we first have to know what we are looking for. We categorise value into three main segments, namely:

1. asset value
2. current earning power value
3. growth value.

These three types of value have also been discussed in many investing books, most notably in Bruce Greenwald's *Value Investing: From Graham to Buffett and Beyond.* However, we would like to elaborate on these values and how they can be found in the context of the stock markets in Asia. And as a bonus, we have also included a section on special situation investments, which is about spotting arbitrage opportunities in the stock markets.

We set up this book as a practical guide to help you in your Asian investment journey. You could start by reading our book chronologically for a better appreciation of the whole process of investing in Asia. When that is done, you can still refer back to any specific chapter to refresh your memory.

In our final chapter, with the help of real life case studies, we will show you how these approaches play out, taking you through our thought process from start to finish. We will start from screening, to getting the right data, to separating the noise from the important data. And lastly, we will look at how to estimate the value of an investment opportunity, more commonly known as finding the intrinsic value of a company.

Asset Value

Deemed the most important investment book by many value investors, Benjamin Graham and David Dodd's *Security Analysis* is probably *the* book that brought value investing to the world. As this book was published in the 1930s (*Hint: Great Depression*), many of their principles came from finding securities selling below their net asset value. The idea was to buy a company so cheaply that even if the business deteriorated, the investor could still stand to profit from the investment. This is how we can look for the first type of value in a company – asset value.

A popular version of this style is known as "cigar-butt" investing. This came from the idea that if you find a lighted cigar butt lying around on the street, it might be unseemly and dirty, but you can still get a free puff out of it. In the context of investing, you might be looking at companies that may not necessary be well run or have great prospects. But they might be trading at such depressed levels that you can make a profit even if the company winds up the next day.

This meant that even if this company stopped operations, liquidated everything and paid off its debts, you could still get back more than what you paid. However, approaching an asset play does not necessary mean ignoring the dynamics or economics of a company. In fact, understanding how the company works gives us a better appreciation for such companies. Let us illustrate this point with a case study of one of our earlier investments.

Case Study: OTO Holdings Limited

OTO Holdings Limited ("OTO Holdings") (now Tempus Holdings Limited) is one of the largest home massage device brand owners. Previously majority-owned by the Yip family, OTO Holdings was present in three key markets, Hong Kong, Macau and China, as a wellness equipment retailer. However, tougher business conditions, mainly due to the slowdown in China and OTO Holdings' divergence from its original IPO plans, led to more than a 60% loss in its market capitalisation in just its first year of its IPO.[7]

Thus the company appeared to be an interesting case when we looked at its balance sheet. For most asset analysis, we focus on their key assets – the things that matter, or stuff that can be converted to cash during a liquidation.

Case Study *(Continued)*

From a company's latest balance sheet, we should be able to estimate the company's residual value. In simple words, if the company was sold today, how much can their assets fetch?

Comparing Its Assets with Its Liabilities

We started by looking at its assets, like cash, inventory, receivables and property, plant and equipment. In investing, we find that it helps to have some scepticism; in other areas, this is known as being conservative. One method is to place a discount on each of the assets that matter. As we are estimating the true value of each asset in the balance sheet, we have to be aware of the assumptions we are making when looking through each line item. Once we have that sorted out, we should be able to have a decent gauge of how much these assets can actually fetch if they were sold at fire-sale prices.

On the other side of the balance sheet are its liabilities. In this case, there is little reason to discount the liabilities. Just think about it: loan sharks don't tend to sympathise when you are in a rut, they just want their money back. *Friendly advice: Don't borrow money from loan sharks.*

Finally, we took what the company owned (assets) and subtracted what it owed (liabilities), arriving at a valuation of the company. Although it looks like there's a whole list of items on their balance sheet, its helps to just concentrate on key items. For starters, we do not have to go through all 12 assets shown on OTO Holdings balance sheet (Figure 5.1).[8]

OTO Holdings traded about HKD0.50 per share in 2012. At that price, OTO was near its net-cash position. If we net off OTO Holdings' total cash with all its liabilities at that time (non-current liabilities were less than HK$0.5 million), we would still end up with close to HKD200 million; more than its then market capitalisation of HKD160 million.[9] This was before even considering the other assets on its balance sheet. With just a single asset – their cash alone, OTO Holdings already appeared to have a rather sizeable margin of safety in place.

Basically, at the trading price of HKD0.50 per share, the market implied that you were "getting paid" HKD40 million for OTO Holdings' profitable massage equipment business. However, when the market looks to be offering something too good to be true, we should always be sceptical and ask, "So what's the catch?"

More often than not, there tend to be legitimate reasons for a company to trade so far below its book value. Some reasons might be:

- A slump in profitability is expected
- Questionable capital allocation skills of the management

Case Study *(Continued)*

OTO HOLDINGS LIMITED BALANCE SHEET DETAILS	30 Sep 2012 (Unaudited)	31 Mar 2012 (Audited)
TOTAL ASSETS	**299,820**	**305,124**
NON CURRENT ASSETS	**29,148**	**25,109**
Property, plant and equipment	9,038	6,462
Investment property	7,650	6,700
Deferred tax assets	989	1,014
Deposit placed at an insurance company	3,061	3,016
Utility and other deposits paid	8,410	7,917
CURRENT ASSETS	**270,672**	**280,015**
Inventories	9,863	7,242
Investments at fair value through profit or loss	0	1,934
Trade and other receivables	31,173	31,972
Amounts due from related parties	48	166
Tax recoverable	1,639	1,572
Pledged bank deposits	15,929	15,918
Bank balance and cash	212,020	221,211
TOTAL LIABILITIES	**35,277**	**37,751**
CURRENT LIABILITIES	**34,838**	**37,573**
Trade and other payables	22,679	21,769
Obligations under finance leases	175	76
Tax payable	871	1,903
Bank borrowings	11,113	13,825
NON CURRENT LIABILITIES	**439**	**178**
Obligations under finance leases	439	178
TOTAL EQUITY	**264,543**	**267,373**
Share Capital	24,960	24,960
Reserves	239,583	242,413

Figure 5.1   OTO Holdings Limited Interim Report 2012/2013 Balance Sheet

Case Study *(Continued)*

- Red flags in their financials, heightening fraud risk
- Questionable reputation of Board members, management or major shareholder.

For asset-based valuations, we start by looking at what can go wrong. Why? Because of Murphy's Law. Before we jumped into the opportunity, here are some issues we considered for the case of OTO Holding:

- The business is cyclical, earnings can be volatile and out of the control of the company.
- Its products are discretionary in nature and sales could suffer during economic downturns.
- The industry has relatively low barrier of entry.
- Its business had seen declining margins in the past few years.
- Its inventory levels were building up.

However, on the bright side, there were also some positive observations about the company:

- Although lumpy, the company has decent operational cash flow.
- It still had positive operating cash inflow matching its profits.
- Given their recent IPO, the bulk of their cash balance is most likely real.
- The business is not too capital-intensive.
- Clean balance sheet, with close to no debt.

At that point in time, at a market cap of HKD160 million, we did feel that the positives in the company outweighed the negatives. In addition, a demise of a business typically happens over a considerable period, giving us the opportunity to monitor the company. Of course, there are certain instances where companies just crash and burn, but in most cases, if businesses are going downhill, it takes quite a while. As the years go by, we would be able to observe if OTO Holdings could, either (1) turn the business around, or (2) see its profitable business go south.

Back in 2012, together with a conservative estimate for their still profitable massage equipment business, we estimated that OTO Holdings might be trading at a 60% discount to our intrinsic value.

Eventually, we invested in the company and continued to monitor its progress. Interestingly, in 2014, its stock price started to shoot through the roof after an acquisition attempt by Tempus Holdings Limited. At its peak, the company saw its share price climbed to almost HKD9, 18 times our initial purchase price![10]

Case Study *(Continued)*

Being conservative, we closed our position somewhere around our valuation of HKD400 million, somewhere in the range of HKD1.25–1.50 per share before Tempus Holdings (Hong Kong) Limited came into the picture. As humans, we still think of what could have been if we had held on. Yet there is not much regret on our part and we did not lose sleep over it. This is because, based on our research and estimation, and after revisiting our thesis post-appreciation, we did not chance upon anything that resulted in a change in our initial thesis. Hence, we divested at our expected value.

In hindsight, there was no way that we could have known the timing of an acquisition which resulted in the share price hitting HKD9. Given the information at that time, we would still make the same decision. That is what we meant by having a process in your investment, having rules on when you buy and why you sell an investment, and revisiting your thesis when something new happens. Always trust in the process.

But wait, not so fast. . .

OTO Holdings is one case study about how we can find investment opportunities through asset plays. However, there are risks involved in this method of investing. Even if we invest in a company that looks "cheap", we have to constantly question ourselves about the probability of potential catalysts to help us realise the full value of our investment.

Many companies that do not appear to be utilising their assets to the best of their potential might be punished by the market, resulting in low valuation. Yet, if they have no immediate plans to change course, this could go on for quite some time. The situation might be worse if the company is in a constant net loss position, this means that whatever "excess value" the company has might be reduced to zero as its loss widens. This is often known as a "value-trap" and we need to be aware of it. As minority shareholders, we have no way of getting to the "hidden" value of the company if it remains in status quo. The practical move is to move on to the next better opportunity.

Hence, not all companies trading "cheaply" relative to their asset base are considered great investments. At the end of the day, investors still have to take note of the company's situation. We might not want to be invested in a pager company even when it might be selling at a discount to its book value.

As a parting note, we would like you to take away the point that, price-wise, cheap doesn't always mean good. We learned this the hard way and we hope you don't need to. With that said, investing through asset plays is still a highly profitable strategy, as shown by the many value investors in Asia following this strategy. Additionally, in order to increase our chances, it would be good to identify the possible catalysts that could help your cause.

Current Earning Power Value

Next, we will be moving on to finding value from a company's current earning power. This is done by appreciating a company based on its current earning power, with not much consideration given to its future growth potential. In short, even without considering any huge future growth, the company should still be attractive as an investment.

Imagine a company priced at $12 per share, with close to no debt and a fairly predictable income stream with earnings of $3 per share. Theoretically, if the company paid out all their earnings as cash dividends, you could break even in less than four years, giving investors a return on capital of 25%. This is without taking into consideration any growth in its current earnings potential. Here is another case study to illustrate how this works.

Case Study: The Cross-Harbour Holdings Limited

This approach is best illustrated with a company with a simple-to-understand operating model. When it comes to a company like The Cross-Harbour Holdings Limited ("Cross-Harbour Holdings"), its business is definitely easy to understand – operating toll roads.

Listed in 1974, Cross-Harbour Holdings operates road tunnels, driving training centres and was also a service provider of electronic toll clearing facilities in Hong Kong. There are other tollgate businesses out there, but why did Cross-Harbour Holdings stand out? *Hint: It was how the market priced their earnings power from their tunnel operations alone.*

To take a look at how much the market was valuing its business in 2014, we can estimate it by subtracting its cash and non-core investments (net of its total debt) out from its market capitalisation. With a market cap of about HK$2.6 billion (September 2014) and net-net cash position (cash less total liabilities) of HK$1 billion, we inferred that the market valued Cross-Harbour Holdings' two road tunnels, three driving training centres and its electronic toll clearing business at HK$1.6 billion.[11] Our next question was, "Is this a fair representation of Cross-Harbour Holdings' earning power?"

We found out that Cross-Harbour Holdings derived most of its earnings from tollgate operations (at its associate level). Hence, we took a closer look at its key operating asset in play – Cross-Harbour Holdings' 50% stake in Western Harbour Tunnel. Basically, there are three main tunnels linking Kowloon to Hong Kong Island: Cross-Harbour, Eastern Harbour and Western Harbour. Western Harbour had 24.7% market share of all vehicular crossings between Hong Kong and Kowloon.[12] From their 2014 Annual Report, Cross-Harbour Holdings' associate – Western Harbour Tunnel Company Limited, the operator of Western Harbour Crossing – reported a profit after tax of HK$786 million, of which Cross-Harbour was entitled to HK$393 million through their 50% interest.[13]

As Western Harbour is an associate rather than a full subsidiary, Cross-Harbour Holdings can only obtain the cash from these earnings through a dividend pay-out. Interestingly, Western Harbour had only started to pay dividends since 2013.[14] At that juncture, we needed to think about whether Western Harbour would continue to distribute its earnings back to Cross-Harbour Holdings.

We had reasons to believe that the distributions were not one-off and were likely to continue in future. Why? This was because, after years of operations, Western Harbour Tunnel had just managed to clear all its bank loans in 2012.[15] Only after that point would Western Harbour have the cash flow to distribute dividends to Cross-Harbour Holdings. And Cross-Harbour Holdings has the right to the earnings of Western Harbour till the end of their franchise agreement in 2023.

Interestingly, Cross-Harbour Tunnel was also operated by Cross-Harbour Holdings prior to the expiration of their franchise agreement; so there is a chance of non-renewal on these contracts. Although the expiration of this franchise agreement is material, we felt that this steady stream of cash flow before expiry would suffice to cover how the market was valuing the company.

Here's some simple maths to show Cross-Harbour Holdings' future earning power from Western Harbour alone. Assuming Western Harbour pays out most of its earnings as dividends, Cross-Harbour Holdings could get, say, HK$350 million. Over the next 10 years, this was a potential income stream of about HK$3.5 billion, if the profit of Western Harbour stayed the same. Western Harbour has demonstrated in the past that it can grow its earnings by raising prices. The expected return from Western Harbour Tunnel was more than its market capitalisation in September 2014, even after discounting the HK$3.5 billion back to present value (assuming 3% discount rate). Also remember that Cross-Harbour Holdings has other profitable businesses.

If we assume that the contribution from Western Harbour holds, it suggests that we could break even in less than five years. After all, we were paying $1.6 for close to $3.5 worth of future earnings.

Up till now, we were only considering one of its tunnel operations. Cross-Harbour Holdings' other tunnel operation had also been a very stable earner and could continue till at least 2018 when the Tate's Cairn Tunnel agreement expires. So there is another income stream for at least the next five years not accounted for in our estimates.

Two years after our investment, we did a review on the company in 2016. Within those two years, Cross-Harbour Holdings' market capitalisation has

Case Study *(Continued)*

increased by more than 50% to about HKD4 billion. The utility of appreciating value through current earning power cannot be understated. This case study shows that if proper research is done, this method of finding value is highly effective due to its directness. Although we cannot eliminate all the unknowns in investing, minimising some of the unknowns with a simple-to-understand business model is a great start.

Growth Value

Our third approach is value through growth. Assessing growth is slightly trickier as we are trying to find value in events that have yet to take place. As no one can forecast the future, you can imagine the difficulty in getting it right all the time in growth investing. Thus, the big risk in growth analysis is in our own expectations and assumptions.

This can be seen time and time again in the market. During the dotcom bubble, any company with any links with the internet, technology or network could be priced at ultra-high valuations (with many not even profitable). This wild expectation was also present before the 2015 Chinese stock market crash. When the A-Share market crashed, it resulted in almost a third of the market value of the A-Shares on the Shanghai Stock Exchange being wiped out.

However, when applied appropriately, this approach can be just as rewarding over the long run. To better understand growth, we are not always talking about high growth. We do not always have to go for companies with sexy double-digit growth rates of 20%, 30% or even 50%. These companies do exist, and if found at the right price, they do have huge investment potential. However, most of the time, their growth might already be priced in and if that growth spurt is unsustainable, your investment might be hit with a double whammy of lower valuations and lower earnings when their growth ends up fading away.

Thus, we must remember that slow growth is still growth. Even companies with sustainable single-digit growth can become one of the pillars of your portfolio. One such company can be found in the realm of consumer staples and today we will be highlighting an easy-to-understand consumer staple with a defensive product range.

In recent years, probably one of the biggest acquisitions in the Asian consumer staple space was when Heineken Holding N.V. took control of Asia Pacific Breweries Limited in 2012.[16] With Asia Pacific Breweries taken off the market, were there any more publicly listed beer companies in Southeast Asia?

Case Study: Heineken Malaysia Berhad

In Malaysia, there were not one, but two listed breweries – Heineken Malaysia Berhad ("Heineken Malaysia") (previously Guinness Anchor Berhad) and Carlsberg Malaysia Berhad, both with a long history of operations in Malaysia. With them having a "duopoly" in Malaysia's legal beer and stout market, you could say that this was a kind of operating environment that we like our investments to be in.

With a market share of close to 60% of Malaysia's legal beer trade,[17] we will be taking a deeper look at Heineken Malaysia, with their principal business in the production, packaging, marketing and distribution of beer, stout and malt-based drinks under world-famous brands like Guinness, Anchor, Tiger, Heineken, Kilkenny and more.

Earlier we mentioned that the beer business was more defensive in nature. Here are Heineken Malaysia's past ten financial years' earnings per share to show it:

Table 5.1: Heineken Malaysia Berhad Earnings Per Share

FY End 30 Jun	2006	2007	2008	2009	2010	2011	2012	2013	2014	2015
EPS (RM)	0.42	0.37	0.42	0.47	0.51	0.60	0.69	0.72	0.66	0.71

From Table 5.1[18] we can see that, over a period of 10 years, Heineken Malaysia's earnings grew at over 6% per year (FY2006–FY2015), even through the 2008 Global Financial Crisis. Notice how its earnings actually increased in 2008 and 2009. It looks as if the Chinese saying 借酒消愁 (essentially translating as "drowning your sorrows through alcohol") really holds true. All of this was done in the face of excise, duties and sales tax of close to 50%.[19]

Another positive for this company is its ability to generate a stream of strong cash flow without the need for large capital expenditure. Apart from more-efficient machinery, beer production and consumption has not fluctuated too much for the past century. Thus, it is safe to assume that in terms of the technology, there might not be anything that would change beer drastically any time soon. What this means is that the company has relatively predictable maintenance capital expenditure. And it would be able to free up more cash to

Case Study *(Continued)*

reward shareholders. Remember, returns are not just made up of capital gains. Dividends matter too. Even with a "low" growth rate of say 5–6% a year, if the bulk of earnings get paid out, this combination of capital gains and dividends could potentially boost your returns to high single digits per annum.

If you had purchased Heineken Malaysia in January 2000 and held on till January 2017, you would have made a total gain of 475% including dividends collected over the period.[20] Not too bad for a non-sexy "low-growth" business.

Growth investing doesn't always have to be investing in the next "in" thing. Slow and steady still works in investing. Even for growth investing. If this is slow and steady, we will take slow and steady any day. The case study of Heineken Malaysia has highlighted how we can find value through growth.

Special Situations

Lastly, we have a bonus category for you – finding value through special situations. This opportunity could encompass any of the above three types of value – asset, current earning power and growth. However, the difference is that a company-specific event is required within a short period of time; a catalyst to unlock this unique value. Typically, a special situation investment is more of a short-term investment.

We seek to benefit from special situations, when we believe the market is behaving irrationally about the odds of the event either taking place or not taking place. These events involve corporate action, from the restructuring of a company to mergers, spin-offs, share repurchases, privatisations, bankruptcy, asset sales and even the sale of the entire company.

Case Study: Fraser and Neave, Limited

A recent example of activist investment in Asia was the investment into Singapore's Fraser and Neave, Limited ("F&N") by Thailand billionaire Charoen Sirivadhanabhakdi.[21] Sirivadhanabhakdi is a well-known billionaire with a majority stake in Thai Beverage Public Company Limited ("Thai Beverage"), the brand owner of Thailand's Chang beer, one of the largest beverage companies in Thailand.[22]

Listed in 1898, F&N is a Singapore conglomerate with over 100 years of history.[23] Before the takeover, F&N was one of the constituents of the Straits

Case Study *(Continued)*

Times Index, the stock market index of Singapore.[24] Through the years, F&N grew as a beverage company, partnering Heineken N.V. to form Malayan Breweries Limited since the 1930s (now Asia Pacific Breweries Limited). It was also the anchor bottler for The Coca-Cola Company for Singapore and Malaysia in the past. Subsequently, F&N diversified into the publishing and property businesses, becoming one of Singapore's largest conglomerates. So, what triggered one of Asia's largest corporate takeovers in 2013?

Majority-owned by Oversea-Chinese Banking Corporation ("OCBC"), a leading bank in Singapore, F&N was considered to be a non-banking business. Due to new regulations, OCBC faced regulatory restrictions concerning the ownership of their non-core businesses. This led to their decision to divest their stake in F&N. At that time, F&N's other significant shareholders included one of Japan's main beverage companies – Kirin Holdings Company, Limited (15%) – and Prudential Asset Management (Singapore) Limited (8%).[25] The fact that F&N was a company with only institutional investors plus the lack of a controlling majority shareholder made it a very interesting proposition. Furthermore, like many conglomerates, F&N was priced in the market with a "conglomerate discount". Thus, it appeared that there was value waiting to be unlocked.

So how can value be unlocked from this company? In essence, given the conglomerate discount, each business segment in F&N might be worth more than its sum. Therefore, in theory, the value could be unlocked by spinning off its different divisions to create three more-valuable assets (beverage, property and publishing) at full value instead of as a single discounted asset.

When the Sirivadhanabhakdi group of companies announced their bid for the 22% stake in F&N from the OCBC Group, it sparked a series of events. Asia Pacific Breweries' ("APB") partner, Heineken, did not want another brewery giant taking control of APB. This led to a buy-out offer for APB separately.

Shortly after, F&N was itself a target after OCBC received a competing offer for its stake from Singapore-listed Overseas Union Enterprise Limited ("OUE"), a property company in Singapore. That triggered a bidding war between OUE and the Sirivadhanabhakdi group of companies.[26]

In the year before the offer, F&N traded in the range of S$6–7 per share. By 2013, share prices soared from the opening bid of S$8.88 (what a nice number) to the final offer of S$9.55 in just a matter of months.[27]

Finally, in 2013, OCBC's stake in F&N was successfully sold by the Sirivadhanabhakdi group of companies. After the purchase, the value-unlocking processes panned out one after another. First, the property business of F&N was spun off into a listed entity, Frasers Centrepoint Limited.[28] Many of the investment properties within the company were later spun off again through the listing

Case Study *(Continued)*

of two Real Estate Investment Trusts (REITs).[29,30] Moreover, there are many initiatives to find synergy between the beverage arm of F&N and Thai Beverage through cross-distribution or new product innovations.

In totality, the Sirivadhanabhakdi group of companies unlocked value by taking control of F&N, breaking it up, finding synergies and "selling" the parts at a higher value.

For investors that understood the logic of this value-unlocking process, they might be able to invest alongside the Sirivadhanabhakdi group of companies during their bid for F&N.

Narrow Your Search – Screening

So how do we go about finding these possible investments in the ocean of thousands of listed companies?

A good way is by screening. Think of it as a funnel where only the best ideas flow through, enabling us to concentrate on the ones we think have better potential. This allows us to make use of our time more efficiently. At least that's the idea.

Maybe an analogy to shoe shopping would make things clearer. Imagine you are looking to buy a pair of running shoes. If we just go ahead without a plan, we would be looking at the entire universe of shoe stores retailing a whole range of footwear, from slippers all the way to high heels, that are not what we were looking for. Now, what can we do to give ourselves an easier time deciding?

Whether you realise it or not, you have already been screening everyday on a subconscious level. Think about it: by deciding on men's shoes you might have already reduced your options by maybe even more than half. And by deciding on running shoes, you might have filtered out a whole range of other shoes stores selling the likes of leather shoes, loafers, boots, etc. This would dramatically reduce the chances of you walking into Timberland or Hush Puppies store to get running shoes! This then allows you to focus your attention on retailers specialising in running shoes, for example ASICS and New Balance. What we want to do is to translate this subconscious process to the investment universe.

Basically, screening gives us the ability to narrow down our search for a possible investment. Consider a stock market with about 1,000 listed companies. You can do a screen with certain criteria to reduce your search down to a workable number of companies. From there you can then start doing a more detailed analysis on each of them before making an investment. How then do we go about this screening process?

There are countless ways, but screens generally fall in these three categories:

1. Quantitative – for when you have things that can be measured:
   - market cap
   - market price (52-week high, low)
   - valuation (P/E, P/B)
   - dividend yield
   - margins (GPM, OPM)
   - leverage (debt to equity, interest coverage)
   - and this list just goes on!
2. Qualitative – for when you have things that are not easy to measure:
   - quality of management
   - width and depth of business moat
   - reputation of company
   - reputation of major shareholder.
3. Thematic – for when you have a certain view of a certain scenario:
   - geographical focus
   - industry focus.

What's great is that there are no hard and fast rules. These three categories can be used separately or in conjunction with one another in any order that you want to use them in!

And to start you off, here are some online screeners that might help you:

- Singapore: SGX Stockfacts[31]
- Malaysia: Stockhut Mobile App,[32] KLSE Screener Mobile App[33]
- Global: Financial Times Equity Screener,[34] Google Finance Stock Screener.[35]

Screen Your Screens

A possible investment idea can come along from anywhere: through mainstream media, books and magazines, conversations with friends and even just from our personal experiences.

However, if we assume that it will take you one full day to analyse one company (very optimistic), this means that it would take you more than four years just to look through all the companies listed in Hong Kong. And with so many listed companies, how can we focus our time on those that are really worth it?

To give an example, one way to narrow down your search is by looking from the top of the economy. Imagine this: if China's growth days are far from over, it might not be too far-fetched to assume that the Chinese appetite for consumer goods – things that people eat, drink, wear and use – is still going strong. Sounds familiar? Yes, it's none other than the China consumer story. Again. So bear with us.

Anyway, with the China consumer story still having certain merits, you might be interested in Hong Kong or China-listed consumer staples with a large market cap, specifically market leaders in the food and beverage industry. If you haven't already noticed, those criteria just about ticked all our three quantitative (large capitalisation), qualitative (market leaders) and thematic boxes (China consumer story – Food and beverage industry).

And with just these factors alone, we would have already narrowed our universe from thousands of listed companies down to a fairly workable list. Some of the companies that might have passed our initial screen included names like Hong Kong-listed China Mengniu Dairy Company Limited, Dali Foods Group Company Limited, Tingyi (Cayman Islands) Holding Corporation, Tsingtao Brewery Company Limited, Uni-President China Holdings Limited, Want Want China Holdings Limited and Vitasoy International Holdings Limited.

To show the versatility and utility of screening, let's stick with our example of the China consumer, but in this case focus on the discretionary consumer industry.

As the general wealth level increases, the Chinese consumer patterns get more sophisticated and demand for higher-quality goods could start to increase. With this train of thought, a decent case for a rise in demand for luxury brands in China could be made.

With that idea, we can perform a thematic and quantitative screen to focus on companies:

- In the consumer discretionary space – jewellery and luxury auto players
- With strong growth over the past decade
- With a huge portion of their revenue from Chinese consumers.

Just for reference, some companies in our list could include names like BYD Company Limited, Chow Tai Fook Jewellery Group Limited, Hengdeli Holdings Limited, Luk Fook Holdings (International) Limited, Prada S.p.A and Zhongsheng Group Holdings Limited.

If we wanted to further narrow down our scope, and were interested in the larger HKEX-listed jewellery companies, we could end up with an even smaller list consisting of companies like Chow Tai Fook Jewellery Group Limited, Chow Sang Sang Holdings International Limited and Luk Fook Holdings (International) Limited.

Another way is to just use a quantitative screen to narrow down your options, and likewise you would also arrive at the desired outcome of a handful of companies worth looking deeper into.

With quantitative screening, it definitely helps if you have an online screening tool at your disposal. Most brokerages should have an online stock screener for investors. In any case, there are many free online screeners available on platforms like Google Finance, Yahoo Finance, Morningstar and Financial Times. Beyond that there are also paid services such Bloomberg, Thomson Reuters and S&P Capital IQ. However, given that most of us might only have access to the free online options, we will attempt a quantitative screen with the *Financial Times* equity screener to show you how it works. Most of these screening tools are quite intuitive to use: input your criteria and let the screener work its magic.

Criteria included with help of the *Financial Times* equity screener:

- companies listed on the Hong Kong Stock Exchange
- Gross Profit Margin (5Y average) > 20%
- Net Profit Margin (5Y average) > 5%
- Net Income Growth (5Y) > 10%
- Return on Average Assets (5Y average) > 10%
- Return on Equity (5Y average) > 10%
- Dividend Yield > 2%
- P/E Ratio < 12×
- Price to Cash Flow (TTM) < 12×
- Total Debt to Capital < 50%.

With these 10 factors, we ended up with a group of 18 companies.[36] Wouldn't you say that this is a much more manageable figure compared with painstakingly combing through a list of over a thousand listed companies?

Furthermore, with less emphasis on the economy-related factors, quantitative screening is associated with the traditional bottom-up style of investing. The bottom-up investor tends to believe that any company, regardless of the industry, might be a good investment so long as it is purchased at an appropriate discount. Or just simply when it is "cheap" enough. Therefore, bottom-up investment strategy emphasises the individual business, looking solely at the merits and valuation of the company.

Additionally, screening is more than just about quantitative values. In fact, depending on the factors we choose, it could give us a rough guide into the qualitative and thematic side of the story. For example, finding companies trading at low Price-to-Earnings and Price-to-Book ratios might be a starting point for us to investigate possible turnarounds or assets plays. Screening for companies with favourable revenue growth trends, good return on capital ratio and trading near 52-week high price might expose us to companies with good growth prospects and positive catalysts. Screens for large cap companies with low leverage ratios coupled with low Price-to-Earnings and Price-to-Book ratios might indicate an industry primed for consolidation.

In any case, the point we are trying to put across is that screening is a very versatile tool. And the objective of screening is always to help you narrow down your search.

The 5-Fingers Rule

After your initial screen, you might still be left with 50–100 companies. At this point you do not want to increase your screening criteria as it might end up being too restrictive. However, focusing on 50–100 companies is still way too many for you to handle. What do we do now?

It's time for the **5-Fingers Rule.**

The 5-Fingers Rule is a simple 10-point checklist to put the short-listed companies through a quick analysis to further narrow down your search to where only the best of the bunch remains. That's the whole idea.

Wondering how this rule came about? Just take a look at your fingers. There's ten right there, five on each hand. Five out of ten is 50% and that's a pass. Thus the idea came about that when companies are able to meet five or more points on our checklists, it would then be worth our time to look into the company in detail.

Our 5-Fingers checklist includes the following ten questions:

1. **Can you understand the business?**

    The single most important factor when it comes to choosing your investment is to find one that you understand. If you cannot even explain how the company makes its money, it will never be a great investment for you as you will not be able to find the confidence to invest in it.

    For us, we have a very simple way to decide if we understand the business. As long as we still find it hard to understand how the business works after three readings of its annual report, and if there is nothing super-compelling about this company, we would place it in our "too hard" pile of companies and move on.

2. **Does the company have a decent track record?**

    Although past performance does not necessarily represent the future performance, a clear observation of the company's track record is still extremely valuable. In particular, it shows us the characteristic of the business, the board and management's response to various challenges and also their treatment of shareholders.

    On the other hand, in the case of a newly listed company, you might only have the management's word to show for things. This is where the risk lies. There is insufficient track record for us to judge if the management behaves fairly towards the shareholders. Again, there is nothing wrong for those who favour this style of operating. But for us, we tend to sleep better when invested in companies with a decent operational track record, a rule of thumb being one business cycle.

3. **Is the company making money?**

    Before all the Captain Obvious jokes come up, we like to say that many people take this fundamental quality for granted. From our experience, many investors still do invest in loss-making companies, in the hopes that they will become profitable. Nothing wrong about this; however it is notable that this approach requires a much higher degree of due diligence from the investor. Given the risk and reward profile, unless we are prepared to do a deep research into the company, to understand the nature of its business, why it is losing money and how it is going to turn the company around, we generally do not recommend investments in consistently loss-making companies. An investor invests to enhance his net worth, and if the company is consistently bleeding, how can its shareholders be enriched? And as Warren Buffett says, "Turnarounds seldom turn."

4. Does the company have worthwhile profit margins?

As an extension of the previous point, we can have a rough gauge of how much pricing power the company has just from its profit margins. Most companies with commodity-like products tend to have low profit margins. On the other hand, companies with a consistently high level of profit margins tend to have some sort of moat in their businesses. (Or are things too good to be true? More on that later.)

To increase our chances of finding better-managed companies with stronger pricing power, we like to focus on companies with a reasonable level of profitability. And although what is reasonable differs from industry to industry, companies consistently delivering operating margins of sub-5% might indicate to us how tough their industry is. And our rule of thumb is that any company with a consistent sub-5% operating margin is considered low for us.

5. Can the company continue profitably in the near future?

This question focuses on the future. This is important as, although track records are good and all, at the end of the day investing is still a forward-looking game. Even for a company with past operating margins of 20%, that doesn't matter if it could fall to 0% due to a shift in technology. So we want to make sure that the company is not operating in an industry that is facing structural decline. You might not want to be invested in a company specialising in the Yellow Pages phone book business.

6. Does the company have a strong balance sheet?

Debt is a double-edged sword. In good times, leverage can be used to boost a company's performance. However, in bad times, they can go downhill way faster and way more painfully than you expect. With this happening since the dawn of capitalism, it's not news to us. Even during the recent 2015 oil crisis, many over-leveraged companies in the oil and gas industry were just a covenant away from defaulting on their obligations.

In our minds, two types of companies employ debt:
- companies that use debt to boost profitability
- companies whose business model is dependent on debt refinancing.

Because downturns are inevitable, we feel much more comfortable with companies with a strong balance sheet position and tend to avoid the latter. Lastly, we like to end this section with one of the 16 factors in Walter & Edwin Schloss Associates LP article "Factors needed to make money in the stock market": "Be careful of leverage. It can go against you."

7. Is there a history of excessive shareholder dilution?

Growth by taking on too much debt might be bad for the company but equal damage can be inflicted through excessive equity financing. This is because every time a company issues new shares to outsiders, it is selling a part of its business.

What this means is that existing shareholders end up owning less of the enlarged group. Shareholders in a company that expands with excessive equity financing might find themselves gradually owning a smaller and smaller part of the pie.

8. Does the company consistently churn out free cash flow?

Free cash flow is a measure of how much cash the company is generating from its operations after all its capital expenditure. If a company is not generating any positive cash flow for a long period, we would pay attention, especially when the company needs external funding to maintain its operations. The funding could come from either additional debt or additional equity, both of which if done too often, and excessively, are not desirable for investors.

At the end of the day, it depends on how much cash the company brings in. Remember this well – cash is a fact, profit is an opinion.

9. Does the company have decent returns on capital?

A good measure of how well a company is making use of its capital comes from looking at its return on capital. One such ratio is the return on equity (ROE). The ROE is calculated as shareholders' net income over the shareholders' equity. This ratio essentially shows well the company performs with the resources it has. Generally, the higher the better.

10. Is the major shareholder fair?

In Asia, there is nothing unusual in a major shareholder owning a controlling equity block in the company. In fact, for smaller cap companies, this might be the norm. *Note: Major shareholders can also be in the form of another company.*

In any case, we aren't implying anything negative just from a major interest by a shareholder. Instead we are looking from the angle that with such a significant block, a major shareholder might have some say in the company, thus it definitely helps to have at least a basic understanding of a company's shareholding structure. From it, we need to see if the major shareholder has done anything unfair to minority shareholders, such as excessive compensation or private placements to themselves at sharp discounts in the past.

The Importance of the 5-Fingers Rule

These ten simple questions that can easily be answered with a quick scan of the company's annual reports. As a quick rule of thumb, we should only investigate deeper if it has at least five positive answers from our checklist. Imagine the ten questions as your ten fingers; if it makes you able to grasp it with one hand or five fingers, then it might be worth your time.

Surely, there are exceptions to the rules and we might miss out some great opportunities with this approach. However, when used conservatively, the benefit of avoiding bad investments should outweigh the possibility of missing out on some good investments.

To end our chapter, we like to share this rather useful checklist from Philip Fisher's *Common Stocks and Uncommon Profits*[37] (Table 5.2). Although we might not be able to answer all his questions (and we do not need to), having the curiosity and answers to some of them is already more than enough for us to help in our investment decisions!

Here are 15 of his questions to check if the company is worth his time:

1. Does the company have products or services with sufficient market potential to make possible a sizeable increase in sales for at least several years?

Table 5.2: 5-Fingers Rule Checklist

S/N	5-Fingers Rule Checklist	✓|✗
1	Can you understand the business?	
2	Does the company have a decent track record?	
3	Is the company making money?	
4	Does the company have worthwhile profit margins?	
5	Can the company continue profitably in the near future?	
6	Does the company have a strong balance sheet?	
7	Is there excessive shareholder dilution?	
8	Does the company consistently churn out free cash flow?	
9	Does the company have decent returns on capital?	
10	Is the major shareholder fair?	

2. Does the management have a determination to continue to develop products or processes that will still further increase total sales potentials when the growth potentials of currently attractive product lines have largely been exploited?

3. How effective are the company's research and development efforts in relation to its size?

4. Does the company have an above-average sales organisation?

5. Does the company have a worthwhile profit margin?

6. What is the company doing to maintain or improve profit margins?

7. Does the company have outstanding labour and personnel relations?

8. Does the company have outstanding executive relations?

9. Does the company have depth to its management?

10. How good are the company's cost analysis and accounting controls?

11. Are there other aspects of the business, somewhat peculiar to the industry involved, which will give the investor important clues as to how outstanding the company may be in relation to its competition?

12. Does the company have a short-range or long-range outlook in regard to profits?

13. In the foreseeable future, will the growth of the company require sufficient equity financing so that the larger number

of shares then outstanding will largely cancel the existing stockholders' benefit from the anticipated growth?

14. Does the management talk freely to investors about its affairs when things are going well but "clam up" when troubles and disappointment occur?
15. Does the company have a management of unquestionable integrity?

Notes

1. Value Partners Group Limited. "2015 Annual Report".
2. Target Asset Management Private Ltd. "Company Presentation". www.targetasset.com. April 2015.
3. APS Asset Management. "Board of Directors & Senior Management". http://www.aps.com.sg/about-us/board-of-directors-n-senior-management. Accessed: 10 January 2017.
4. Aberdeen Asset Management Asia Limited. Thailand. "Hugh Young". http://www.aberdeen-asset.co.uk/aam.nsf/thailand/hughyoung. Accessed: 10 January 2017.
5. Pheim Asset Management (Asia) Pte Limited. About Us. Structure. "Our Team". http://www.pheim.com.sg/about_us/staff_singapore_team.html. Accessed: 10 January 2017.
6. Yeoman Capital Management Private Limited. Corporate Presentation. http://yeomancapitalmanagement.com/. Accessed 10 January 2017.
7. OTO Holdings Limited. "Annual Report 2011/2012".
8. OTO Holdings Limited. "Interim Report 2012/2013".
9. OTO Holdings Limited. "Annual Report 2012/2013".
10. Google Finance. "Tempus Holdings Limited". https://www.google.com/finance?cid=1065337311517219. Accessed: 10 January 2017.
11. The Cross-Harbour (Holdings) Limited. "Interim Report 2014".
12. The Government of the Hong Kong Special Administrative Region. Transport Department. "The Annual Traffic Census 2013". June 2014.
13. The Cross-Harbour (Holdings) Limited. "Annual Report 2014".
14. The Cross-Harbour (Holdings) Limited. "Annual Report 2013".
15. Ibid.
16. Heineken Holdings N.V. "Annual Report 2012".
17. Star Media Group Berhad. The Star Online. Business News. "Cheers to brewery stocks, shares rise on price increase". http://www.thestar.com.my/business/business-news/2016/07/06/cheers-to-brewery-stocks/>. July 2016.
18. Guinness Anchor Berhad Annual Report 2010 & 2015.

19. Guinness Anchor Berhad. "Annual Report 2015".
20. Authors' Calculation with Data from Yahoo Finance; https://goo.gl/4P8kMG.
21. Joyce Koh. Bloomberg. "Thai Billionaire Charoen Wins Control of Fraser & Neave". https://www.bloomberg.com/news/articles/2013-01-30/thai-billionaire-charoen-wins-control-of-fraser-neave. 31 January 2013.
22. Thai Beverage Public Company Limited. "Annual Report 2016".
23. Fraser and Neave, Limited. "Annual Report 2016".
24. Alvin Foo. *The Straits Times*. "Hutchison Port Holdings Trust to replace F&N on Straits Times Index next month". http://www.straitstimes.com/business/hutchison-port-holdings-trust-to-replace-fn-on-straits-times-index-next-month. 26 March 2013.
25. Fraser and Neave, Limited. "Annual Report 2011".
26. Eveline Danubrata and Saeed Azhar. Reuters. "Thai Tycoon Trumps Overseas Union bid for F&N, setting up showdown". http://www.reuters.com/article/us-fraserandneave-takeover-thais-idUSBRE90I03T20130119. 18 January 2013.
27. Ibid.
28. Fraser and Neave, Limited. "Annual Report 2013".
29. Sudhan P. The Motley Fool Singapore Private Limited. "What Investors Need to Know About Frasers Hospitality Trust's Initial Public Offering". https://www.fool.sg/2014/06/24/what-investors-need-to-know-about-frasers-hospitality-trusts-initial-public-offering/. 24 June 2014.
30. Esjay. The Motley Fool Singapore Private Limited. "Frasers Logistics and Industrial Trust's IPO: What Investors Should Know". https://www.fool.sg/2016/06/06/what-investors-should-know-about-the-upcoming-ipo-of-frasers-logistics-and-industrial-trust/. 6 June 2016.
31. Singapore Exchange Limited. Company Information. "StockFacts". http://www.sgx.com/wps/portal/sgxweb/home/company_disclosure/stockfacts. Accessed: 12 January 2017.
32. StockHut. http://www.stockhut.com.my/. Accessed: 6 April 2017.
33. KLSE Screener. https://www.klsescreener.com/v2/. Accessed: 6 April 2017.
34. *Financial Times*. Equities. "Equity Screener". https://markets.ft.com/data/equities. Accessed: 12 January 2017.
35. Google Finance. "Stock Screener". https://www.google.com/finance/stockscreener. Accessed: 12 January 2017.
36. *Financial Times*. Equities. "Equity Screener". https://markets.ft.com/data/equities/results. Accessed: 12 January 2017.
37. Philip A. Fisher. Published by John Wiley & Sons, Inc. *Common Stocks and Uncommon Profits*. Copyright 1996, 2003.

CHAPTER 6

Research Like a Businessman

In God We Trust, All Others Must Bring Data
— William Edwards Deming

Once we run our screens together with our "5-Fingers Rule", we should be left with a manageable number of companies. But before rushing in to buy any of these investment opportunities, we always have to ask ourselves these key questions:

- What is the key value of the company? Is it based on assets, earning power or growth?
- What are the key opportunities?
- Do I understand the business model?
- What are the key risks?
- Is our margin of safety sufficient?

Humans are emotional creatures. However, to make good investment decisions, we have to take our emotions out of the picture. That is why we need to have a structured investment process. These questions are a critical part of that process as they force us to form the investment thesis for the company in a logical manner.

At the end of the day, what we are doing is to convince ourselves both quantitatively and qualitatively that this is a worthy investment opportunity for us to act upon. Moreover, it always helps when we are supported by facts and logical reasoning, and not based on "what a little bird told me" or that "this feels right". Investment decisions are best made without the presence of emotions.

To make such informed decisions, we need to use good data. And in order to use good data, we need to know how to obtain good data. Otherwise it might end up being a case of "garbage in, garbage out" – incorrect or poor-quality input will produce faulty output. And that's definitely not something we want.

To avoid poetic justice (Figure 6.1),[1] we will proceed to outline our investment processes, which is something you can use as a framework to arrive at your very own investment style and processes.

Having a good process does not mean that you will totally avoid "bad breaks". Sometimes, even with a good process, we might end up with a "bad break" for reasons beyond our control. However, a good process is needed for us to increase our chances of finding better investments and avoiding bad ones. Knowing what to avoid is half the battle won.

Getting the Right Data

With the need for good data firmly established, let's show you where to get good data.

Useful external data sources:

- Data service providers: Bloomberg, Thomson Reuters, S&P Capital IQ and Factset
- Google: your best friend
- industry studies: market research reports
- conversations and interviews: company, competitors, customers, suppliers, investors, people in the industry
- investor forums: Seeking Alpha, Value Investors Club, Value Chambers
- newspapers and magazines: CNBC, Bloomberg, Channel News Asia, *South China Morning Post*, The Edge (Singapore and Malaysia)
- other publications: biography, books and documents on the company

Decision Matrix	Good Outcome	Bad Outcome
Good Process	Deserved Success	Bad Break
Bad Process	Dumb Luck	Poetic Justice

Figure 6.1   Decision Matrix

- personal observations: taking note of the latest trends and products
- research reports: sell-side brokerages
- top holdings of funds: reports and disclosures by fund managers.

Useful internal data sources:

- Annual General Meeting
- company presentations
- company prospectus
- investor relations.

And finally, *the* single most important piece of documentation:

- annual reports.

Remember what famous investor, Michael Burry, said in the movie *The Big Short.* He was able to detect mispricings in mortgage securities because he *actually* read the thousands of pages of mortgages. We might be oversimplifying this part but many people look at the thickness of documents and take things for granted. Newsflash: You actually have to read it.

Now that we know where to get the data, here's how to use the data, starting with the annual report.

Annual Reports Are Your Best Friend

Here are three reasons why we should start with the annual report.

1. The annual report is pretty much the most comprehensive piece of documentation that a listed company is required to publish on an annual basis.
2. The financials are audited.
3. It is publicly available.

The keywords here are "required", "audited" and "publicly available".

Annual reports are a great starting point that we can work from, especially true for companies we have no prior knowledge of. Not only do annual reports provide valuable knowledge about how the company goes about its business, they also provide you with the financial numbers. We can also compare annual reports from different financial years to double check if management really walked the talk.

To reinforce our earlier points, we have to, at a minimum, understand the basic operation and business model of the company before we even consider it as an investment. This is because understanding the company and the business model allows us to be more comfortable when investing in the company and not succumb to fear or greed in the face of Mr Market's mood. And annual reports help us do this.

Making Sense of an Annual Report

Most annual reports are filled with legal jargons and may cause information overload for most investors. That is why it is important to know the key sections to focus on and why.

Apart from being an information pack for companies, annual reports are also powerful marketing tools for them. Thus, most annual reports tend to have positive upbeat remarks surrounding the description of the business. But as Rocky Balboa says, "The world ain't all sunshine and rainbows."

When reading an annual report, it helps to keep in mind this single piece of advice: Don't just focus on the positive statements and nice pictures, but on the quality of information – things that will help you make investment decisions. Here are the key segments to focus on.

Letter to Shareholders

Here is where we can get a summary of what the company accomplished in the past year. It usually starts with a summary of the financial performance of the year. It might be followed by a brief discussion of the company's operations. This part should also cover some of the achievements and mishaps that occurred during the year. Finally, this section normally wraps up with a discussion of the future plans of the company.

Companies with detailed and informative letters to shareholders are beneficial for shareholders. For example, Warren Buffett, chairman of conglomerate Berkshire Hathaway Inc., typically publishes detailed letters to shareholders. You could say that a letter of such detail is not the norm. On the other hand, there are also companies that go with a minimalistic approach.

In either case, we should be wary when:

- the tone of the letter is overly optimistic
- their plans seem too out-of-this-world
- the company's past actions contradict what they write.

A sign of an informative letter is when the company discusses what they did well and also their missteps in detail. However, it is important that the company learns from the mistakes rather than just repeating the same mistakes year after year. Also, if the company is a serial mistake maker, you might want to spend your time elsewhere.

When reading the letters to shareholders, do take note of:

- Tone: Language and expectations compared to previous years
- Strategy: Does it sound possible and how does it compare to previous years?
- Outlook: Do their future plans sound possible and is it consistent throughout the years?
- Shareholder action: Dividends and share buybacks?
- Execution: Has the company been able to do what it says?

Management Discussion and Analysis ("MD&A")

If you are wondering where to look in order to have a better understanding of the company's operations, the MD&A (also known as Operational and Financial Review in Asia) would be your choice. If the Letter to Shareholders represents the big picture appetiser to how the company works, the MD&A is the main course when it comes to understanding the company's operations.

If we think of a company as a plane, the shareholders are the passengers, management are the staff ensuring that the plane is running properly and the board of directors are the ones plotting the course as well as keeping an eye on the pilots – in this case the top management. Hence when it comes to operational details, the MD&A (by the management) might be more helpful when it comes to understanding the business. Think of it as tapping directly into the minds of the management team, with a highlight on both their objective and priorities, at least to the extent that they want us to know.

Reading an insightful MD&A should give us the information to perform a SWOT analysis on the company.

SWOT stands for:

- Strengths: What is their economic moat?
- Weaknesses: What are they struggling with and how they can do better?
- Opportunities: What are their future plans?
- Threats: What are the key risks faced by the company?

Let's run through one example of what to look out for in the MD&A with Singapore-listed Super Group Limited ("Super Group"). The company's 2014 Annual Report's Operations and Financial Review provided quite a comprehensive discussion of its business.[2] Taking it from the top, Super Group came out with the painful truth that their operating environment in the past year was tough. However, they were clearly still profitable and still looked to be headed in the right direction in the near future. Next was a brief on their two core operations – what they sell, where they sell and who their customers are.

Subsequently, Super Group took it one step further with a breakdown of their core operating segments both geographically and by product. This was also presented during the review of their financial position. In our opinion, the part that gave us the greatest value-add were the in-depth discussions provided behind major significant events.

Next, when it came to their growth, Super Group gave a series of clear and actionable steps on how they were looking into the future. The keywords here are "clear" and "actionable". We often hear management speak of expansion plans. But if it was left as vague as "the company is looking to expand overseas", that's pretty much as useful as a toothpick in a gunfight.

All in all, even though we still had some unanswered questions (surprising if we didn't) after reading through the reports, we could see the effort taken by Super Group to communicate with their shareholders. Thus, we felt that Super Group's MD&A was definitely above average.

Here is also where our three-reads rule comes into play. It really is a pretty useful rule. As a rule of thumb, if you are unable to even have a basic grasp of how the company makes money after three reads, then the issue might not be you. Either the business is too complicated or someone is trying to confuse you. In any case, it might be better to move on.

Always keep in mind that, no matter how detailed the MD&A is, it is not audited. We should verify what was said in the MD&A with the financial statements and footnotes. If the management says one thing but the numbers show another, go with the numbers.

When reading the MD&A, do take note of:

- track record – does management walk the talk?
- how the company made money – the process and operations
- key products, operating segments and assets
- how the company did in the past year
- the company's economic moat over their peers
- how the industry is doing
- significant events during the year (acquisitions, divestments, reorganisation)
- feasibility of future plans.

Auditor Opinion

The role of an auditor is to form an opinion about whether the information presented in the financial statements is fair and whether the financial statements are prepared according to the country's accounting standards. At the end of an audit, the auditor issues the opinion about the financial statement for that year. Also, it is not an auditor's job to detect fraud.

An Enron tale comes to mind. We can use this example to illustrate to you just how ridiculous the Enron saga was. Imagine that your company has a dog as an asset but you need a duck to appear on your financial statements. Fortunately, there are specific accounting rules for what defines a duck. The rules state that a duck is something that is white, with yellow feet and an orange beak. So what you do is you take this dog and paint it white on the body, yellow on the feet and paste a bright orange beak on its nose. Next you say to your auditor: "This is a duck. Look at its yellow feet, white covering and orange beak! Don't you agree that it is a duck?" And the auditor says: "Yes, according to the rules, this is a duck." Basically, everyone knows that it's a dog and not a duck. But it doesn't matter because it met the rules to be a duck.[3]

When the entire saga blew open, both Enron and its auditor, Arthur Andersen, went under.

Despite what we've just said, auditors in general do play a very important role by providing us with a basis to assess companies. And unless the auditor comes up with a qualified or adverse opinion, we tend to go with them.

Basically, an auditor can issue either three types of opinions or a disclaimer:

- unqualified: things are all good
- qualified: things are not so good
- adverse: things are not good at all
- disclaimer: unable to even give an opinion.

As a rule of thumb, we only look at companies with unqualified financial statements. Taking Singapore-listed companies for example, some companies that were given qualified opinions included Great Group Holdings Limited[4] and Metech International Limited.[5]

If you think that this only affects smaller companies, think again. Hong Kong-listed Tianhe Chemicals Group Limited ("Tianhe Chemicals"), with its market capitalisation of over HK$40 billion during their IPO,[6,7] saw its auditor resign after the audit committee refused to accept the auditor's disclaimer opinion.[8] As at January 2017, Tianhe Chemicals was suspended and has not traded since March 2015.[9]

When looking at the auditor opinion, do take note of:

- the reputation of the Auditor
- when the Auditor gives a qualified opinion – watch out!
- when the Auditor suddenly resigns – not a good sign.

Financial Statements

The financial statements are a treasure trove full of useful information and we should always investigate them. The financial statements alone can give us a decent idea of how the company is. Not only can the financial statements tell you how well the company is operating, but more importantly you can use the audited information to cross-check what the company mentioned in its Letters to Shareholders and MD&A.

Think of the company's financial statements as its yearly health screening. You might not know the character and lifestyle of the person from just the screening report, but you could be able to get a good idea on his present condition.

Typically, excluding the notes, financial statements consist of four main parts:

- income statement: how good the company is at making money
- balance sheet: what the company owns and owes
- cash flow statement: how much cash really went in and out of the company
- statements of changes in equity: showing the movement in reserves within the shareholders' equity. *Note: Statement of Changes in Equity is an accounting necessity, but seldom used by investors.*

So, in order for this story to come together, it is important for us to read at least the first three parts together. For instance, you do not have to be a sophisticated investor to notice higher revenue. Your first thought might be a good thought; how can more revenue be a bad thing?

However, there is always more to things than meets the eye. Apart from the revenue, we need to monitor other factors. Imagine that, apart from higher revenue, the company also experienced:

- ↓ Gross Profit Margin (Income Statement)
- ↓ Operating Margin (Income Statement)
- ↑ Trade Receivables (Balance Sheet)
- ↑ Inventory (Balance Sheet)
- ↑ Borrowings (Balance Sheet)
- ↓ Operating Cash Flow (Cash Flow Statement)
- ↑ New share issue (Cash Flow Statement).

What do all these mean? Historically, these points indicated that the company might be:

- ↓ Margins: selling more commoditised products, experiencing more challenging operating conditions
- ↑ Trade Receivables: having trouble collecting payment from customers or having laxer credit terms
- ↑ Inventory: having trouble selling their products
- ↑ Borrowings: having worsening cash flow or liquidity issues

- ↓ Operating Cash Flow: having trouble generating cash
- ↑ New share issue: having liquidity or funding issues.

In summary, the three main statements have to be read together. With that said, the financial statements by themselves are not enough for us to make an investment decision. No analysis is complete without reading the financial footnotes of the annual reports, which is next on our list.

When reading the Financial Statements, do take note of:

- How the company makes money
- How good are they at making money?
- Are they conservative or aggressive – industry-specific?
- Net profit is opinion, cash is fact
- Do the numbers tally with the Letter to Shareholders and MD&A?

Notes to the Financial Statement

Financial statements are based on accounting assumptions and they alone do not tell us what these assumptions are. Therefore, we need to investigate the financial footnotes to better understand the story from the company's financial statements. The phrase that best describes the notes is: "The devil is in the details."

First of all, why are these called the notes to the financial statements? This is simply because there isn't enough space to expand on what each line item means in the financial statements itself. Hence, next to each significant line item there will be a number pegged to it. In order to make more sense of this line item, we can flip to the corresponding note in the notes section.

Looking at Want Want China Holding Limited's ("Want Want China") annual report 2014, Revenue was reported as US$3.78 billion with a Note 5 at the side. So far, all we know is that the company had sales of US$3.78 billion for the year ended December 2014.[10] However once we go to Note 5, a whole new world awaits us. Under Note 5, we find out:

- Want Want China's three core operations in detail
- the three core operations that made up over 99% of revenue
- that over 90% of revenue and business activity was done in the PRC
- the revenue, operating profit and operating margin of each of the core operations

- the assets, liabilities and equity of each of the core operations
- the same information for the previous year (FY2013) for comparison.

It is safe to say that we have learned more about Want Want China's operations from Note 5 compared to knowing that they had a revenue of US$3.78 billion. Not only do we know how much they made, we also know where they made it, how efficient they were at making it and how they did compared to a year ago.

So you see, the notes to the financial statements contain a large amount of useful information for investors. Here are some common information you can find within the notes:

- one-time gains
- the breakdown of expenses
- the remuneration of management
- shares outstanding of the company
- risks
- any other contingent liabilities not mentioned in the financial statements.

Sometimes you will come across very interesting information within the notes of the financial statement that will give you a better idea of how the company is really being managed. Once in a while, you might find golf club memberships, private jets, paintings or even mansions in exotic places disclosed in the notes. If you come across such items, that might give you an idea of how the company is being managed.

When reading the Notes to the Financial Statements, do take note of:

- consistency – any change in accounting practices
- how transparent the company is
- breakdown of each line item on the financial statement
- large hidden assets
- contingent liabilities
- operating leases
- cross-checking what was mentioned in letters to shareholders and the MD&A
- notes that do not make sense.

Directors and Key Management

Directors and key management are the head of the company, the ones leading the charge. As stewards of the company, you want your leaders to have good character and be held in high regard – or, at the very least, not to appear on the front page of the newspaper for the wrong stuff.

On a positive note, Asia-listed companies tend to have a rather comprehensive directors' profile section, with a good record of their professional experience and professional commitments in other companies. And although investment decisions are not made solely on the basis of the involvement of a particular person, they do matter. A recent example is Singapore-listed Wilmar International Limited's two recent additions in 2014 and 2016, George Yong-Boon Yeo and Pua Seck Guan respectively.[11] Both are distinguished businessmen in their own right.

On the other hand, you might think twice about investing in a company if:

- some of the directors are also directors of another company under investigation by the authorities
- directors and key management abruptly leave the company within a short period of time – if there is a mass exodus of key personnel, things within the company might not be that rosy.

When looking at the list of directors and key management, do take note of:

- reputation of the directors
- any significant changes in directors' composition within a short period of time
- any significant changes in key management team within a short period of time.

Shareholders

We do not find it unusual for a major shareholder to own a sizeable equity block in an Asia-listed company. As the decisions of an influential shareholder might be able to make or break a company, it definitely helps to take some time to appreciate the major shareholders. If they have a track record of value creation, that's definitely a positive for us. Take, for instance, REITs. If the REIT has the backing of a strong sponsor or majority shareholder, the company might have easier access to both liquidity and potential assets to grow its income stream.

However, if this particular shareholder is outrightly treating minority shareholders unfairly, we should reconsider investing in the company.

When looking at the shareholding list (Table 6.1), do take note of:

- the reputation of the major shareholders
- any sudden changes in the major shareholders
- the past actions of the major shareholders, both privately and within the company.

Don't Stop at One

Now that you have finished reviewing one annual report, pat yourself on the back. However, it is important to continue with your momentum and start reading another annual report.

This is because an annual report only details what the company did over the past year. In the grand scheme of things, a year is a very short period – Rome wasn't built in a day. One annual report is just one chapter of the company's story.

Most significant business decisions have a high possibility of needing many months to be agreed on (just ask any manager out there). In addition, big decisions may also take many years before having a sizeable effect on the company. Therefore, we need to read the annual reports in a chronological order to give a sense of how past decisions are having an impact on a company in the present day.

Some examples of these decisions include:

- construction of new factory
- implementation of new software
- integrating post-acquisition employees
- overseas expansions
- new business segments
- ramping up of a new facility.

All these decisions would take years before you can see the full effect it would have on the company. The point we are trying to put across is this – with business decisions taking time to have an impact, it makes perfect sense that you might need to read more than a few

Table 6.1: Annual Report Checklist

S/N	Making Sense of the Annual Report Checklist	✓|✗
1	**Letter to Shareholders**	
	i Tone	
	ii Strategy	
	iii Outlook	
	iv Shareholder action	
	v Execution	
2	**Management Discussion & Analysis ("MD&A")**	
	i Track record	
	ii How company made money	
	iii Key products, operating segments and assets	
	iv How the company did in the past year	
	v Advantage (moat) over their peers	
	vi Industry analysis	
	vii Significant events	
	viii Feasibility of future plans	
3	**Auditor Opinion**	
	i Reputation of Auditor	
	ii Qualified opinion	
	iii Auditor resigns	
4	**Financial Statements**	
	i How the company makes money	
	ii How good are they at making money	
	iii Conservative or aggressive	
	iv Net profit is opinion, cash is fact	
	v Do numbers tally with the rest of the report?	
5	**Notes to Financial Statements**	
	i Consistency	
	ii Transparency	
	iii Common sense	
6	**Directors and Key Management**	
	i Reputation	
	ii Significant changes in directors	
	iii Significant changes in key management	

S/N	Making Sense of the Annual Report Checklist	✓|✗
7	**Shareholders** i Reputation ii Significant changes in major shareholders	

years of the company's annual report to understand how things work. Doing so will allow us to have a better idea of the company's track record and, more importantly, to make sure that the company really does walk the talk.

However, many would argue that investing is all about the future, so why should we be worrying about the past?

This is because, in order to gain a better understanding of the future, we must keep track of the rear-view mirror to give us an idea of how the company might decide what to do in the future. Reading at least a business cycle's (typically five to ten years') worth of a company's annual reports allows us to see how the company performed through good and bad times.

In this section, do take note of:

- how the past decisions of the company are affecting the company now
- whether the management are consistent with their promises and discussion about the business
- whether the management are candid when discussion challenges
- whether the management have kept their promises in the past.

Why Should I Read a Competitor's Annual Report?

If you think that reading a ten-year history of a company is not enough for you, you will be delighted to read this next section.

We would advise serious investors not just to consider the annual reports of the company you are interested in; you should also be reading annual reports from its competitors as well.

Scuttlebutt – a phrase made famous by Phillip Fisher's *Common Stocks and Uncommon Profits*[12] – is a very important activity for an investor. When conducting his research, Phillip Fisher, went around everywhere, talking to everyone to find out stuff about the company, working through their entire value chain from their suppliers, competitors and even the customers.

However, we understand that doing that might not be a practical option for most investors. What is the next best alternative? At a minimum, you should most definitely read up on their competitor's annual report; the more the merrier.

Think of the competitors' annual reports as points of comparison. With one company, you might know how the company is operating; but you might not have a clue as to how good the company is compared to its industry, or its competitors. Understanding how its peers work might enable you to appreciate the company from another perspective.

For example, imagine you came across a company, company A, which has an operating margin of 10%. By itself 10% seems decent, but how do you know if that is a great margin? If its competitors, company B and company C, have operating margins of 18% and 20% respectively, then company A might be underperforming its peers.

Besides using competitors' reports as a source of confirmation regarding what management is saying, they are a great place to learn about the industry. This is because the competitor will most likely have a different viewpoint on what is happening in the industry and how it is handling this as a company. By reading more than one side of the story, we can get a better picture of the industry.

Who Do I Speak To?

For many investors, contacting the company directly seems like a mountainous task. However, speaking to management or an investor relation officer might give you valuable information about the company you are interested in.

Reaching out to the company includes:

- emailing and calling investor relations department
- face-to-face meeting with the management or investor relations officer
- attending annual general meeting as a proxy or shareholder
- attending investors' day events or brokerage events.

Meeting management face to face might provide clues for investors about the company. It even gives us an opportunity to size up the management on non-verbal cues. For example, the manner in which they reply to questions might show their willingness to engage shareholders. We should observe whether the management talks freely about current challenges facing the company, or tries to cover up bad news. In most cases the Annual General Meeting serves as a platform for such interactions.

Things to observe if you are meeting with management include:

- Does management have a short- or long-term outlook? If management constantly discusses its quarterly targets, it might imply that management is more focused on short-term profitability than the long-term future of the company.
- Are management candid?
- Do the management have a clear plan for the company?
- How do the management react to questions about competitors; are they fearful, dismissive or respectful of their peers?

Contacting management or an investor relation officer is a highly debatable investing strategy. Many people, and even some professionals, make investment decisions without any interacting with the company at all. Some even avoid management contact at all cost. This is because management can sometimes be overly optimistic, and if they are highly charismatic individuals, meeting with them might affect our own emotional state.

From our personal experience, we find that although contact with either the management or investor relations officer might not always be crucial in your investment decision, every now and then you might be able to find out valuable information not easily detected in an annual report. When that happens, it might make your effort worth the while.

It is More Than Just the Numbers

Most of the time, there's a story behind the company. Companies will sell you a story, be it the launch of a new product, a new investment, a new development, a turnaround, new markets, new customers and much more.

What is an investor's role? Do we just read the story and believe it at face value? No.

Our role is to check whether the story is credible, whether management is making sense, whether they are doing what they are saying. That's our job.

At this point, we would like to reinforce that this book does not tell you of specific companies to dig into. However, some good advice for investors who are just starting out is to focus your attention on simple-to-understand companies, businesses where you are able to explain their business model in one simple sentence.

Let's take a look at these companies:

- AirAsia Berhad (KLSE): budget airline
- Ajinomoto Malaysia Berhad (KLSE): monosodium glutamate (MSG) and food seasonings
- Dutch Lady Milk Industries Berhad (KLSE): dairy products
- ComfortDelGro Corporation Limited (SGX): transportation
- Hengan International Group Company Limited (HKEX): hygiene and sanitary products
- The Hour Glass Limited (SGX): luxury watches
- Kweichow Moutai Co., Limited (SHSE): alcoholic beverages
- Q & M Dental Group (Singapore) Limited (SGX): dental services
- Sands China Limited (KLSE): casino operations
- TaoKaeNoi Food & Marketing PCL (BKK): snacks.

In fact, among the examples above, some of these companies operate in simpler and less competitive environments than others. All things being equal, which do you think would be more prone to operational challenges, a budget airline company or a dairy beverage company? Think about it. However, we have to be aware that having a simple business model is not the same as having a great business.

Although we highlight simple-to-understand businesses, it does not mean that these companies are always good investments. As discussed in other chapters, there are many other things to consider.

One way to start researching on a company is to find a company with a business model which you can understand. However, we accept that, given the unique background and knowledge we each have, what is complicated to someone else might be easy for you and vice

versa. For instance, here are certain industries that might be complicated for the general public to understand in the traditional sense,
but not for those who deal with them on a daily basis:

- for a doctor or scientist, healthcare companies might be
  familiar to you
- for an oil and gas engineer, offshore marine, upstream and
  downstream companies could be their forte
- for a head of a cybersecurity firm, software companies might
  be easy to understand
- for a manager of a property agency, property companies could
  be second nature.

To sum things up, we do not plan to point you to any particular industry, or genre of companies. So long as you are comfortable
enough with the company, that could be a good starting point.

Once you have decided on your screening criteria, we hope to
pass you the tools to:

- make your list even more focused
- identify the type of value that exists
- know where to look for useful information
- know how to use this information to understand the story of
  the company
- be able to tell if the numbers make sense
- arrive at a reasonable estimation of the business.

What we will be doing next is something rather unique. Assuming
you have already screened these companies quantitatively, and they
have passed our 5-Fingers Rule, we will be looking at three companies
from a qualitative perspective on how they stood out from the crowd.

Company 1: Dairy Farm International Holdings Limited

Founded in 1886, Dairy Farm International Holdings Limited
("Dairy Farm International") was literally a dairy farm (with 80 head
of cattle) with an objective to supply clean and uncontaminated cow's
milk. In 1972, Dairy Farm International was acquired by Hongkong
Land Holdings Limited, also part of the Jardine Matheson Group.[13]
Today, with over 6,500 outlets and ranked one of the top retailers

in Asia, it's not too far of a stretch to say that Dairy Farm International is the leader of Asia's modern retail business.[14]

1. Well-oiled rolled-up vehicle: Between 2008 and 2014, Dairy Farm International accumulated sizeable stakes in modern retail businesses throughout Asia, from Indonesia (PT Hero Supermarket), Singapore (MCP Supermarket), Cambodia (Lucky Supermarket), and the Philippines (Rose Pharmacy and Rustan Supermarket) to Malaysia (Bintang Retail Industries and Jutaria Gemilang Sdn Berhad). From 2008 to 2014, Dairy Farm International reported a 64% increase in revenue, 38% increase in operating profit, 53% increase in net profit and 30% increase in operating cash flow.[15] This was achieved from both organic and acquisition growth. This indicates that not only is Dairy Farm International adept at integrating new businesses, they also appear to be good at organic growth.

   These investments (2015–2016) were less than half of Dairy Farm International's close to US$1.1 billion investment in Yonghui Superstores Co., Limited ("Yonghui Superstores") in China.[16,17] This investment into Yonghui afforded the company less operational risk in terms of its China expansion. Many foreign retailers have failed in China and one way in which Dairy Farm International avoided that is by investing in a successful local player. Moreover, the investment gives Dairy Farm International other benefits as well. For example, Yonghui is very strong with its fresh produce business. The investment makes Dairy Farm International improve on its own fresh produce business as well. Second, Yonghui's network might be able to help the company with its own operations (Mannings expansion) in China. Lastly, Dairy Farm International is part of the Jardine Matheson Group – a group with a long track record.

2. Integration commitment: For many companies, integration is a tough challenge. And one key challenge is the integration of the back-office operations.

   Dairy Farm International has also been consistently integrating its international business. For example, it has pushing for SAP system implementation in:
   • 2010: Malaysia
   • 2011: Indonesia.

Possibly totalling millions of processes to implement, this showed Dairy Farm's commitment for integration.

A fully integrated and software-controlled system should greatly standardise the Group's operational controls. Implementing such a system may also lead to the company finding out more about where its weak controls are. For example, in Malaysia, the implementation led to Dairy Farm International uncovering an operation fiasco back in 2012. This also led to management changes in their Malaysian operations as well as a review of the Group's other principal operations. With these actions taken, it's unlikely that the same issue would resurface.

3. Operational discipline: Not everything a business touches becomes gold. But that is part and parcel of doing business. As Peter Lynch said, "In this business, if you're good, you're right 6 out of 10. You're never going to be right 9 out of 10". Dairy Farm International was not always successful in every market it entered. However, it also decided to call it quits when things were not improving.

Markets exited:
* 2007: Thailand
* 2007: South Korea
* 2014: India.

On the bright side, this implied that they were willing to take hits and not afraid of divesting those that do not fit into their playbook. Just two years into the business, Dairy Farm International closed their Thailand health and beauty operations as they did not meet the Group's expectations of being able to achieve rapid scale. Instead of throwing good money after bad, Dairy Farm International bit the bullet to concentrate on more promising markets.

As the saying goes, it is okay to be wrong, but not okay to stay wrong.

Company 2: Heineken Malaysia Berhad

Heineken Malaysia Berhad ("Heineken Malaysia") (previously Guinness Anchor Berhad) is the largest alcoholic beverage company in Malaysia. It was formed after Heineken N.V. acquired Diageo Plc's stake in GAPL Private Limited, the parent company of Heineken Malaysia, in 2015.[18] The company has a long history in Malaysia, dating back to the pre-World War II period.[19] How many companies can say that they have been in business since the 1930s?

Even so, Heineken Malaysia is still growing and has recorded amazing growth over the past decade, with revenue and net profit increasing by 6.3% and 7.1% annually respectively from 2005 to 2015.[20] The following three observations, not directly evident from a read of its financial statements alone, might give you a better appreciation of the strong economic moat of Heineken Malaysia's business.

1. **Pricing power:** The largest cost component of Heineken Malaysia by far was the excise duties and tax payable to the government. In 2015, excise, custom duties and sales tax made up 48% of revenue![21] Yet in times when the government raises the excise duties, Heineken Malaysia appears to be able to pass these increases down to consumers fairly easily.

   In fact, during the last excise duties hike, the company raised the price of its product on the very same day the new duties took effect.[22] Moreover, during the next three months of operation, the company actually experienced a 15.6% jump in its revenue compared to last year.[23] This highlighted the strong pricing power of the company and how Heineken Malaysia can maintain margins without affecting sales volume.

2. **Shareholder support:** As a listed subsidiary to one of the largest breweries in the world, Heineken Malaysia, without a shadow of a doubt, has a world-class support infrastructure. Throughout the years, the company has been able to leverage the expertise of its parent company to grow its business. A clear example is the potential of its parent company, Heineken N.V., with a product arsenal of over 250 products.[24] The product portfolio of Heineken Malaysia is still less than 20 brands.[25] Think of the potential as the company decides to add more products into its range.

   Thus Heineken Malaysia can easily add more products to its sales channel without much research and development. That is certainly a huge advantage over a smaller brewery which lacks this strong support from a global parent.

3. **Competitive landscape:** Finally, when we look at the competitive landscape for the beer market in Malaysia, Heineken Malaysia, together with Carlsberg Brewery Malaysia Berhad, have the lion's share of the country's legal beer trade. With a less fragmented market, these two companies have enjoyed a certain degree of pricing power.

Company 3: Super Group Limited

Founded in 1987, Super Group Limited ("Super Group") is an Asia-centric instant F&B player with Super, Owl and NutreMill as standout brands in their portfolio. What makes them stand out from their 3-in-1 instant beverage peers like Food Empire Holdings Limited, Nestlé (Malaysia) Berhad, OldTown Berhad and Power Root Berhad is their big push into the food ingredient business in 2010.

In 2015, Super Group's food component contributed 33% of its group revenue,[26] up from 16% back in 2010.[27] And this capital-intensive move inevitably involved the development of the corresponding infrastructure to support it, bringing us to our first point...

1. Execution track record: If you have been around construction management, things don't always go on schedule. So how was Super's track record when it came to delivering on their execution?

    From their track record (Table 6.2)[28] over the five-year period from 2010 to 2015, Super Group appeared to walk the talk. Most of what the management promised to deliver was achieved. What this does is to give us the confidence that they are able to deliver on their promises.

2. Succession planning: In recent years, the theme for Super Group has appeared to be moving into a new phase of growth, and the taglines for their Annual Reports in 2012 and 2015 of "A New Era" and "Building our Future" appear to correspond with that.

    Other than the business side of things, highlighted by their track record of timely delivery of projects, a key concern for businesses in Asia is the issue of succession planning. In many companies, it is even sort of a taboo to even talk about it sometimes. However, in the case of Super, it seems that succession planning is well in play.

    From 2010–2016:
    - Four executive directors stepped down, with two being direct family members
    - Three members of the younger generation came into the company, with one as a director
    - Prior to appointment, this individual was in a senior management position for four years
    - Four out of six new additions to senior management appeared to be non-family members.

Table 6.2: Super Group Limited Major Capital Expenditure 2010–2015

S/N	Announced	Project	Expected	On Track	Actual
1	1Q10	Add 25k MT NDC Capacity in Wuxi	2H2010	✓	2H2010
2	1Q11	Add 25k MT NDC Capacity in Wuxi	3Q2011	✓	3Q2011
3	2Q2011	Add 25k MT NDC Capacity in SG	3Q2011	✓	3Q2011
4	3Q2011	New 1.5k MT Freeze Dry SC powder	2H2012	✓	2H2012
5	4Q2011	New 3k MT BHE Plant	4Q2013	✗	2H2014
6	3Q2012	Rebranding of Super Brand	1H2013	✓	1H2013
7	1Q2014	Add 5k MT to SC plant in Malaysia	2Q2014	✓	2Q2014
8	4Q2013	100MT LGSS Facility in Wuxi	2015	✓	2015

Interestingly, among Super Group's key management positions in 2015, there were certain individuals (non-family) that stood out. Two individuals previously started in Super then left for another company before rejoining the Super Group. It looks as if going into the "new era" is more than just words. Super Group appeared to be able to attract and retain younger talent to work for them.[29]

3. Share buybacks and insider purchases: This brings to mind the words of Peter Lynch, "Insiders might sell their shares for any number of reasons, but they buy them for only one: they think the price will rise."

Of course, there are exceptions. However, in most cases, when insiders with the company are repurchasing shares, it might indicate that those closely linked to the internal workings of the company do see value – a positive signal for us to dig deeper.

Between August 2015 and August 2016, not only has the family increased their stake,[30] but both the company itself[31] and a non-executive director (deemed a substantial shareholder)[32] have all bought shares of the company in the open market.

To conclude, we would like to emphasise that this is just the view of the insiders, and not yours. Although by itself this is a positive sign, you still have to do your own research to see whether the company fits with both your investment approach and objective.

Notes

1. J. Edward Russo and Paul J.H. Schoemaker. Doubleday. *Winning Decisions.* 1st Edition: January 2002.
2. Super Group Limited. "Annual Report 2014".
3. Bethany McLean and Peter Elkind. Portfolio, a member of Penguin Group. *The Smartest Guys in the Room.* Updated paperback published: 2004.
4. Great Group Holdings Limited. "Annual Report 2014".
5. Metech International Limited. "Annual Report 2014".
6. Tianhe Chemicals Group Limited. Announcement and Circulars. "Global Offering". 17 September 2015.
7. Tianhe Chemicals Group Limited. "Interim Report 2014".
8. Tianhe Chemicals Group Limited. Announcement and Circulars. "Resignation of Auditors". 17 September 2015.
9. Tianhe Chemicals Group Limited. Announcement and Circulars. "Delay in Publication of the 2014 Annual Results Announcement and Suspension of Trading". 26 March 2015.
10. Want Want China Holding Limited. "Annual Report 2014".
11. Wilmar International Limited. "Annual Report 2015".
12. Philip A. Fisher. John Wiley & Sons, Inc. *Common Stock and Uncommon Profits.* Originally published: 1958.
13. Dairy Farm International Holdings Limited. Our Company. "Our History". http://www.dairyfarmgroup.com/en-US/Our-Company/ Our-History. Accessed: 25 January 2017.
14. Dairy Farm International Holdings Limited. "Annual Report 2015".
15. Dairy Farm International Holdings Limited. "Annual Reports 2008 to 2014".
16. Dairy Farm International Holdings Limited. Press Release. "Dairy Farm Completes Further Investment in Yonghui Superstores". 10 August 2016.
17. Dairy Farm International Holdings Limited. Press Release. "Dairy Farm Investment in Yonghui Superstores Receives Regulatory Approval". 10 August 2016.
18. Guinness Anchor Berhad. Circular to Shareholders. "The Proposed Change of Name of the Company from 'Guinness Anchor Berhad' to 'Heineken Malaysia Berhad'". 29 March 2016.
19. Heineken Malaysia Berhad. About Us. "Milestones". http://www .heinekenmalaysia.com/milestones/. Accessed: 25 January 2017.
20. Guinness Anchor Berhad. "Annual Report 2005 to 2015".
21. Guinness Anchor Berhad. "Annual Report 2015".
22. *The Sun Daily.* "Guinness Anchor adjusts product prices after excise duty hike". http://www.thesundaily.my/news/1717098. 3 March 2016.

23. Heineken Malaysia Berhad. Announcement. "Condensed Consolidated Financial Statements for the Quarter and Period Ended 30 June 2016". 18 July 2016.

24. Heineken N.V. "Brands". http://www.theheinekencompany.com/brands. Accessed: 25 January 2017.

25. Heineken Malaysia Berhad. "Our Brands". http://www.heineken malaysia.com/our-brands/. Accessed: 25 January 2017.

26. Super Group Limited. "Annual Report 2015".

27. Super Group Limited. News Release. "Super Achieves Record Revenue of S$440.9M and Net Profit of S$63.9M for FY2011 with a Full year dividends of 5.8 cents per share". 23 February 2012.

28. Super Group Limited. Data from Annual Reports and Company Presentations from 2010 to 2015.

29. Super Group Limited. "Annual Reports 2010 to 2015".

30. Super Group Limited. Securities and Futures Act. Form 1. "Notification Form for Director/Chief Executive Officer In Respect of Interest in Securities". 13 August 2015.

31. Super Group Limited. Singapore Exchange Limited. "Daily Share Buy-Back Notice". 29 September 2015.

32. Super Group Limited. Securities and Futures Act. Form 1. "Notification Form for Director/Chief Executive Officer in Respect of Interest in Securities". 31 August 2016.

Finding Red Flags

Fool me once, shame on you; fool me twice, shame on me.

— Proverb

When it comes to investing, knowing what to buy is just half the equation. Given our investment criteria, it is not often we come across a company with a perfect score. This means that we often research a company which ends up not being an investable opportunity. After a while, many investors might get impatient and rush into investing in a sub-par company. Remember: as much as being able to find winners, investing also greatly depends on your ability to avoid losers. Thus, knowing when not to put your money in is more than half the battle won. Let the last part of the statement sink in.

We repeat, knowing what not to buy is more important than knowing what to invest in. After all, in the stock markets, ideas are almost unlimited while our investable capital is always limited. And statistically, it is far harder to gain back our losses. Remember, if you are down 50%, you need a gain of 100% just to break even.

For simplicity, you can look at "knowing what not to buy" as a form of screening. Earlier we used screening to filter for companies with positive traits. In this case, we are adding an additional layer to filter out companies with negative traits.

Let us find out how to uncover red flags in a company.

What are Red Flags?

A red flag is a sign that warns us of incoming danger. However, we like to point out that the presence of red flags does not always mean that things are 100% shady. In most cases, red flags just serve as canaries in the coal mine, pointing us towards unfavourable headwinds that the company might be facing. These headwinds could be temporary issues, where a potential turnaround could be on the cards. Or it can be structural concerns, pointing us to the long-term unattractive prospect of the company. Red flags can range from the market or the company showing unwarranted optimism, liquidity and solvency issues within the company, business and industry slowdowns, and even to questionable business practices. When it gets too quiet, it might be time to clear the tunnel.

In the words of Warren Buffett, "In the world of business, bad news often surfaces serially: You see a cockroach in your kitchen; as the days go by, you meet his relatives".[1] Or more commonly, there's never just one cockroach in the kitchen. If we look closely enough, once we find something that "doesn't look right", it might just be a matter of time before more red flags join the party. And if you are not careful, it might result in a big fat red mark on your portfolio.

There are numerous types of red flags out there. Our aim here is not to uncover every single red flag, but rather to give you a better appreciation of how to recognise some of the more common ones. You don't have to uncover every single detail about a company before deciding *not* to invest in the company. When a company ticks most of the red flags from our list, then it might be time to move on.

Spotting red flags does require some experience. But don't worry, this will come with time. Having lived through some of these red flags, we thought that it would be good to share our experiences. We really think that it is very much worth your while to pay attention to some of these red flags in the hope that you will learn from our experiences and not be oblivious to the following warning signs. With that in mind, we will bring you up to speed with our analysis of some of the common red flags; think of it as a fast track, without the pain of experiencing it for yourself.

First, think of yourself as a detective. Instead of solving cases with tools like fingerprints or DNA analysis, we rely on making sense of the financial statements. Financial statements are to investors what DNA analysis is to crime scene investigators. Due to the standard formatting of most financial statements, we tend to use them as our starting point.

Our first step is, of course, to check the legitimacy of the financial statements. Most of us take for granted that when Annual Reports are published, all is good, and we do not even bother checking the auditor's opinion. The auditor's opinion is a written statement by the auditors, stating what they think about the audited report.

Auditor's Opinion

There are four types of auditor's opinion:

1. **Clear, unqualified:** The auditor deemed the report to be fair and accurate, or "All is good, let's move on".
2. **Qualified:** There are some areas which the auditor does not agree with, or "Almost all is okay, except for certain parts".
3. **Adverse:** The auditor does not agree with the report, or "Things are not that good".
4. **Disclaimer:** The auditor is removing itself from what is reported in the financial statement, or "No one is saying anything".

As a rule of thumb, we would stay away from anything other than a clear and unqualified statement. If we cannot even rely on the legitimacy of the financial statements, it does not even matter how nice the numbers look, the risk is too high for us to handle.

Once getting the all-clear signal from the auditor's opinion section, we have to differentiate between the types of red flag we might encounter during our research. We found that separating these red flags between financial and non-financial concerns gave us a better appreciation of this issue and we will be starting with the more quantifiable financial red flags.

Financial Red Flags

As they are measurable, financial red flags tend to be easier to spot as compared to non-financial red flags. To put it crudely, it does not matter how optimistic the picture painted by the company is if its financials show a picture of a company in the dumps.

Financial red flags are quantifiable factors and commonly stem from the overstatement of the following two items:

1. Profits – making others think that you are earning more money than you actually do:
   - inflate revenue
   - deflate expenses.
2. Assets – making others think that you have more net assets than you actually have:
   - inflate assets
   - deflate liabilities.

What is interesting is that the Income Statement, Balance Sheet, Cash Flow Statement and Notes to the Financial Statements tend to come together nicely to give you a decent report on the health of the company, just like a proper health screening report.

Here are some of the things you might want to look out for.

Abnormally High Margins

Who doesn't like a high-margin business? Theoretically, the higher the margins, the better the business. However, it might also be a warning sign.

When a company is enjoying a much higher margin than its peers, we need to find out the reason behind it. The company might have good reasons for its higher margin, such as serving a very niche market or having some special technology or process unknown to its peers.

However, if you cannot seem to find any apparent advantage the company has for enjoying such a wide margin, things might be too good to be true. After all, if the company is not operationally superior to its competitors, its margins should not be too different. At the end of the day, businesses with the same capital outlay, customers, suppliers, workforce and selling price should have similar profit margins as well.

We refer to a 2012 report by Anonymous Analytics on Huabao International Holdings Limited ("Huabao International") titled "Smoke and Mirrors".[2]

In their analysis, Huabao International was detailed as China's largest flavour and fragrance company, supplying fragrances to food and beverages, cosmetics, detergent and tobacco products, with the highest gross margins (upwards of 70%) compared to its peers (in the range of 40–50%). This was in the absence of any notable advantage of Huabao compared to its peers. Additionally, Huabao International was also one of the lowest spenders in research and development as a percentage of revenue compared to its peers.

Yet, Huabao International had been experiencing the fastest growth in the industry.[3] So Huabao is a company that spent little on research and development, but still managed to generate the fastest growth and highest margins in the industry. From Anonymous Analytics' perspective, this story did not seem to add up.

Trade Receivables Growing Faster than Revenue

Investors must understand that there is a timing difference between when a sale is recorded on the income statement, when the cash is actually collected, and when the inflow is recorded in the cash flow statement. Or as Alfred Rappaport, the author of *Creating Shareholder Value: A Guide for Managers and Investors*, says, "Remember, cash is a fact, profit is an opinion."

For most companies, business is done by giving out credit to customers, so the cash might only be received some time after the revenue has already been booked. This gap between recording the revenue and receiving the cash flow is recorded as trade receivables – nothing uncommon about that.

Generally, it is also perfectly normal for businesses to report an increase in trade receivables with an increase in revenue. As a company generates more sales, it is reasonable to expect a corresponding increase in trade receivables. However, we should start taking notice when trade receivables increase at a much higher rate than revenue growth. Why? Because this could mean that the company might be:

- having a poor credit control
- facing tougher times in the industry (compared with peers)
- giving laxer credit terms to customers to boost revenue.

For this chapter, we can use the top players in the China sportswear industry back in 2010 as an example. Although China has many local sport brands, Hong Kong-listed Li Ning Co Limited ("Li Ning") and Anta Sports Products Limited ("Anta Sports") stood out as two of the key players in the industry.

In 2010, both companies were still recording good revenue growth. However, their rates of increase in trade receivables were foreshadowing issues that the sportswear industry might be in for.

- Li Ning: Revenue: ↑ 13%; Trade receivables: ↑ 51%[4]
- Anta Sports: Revenue: ↑ 26%; Trade receivables: ↑ 82%.[5]

The data implied that the growth in revenue was questionable. The two companies, or maybe even the entire industry, might be faced with an oversupply issue.[6] Products are being pushed to the retailers but the retailers are either unable to sell the product or requiring longer credit terms from the brand owners. In short, things are not looking good, and typically trouble does not travel alone. We could spot other warning signs during this period in the Chinese sportswear industry. Aggressive marketing by many retailers was a common sight. Examples are the "Buy one, get one free" offers or "Buy one, donate one" offers that many retailers used during that period.[7]

Another tell-tale sign comes from the impairment or write-off of trade receivables. As trade receivables represent cash supposed to be received from an earlier sale, a write-off meant that that sale had literally vanished into thin air. If it was a one-time event and the impairment made up only a small portion of the company's trade receivables, we need not be too worried about it. However, if it happens too often, it might be a red flag to take notice of.

In the case of Singapore-listed InnoPac Holdings Limited ("InnoPac"), it was more than a one-off case. Between 2014 and 2015, InnoPac reported impairment charges of S$29.5 million (2015) and S$26.7 million (2014), while only recording revenue of S$817,000 and S$330,000 respectively. Its impairment in 2015 was over 97% of its gross trade receivables[8]. *Side note: This contributed towards a qualified opinion from its auditor for 2015.*

Inventory Growing Faster than Revenue

This red flag might be easier to spot for industries with bricks and mortar operations, compared to software or service companies. This is because a company that manufactures or sells physical goods needs to record an inventory on its balance sheet. For example, a retailer needs to keep track of its inventory at a particular point, and the direction that its inventory level is going in compared to its revenue will tell us a lot about the business. The consumer goods industry is a perfect industry to explain this concept.

Let's take an apparel retailer as an example. To make money, it must sell clothes; hence clothes are its inventory. Similar to our discussion on trade receivables, inventory should generally be growing in tandem with its revenue. Additionally, if finished goods are increased at a higher rate than the overall inventory level, it indicates that the company might be stuck with old products. In this business, inventory is not like wine; it doesn't get better with age.

One such example is Hong Kong-listed Bossini International Holdings Limited ("Bossini"). In 2011, Bossini's inventory level went up 37% to HK$412 million, of which its finished goods increased by HK$108 million to HK$405 million. In the same period, its revenue only rose by 15%.[9]

Another metric we can watch is its inventory turnover days. This is basically a gauge of the time required for a company to turn over one cycle of its inventory. This gives us an idea of how fast a company turns its inventory into cash. And, of course, the faster the better.

$$\text{Inventory turnover days} = \frac{\text{Average Inventory}}{\text{Cost of Goods Sold}} \times 365 \text{ days}$$

Since 2005, Bossini's inventory turnover days gradually increased from 71 days to 2011's 101 days.[10,11]

Consistent Excessive Fair Value Gains

Fair value is an accounting gain that companies might need to record due to accounting standards. By itself, fair value gains are not inherently a negative thing. Fair value gain allows a company to restate its legacy assets at current market value instead of them remaining at cost. This allows investors to have a clearer understanding of the true value of the assets in a company. For example, Singapore-listed Haw Par Corporation Limited ("Haw Par") holds long-term investments, mostly in its related company, United Overseas Bank Limited. From its 2004 annual report, these investments were booked at just S$311 million on its balance sheet. Yet, just by turning a few pages to Haw Par's notes to the financial statements, we would discover that these investments had a market value of S$761 million back in 2004.[12] In 2015, these investments were reflected at fair value on Haw Par's balance sheet.[13] Valuation of marketable securities is relatively easily justified and restating it gives investors a good sense of the current worth of the company. This is fair value used appropriately.

However, for certain illiquid assets, the estimation of fair value can be rather subjective. What we mean by subjective is that these estimations might be dependent on management's assumptions. Things might not be that simple for other cases; fair value accounting might be involved with assets with more ambiguous valuations – especially for biological assets if no intermediate market exists during its growth stage. Think immature crops and livestock like pineapples, oil palms, rubber trees, poultry, cows and not forgetting abalones! Per accounting standards, these need to be valued on the balance sheet and yet the valuation of these items is hugely dependent on the assumptions that management made.

Therefore, fair value gains of certain illiquid assets might not be very useful for an investor. And if these gains consistently contribute to a large portion of the overall profitability of a company, we as investors should be cautious when analysing such companies.

Apart from biological assets, a common class of asset that appears with fair value gains is property. Property revaluation can also be subject to some assumptions from the management. Most notably, the discount rate, known as the cap rate, used to value a property can be subject to management's discretion. A lower cap rate will result in a higher value for the property. It is important for investors to know the assumptions of the management when they are recording fair value gain items. Moreover, some properties might not be up for sale by the company. In such cases, the fair value gain of the property might not be that important to an investor as compared to the actual net revenue coming from the property.

Companies in a Dilutive Mood

One way a dilution happens is when a company issues new shares to fund its expansion. The company might have spotted an awesome investment opportunity and require more funds to grow the business. If the company manages to put your new funds to good use in growing the business, and if existing shareholders have an equal opportunity, why not?

But what if the benefit from the expansion was not for existing shareholder and it also did not justify the cost of issuing new shares? Here we have Company A in Year 1 with:

- Revenue: US$1.0 billion
- Net income: US$100 million
- Shares outstanding: 100 million
- Earnings per share: US$1.00
- Current price-to-earnings ratio (P/E): 10
- Share price of the company: US$10.00
- Value of the company: US$1.0 billion

If this company A decided to raise another US$1.0 billion at current valuation, it would be issuing another 100 million shares to new investors. With this equity injection, the value of the company would stand at US$2.0 billion. To illustrate a case where the cost outweighs the benefit, let us assume that the additional funds allowed the company to expand and grow its revenue and net income by 50% in the next year.

Now, Company A in Year 2 reports:

- Revenue: US$1.5 billion
- Net income: US$150 million
- Shares outstanding: 200 million
- Earnings per share: US$0.75
- Current price-to-earnings ratio (P/E): 10
- Share price of the company: US$7.50
- Value of the company: US$1.5 billion

In this case, although the company had grown by 50%, the end result for the shareholder is a negative 25% loss. This means that the growth of the company has not justified the cost of the additional share issuance, thus resulting in dilution to its existing shareholders. This is an important concept for investors to understand. Not all growth is created equal.

In the six-year period between 2010 and 2015, Singapore-listed Innopac Holdings Limited's ("Innopac") shares outstanding increased from 1.4 billion (2010) to 4.4 billion (2015) – a 204%

increase![14,15] Also, back in 2014, Innopac proposed the issuance of two rights shares for every one existing ordinary share, totalling 6.9 billion rights shares, and up to 3.5 billion free warrants, with each warrant carrying the right to subscribe for one new share.[16] The company would need considerable growth to justify the degree of this equity financing.

Yet, in the same period, Innopac hardly generated any free cash flow. Instead of growth, revenue fell drastically, resulting in sizeable losses.[17] Even after tapping shareholders for capital, Shareholders' equity tumbled 66%, from S$44 million (2010) to S$15 million (2015).

Even after tapping shareholders for capital, Shareholders' equity tumbled 66%, from S$44 million (2010) to S$15 million (2015). In summary, it could be described as paying more for a shrinking pie.

Leverage – The Double-Edged Sword

Debt is a double-edged sword – one which could make or break a company. On the one hand, leverage can increase a company's return on equity (ROE). Based on the DuPont formula, return on equity of a company is:

$$ROE = Profit\,Margin \times Asset\,Turnover \times Leverage$$

$$Profit\,Margin = \frac{Net\,Income}{Revenue}$$

$$Asset\,Turnover = \frac{Revenue}{Asset}$$

$$Leverage = \frac{Asset}{Equity}$$

$$Therefore,\,ROE = \frac{Net\,Income}{Revenue} \times \frac{Revenue}{Asset} \times \frac{Asset}{Equity} = \frac{Net\,Income}{Equity}$$

Intuitively, if a company takes on more and more debt, its leverage would increase, and, holding all else constant, this should generate a higher ROE for the company. However, things are not always so straightforward; with great debt comes great risks. If things go south, the company could even end up being unable to service their interest payments, leaving the company in a vicious spiral of debt.

The degree of leverage that might be considered safe depends largely on both the industry and the nature of business. For example, utility companies with a steady demand for their services tend to employ leverage to boost returns. However, the debt level must still be manageable for the company. The key word is "manageable". Companies with manageable debt levels might not necessarily be that bad a thing.

$$\text{Interest coverage ratio} = \frac{\text{EBIT}}{\text{Interest Expenses}}$$

EBIT = earnings before interest and tax, or operating profit

The interest coverage ratio shows us how many times a company's operating profit covers its annual interest expenses. A company with an interest coverage ratio of just one time means that it is spending 100% of its operating profit just to service its loans. From our experience, we consider a company with an interest coverage ratio of five times as conservative (in a good way).

Commodity-linked companies, on the other hand, might need a higher margin of safety when it comes to debt management. In the commodity world, when it rains, it pours. Given that most commodity-linked companies have very limited pricing power, if they are caught during a downturn in their sector with a highly leveraged balance sheet, it might lead to disaster. A case in point is Korea-listed Hanjin Shipping Co., Limited ("Hanjin"). The company had a net debt to equity of 6.7 times. More importantly, in 2015, the company's net finance costs of KRW28 billion alone were more than its operating income of KRW21 billion.[18] Thus the company had operating income that was not even enough to cover its interest payments, contributing towards their eventual bankruptcy.[19]

Singapore-listed Del Monte Pacific Limited ("Del Monte Pacific") is also a great example when it comes to leverage management. The current company structure came into effect after a reverse merger (smaller company acquiring larger company). In 2014, Del Monte Pacific acquired US Del Monte Foods, Inc (separate company) from private equity firm, KKR & Co, for US$1.65 billion. With this, Del Monte Pacific quadrupled their revenue to US$2.2 billion.[20]

However, how did Del Monte Pacific, a company with a pre-acquisition shareholders' equity of just US$231 million, pull off such a large acquisition?[21]

Simple: the answer is debt, a whole lot of debt. From total borrowings of US$0.3 billion in 2013, Del Monte Pacific's total borrowings in 2015 went up by over six times to US$1.7 billion. In perspective, this is in comparison to a market cap of just US$0.4 billion during that period.

In theory, this strategy, more commonly known as a leveraged buy-out, is simple:

- A company uses debt to acquire cash flow-generative business.
- This company then uses the cash flow generated from the new business to pay down debt.
- The company ends up owning a new business without a huge investment from its shareholders.

The saying goes, "In theory there is no difference between theory and practice. In practice, there is." Del Monte Pacific's underlying idea still made sense and, if given time (and some luck, as with most things in life), it could work out in the company's favour. Yet, as with all issues associated with debt, it reduces the margin of error a company can tolerate. Everything would have to go according to plan for the company to generate that return. If something happens that throws a spanner into the works, it could very easily lead to a vicious cycle. From the looks of both its income statements and statements of cash flows in 2016, it appears that a significant portion went towards servicing their loans. The company had an interest coverage ratio of 1.7 times in 2016.

If there is any reduction in profitability or cash flow from the business, management might need to either (1) dilute shareholders and raise more funds, (2) borrow more or, in the worst-case scenario, (3) declare bankruptcy. All the above hold significant risks to its shareholders.

Seemingly Unnecessary Borrowings

This can be simplified to the question of, "Is the cash really there?"

We tend to assume that cash is fungible: $1 of cash = $1. Moreover, many investors also assume that auditors can easily verify cash balances through a simple bank statement. However, is this as foolproof as it seems?

Most of the time, we don't see much of a need to ask much questions about a company's reported cash values. But there are instances that led us to question the reported value of the company's cash balance. Our earlier case study of Singapore-listed Eratat Lifestyle Limited ("Eratat Lifestyle") comes to mind.

Back in 2012, Eratat Lifestyle traded close to their net cash (less total liabilities) level of RMB283 million (about S$57 million) or S$0.12 per share. To place things in perspective, Eratat Lifestyle's shareholders' equity was RMB949 million, indicating that the company was only trading at 0.3 times its book value.[22] In its Q1 2013 report, even with a huge cash balance on its book, Eratat Lifestyle issued a RMB103 million bond with an effective interest rate of about 17%[23] (Hint: this was expensive).

Why would a company with an extremely strong balance sheet raise a bond at such a high interest rate (in a low interest-rate environment), when it is still profitable? Why would they need to do that? We could not arrive at a logical explanation for this action. Unless for some reason, its cash position wasn't where it was supposed to be.

In 2014, our suspicions became reality. Eratat Lifestyle was suspended after defaulting on their bond interest payments. This is a company with RMB584 million in cash, and yet could not even afford to pay its bonds' semi-annual interest of just RMB8 million.[24]

As we mentioned before, red flags very rarely travel alone. As we like to say, red flags are social animals – they like gathering together. In Eratat Lifestyle's case, we also found out that the company's trade receivables were over 50% of revenue – implying it took more than half a year to collect cash from customers.[25] That is an extremely high figure and one that does not bode well no matter how you see it.

Shortly after defaulting on their bond, both Eratat Lifestyle's shares and CEO were suspended.[26] A short while later, the Chief Financial Officer (interim Chief Executive Officer) also resigned.[27] Ironically, the company was awarded with a corporate governance award just two months before this news went public.[28] This is a cautionary tale to investors that it is important to do our own research instead of relying too much on the opinions of others.

Non-Financial Red Flags

Now for the qualitative stuff. Compared to financial metrics which are more quantitative, qualitative factors are slightly more ambiguous, allowing you to look at the matter from a different perspective.

Done right, and used together with quantitative analysis, these would allow you to arrive at a better appreciation of the company.

When we talk about quantitative factors, it is all about the numbers. For qualitative analysis, it's a whole different ball game. Basically, it is everything else, the intangibles, and the things that cannot be measured. Some people say that qualitative analysis is like listening to your gut, or intuition. For beginners, it might look as such. However, qualitative analysis is not magic. When something feels off, it might be from our experience from similar situations in the past. Take it from us, when we say that this will get better with experience.

To kick-start your journey and not to start from ground zero, here are some of the non-financial red flags you might want to look out for.

Massive Reshuffling of the Company's Officers

When we talk about company's officers we are referring to its directors, executives (Chief Executive Officer, Chief Finance Officer and key management) and the company secretary. It is part and parcel for personnel changes in a company, it is part of a natural succession process. However, when we see a massive exodus of the company's management, or even the auditors (before their term is up), it might be a sign of trouble within the company that warrants deeper research.

Here is one such example. This is what took place at Hong Kong-listed Chaoda Modern Agriculture (Holdings) Limited between 2003 and 2007:

- 2003: Auditor PricewaterhouseCoopers resigned[29]
- 2003: Independent Director resigned[30]
- 2004: Executive Director (co-founder) resigned[31]
- 2005: Executive Director resigned[32]
- 2005: Chief Finance Officer resigned[33]
- 2006: Company secretary resigned[34]
- 2007 Auditors Baker Tilly Hong Kong Limited and CCIF CPA Limited resigned.[35]

Subsequently, the company was targeted by Anonymous Analytics. Anonymous Analytics released a report *11 Years of Deceit and Corporate Fraud.*[36]

Infamous Directors and Major Shareholders

We know that most major shareholders have considerable influence over a company. How about its directors?

The directors are the ones setting the direction and policies for the company. We think that is pretty important too. Hence directors with a good reputation on the company's board are always welcomed.

On the flip side, investors invested in companies where their directors or major shareholders do not have that great a reputation might find themselves in a different position. Therefore, we should investigate the directors and/or major shareholders on the companies we are interested in. *Note: Major shareholders also include corporates.*

Some points to look out for are directors and major shareholders:

- that are consistently making seemingly value-destructive moves
- that are repeatedly on the board of other companies that have been suspended or delisted
- who do not have a good reputation
- with frequent regulatory brushes
- that overpay themselves despite poor performance in the company.

When Things Vanish into Thin Air

When it comes to vanishing financial documents, it seems like fires and grand theft auto are the way to go. This puts the "dog ate my homework" reason to shame.

Just a week after the auditor flagged certain discrepancies in their invoices, there was a fire at Singapore-listed Sino Techfibre Limited's office and administrative premises in the early hours of the morning. In the company's statement, the fire "destroyed the Company's books and financial records which were kept in the affected office premise".[37]

In another case, in the middle of a forensic audit ordered by regulators, Hong Kong-listed China Animal Healthcare Limited ("China Animal Healthcare") had their lorry stolen while the driver was having lunch. You might ask, "What was so special about this truck?" It just so happened that this very truck was carrying five years' worth of the China Animal Healthcare's original financial documents.

Interestingly, a week later, the truck was found. However, the documents were nowhere to be found.[38] In most vehicle thefts, you would expect the truck to be the main target. Maybe not this time.

Substantial Shareholder Divesting Significantly

When shareholders divest their shareholdings, it can be for a variety of legitimate reasons. In our opinion, substantial shareholders paring down part of their stake is not that big of a deal – it happens all the time. But if the quantum is significant, then something might be up.

A general rule of thumb is that when a major shareholder starts selling down its stake fast, especially in the open market and without a logical reason, it might be worth taking note of.

Significant Related Party Transactions

Like leverage, related party transactions on their own are not necessarily negative – as long as they are properly disclosed and the deal is fair. As a matter of fact, we think that, if done properly, related party transactions can be a good thing – the company can get better terms compared to those out in the market. In addition, we also should not be too concerned if the amount of these transactions is not that significant to the company as a whole.

But if related party sales take up over 50% of your sales, it should be a significant deal worth investigating. As Singapore-listed Kingboard Copper Foil Holdings Limited ("Kingboard Copper Foil") was recently in the spotlight, let us explore the issues that its shareholders are concerned about. In their 1999 IPO prospectus, it was highlighted that Kingboard Copper Foil sold the majority of their copper foils to the Kingboard Group, at discounts ranging from 5% to 30%. This meant that almost all Kingboard Copper Foil's income came from their parent. In the same document, Kingboard Copper Foil also mentioned that they were looking to diversify their customer base.[39] Fast forward to FY2010, and Kingboard Copper Foil's sales to their parent group still made up 89% of revenue.[40] In other words, Kingboard Copper Foil was a captive manufacturer with little ability to raise prices and serving only its parent company.

What made some minority shareholders concerned was the alleged negative impact on the company's profit margins. This led to certain shareholders voting down the renewal of the interested party transaction mandate, risking almost all of Kingboard Copper Foil's revenue.[41]

When Taxi Drivers Become Your Portfolio Advisor

APS Asset Management is one of the largest and most successful fund management companies in Singapore. During an interview, Wong Kok Hoi of APS Asset Management Private Limited once mentioned that during a business trip in Switzerland, a taxi driver started to brag to him about his Japanese stocks' performance. That was the point when Mr Wong decided that the market had gone too far. Shortly after, the fund manager unloaded most of his Japanese stocks. Just weeks later in December 1989, the market crashed.[42] Is that coincidence? It might be. Or is it?

The key takeaway is not to blindly follow the crowd. When the man on the street is freely providing you with stock tips, it might just be the sign to head for the exit.

Innovative Business Deals

When a company starts using customised business deals to boost income, it is worth taking note of. For example, in 2016 an operator of one of the largest number of dairy farms in China sold about a quarter of their cows. Although this was operationally significant, it was not the issue which made us do a double take. What was so special was that they were leasing them back in a sale and leaseback agreement.[43] I am sure that we have heard sale and leaseback deals that involving property. But cows? Now that's a first. This brings a whole new meaning to the term "cash cows". Analysts commented that it was not very common to use cows as collateral. We agree.

Viewed financially, the deal helped the company to lower their debt levels considerably. However, this type of off-balance sheet financing model might be more about financial window dressing than effecting any real improvements in operation. *Side note: We are more interested to find out more about the party that bought all of their 50,000 cows!*

If you are interested to know more about financial irregularities, we highly recommend Tan Chin Hwee and Thomas R. Robinson's *Asian Financial Statement Analysis*.[44]

Table 7.1 shows a checklist of the red flags covered in this chapter.

Table 7.1: Red Flag Checklist

S/N	Red Flags	✓|✗
1	**Auditor's Opinion**	
2	**Financial Red Flags**	
	i Abnormally high margins	
	ii Trade receivables growing faster than revenue	
	iii Inventory growing faster than revenue	
	iv Consistent excessive fair value gains	
	v Companies in a dilutive mood	
	vi Leverage – the doubled-edged sword	
	vii Seemingly unnecessary borrowings	
3	**Non-Financial Red Flags**	
	i Massive reshuffling of the company's officers	
	ii Infamous directors and major shareholders	
	iii When things vanish into thin air	
	iv Substantial shareholder divesting significantly	
	v Significant related party transactions	
	vi When taxi drivers become your portfolio advisor	
	vii Innovative business deals	

Notes

1. Berkshire Hathaway Inc. "2014 Annual Report".
2. Anonymous Analytics. "Huabao International". http://www.anonanalytics.com/2013/04/initiating-coverage-huabao.html. Released: 24 April 2012.
3. Ibid.
4. Li Ning Co Limited. "Annual Report 2010".
5. Anta Sports Products Limited. "Annual Report 2010".
6. Simon Rabinovitch. *Financial Times.* "China hit by demands of oversupply". https://www.ft.com/content/8e2a74e4-eac0-11e1-984b-00144feab49a. 21 August 2012.
7. Donny Kwok and Rachel Lee. Reuters. "China's sportswear brands nurse Olympics hangover". http://www.reuters.com/article/uk-china-sportswear-idUKBRE8600KH20120701. 1 July 2012.
8. Innopac Holdings Limited. "Annual Report 2015".
9. Bossini International Holdings Limited. "Annual Report 2010/2011".
10. Ibid.
11. Bossini International Holdings Limited. "Annual Report 2004/2005".
12. Haw Par Corporation Limited. "Annual Report 2004".

13. Haw Par Corporation Limited. "Annual Report 2015".
14. Innopac Holdings Limited. "Annual Report 2015".
15. Inno-Pacific Holdings Limited. "Annual Report 2010".
16. Innopac Holdings Limited. "Annual Report 2014".
17. Inno-Pacific Holdings Limited. "Annual Report 2010 to 2012" and Innopac Holdings Limited. "Annual Report 2013 to 2015".
18. Hanjin Shipping Co., Limited. "2015 Business Report".
19. Xiaolin Zeng. JOC.com. "Hanjin Shipping will enter receivership after bank support lost". http://www.joc.com/maritime-news/container-lines/hanjin-shipping/hanjin-shipping-will-enter-receivership-after-bank-support-lost_20160831.html. 31 August 2016.
20. Del Monte Pacific Limited. "Annual Report FY 2015".
21. Ibid.
22. Eratat Lifestyle Limited. "Annual Report 2012".
23. Stanley Lim Peir Shenq. The Motley Fool Singapore. "How Investors Can Protect Themselves Against Fraudulent S-Chips Such as Eratat Lifestyle Limited". https://www.fool.sg/2014/08/19/how-investors-can-protect-themselves-against-fraudulent-s-chips-such-as-eratat-lifestyle-limited/. 19 August 2014.
24. Eratat Lifestyle Limited. SGX Announcements. "(A) default on Bond Interest Payment; (B) Suspension of Trading Pending Verification of Group's Cash Balance; and (C) Suspension of CEO and Appointment of Interim CEO". 29 January 2014.
25. Eratat Lifestyle Limited. "Annual Report 2012".
26. Eratat Lifestyle Limited. "(A) default on Bond Interest Payment".
27. Eratat Lifestyle Limited. SGX Announcements. "Change – Announcement of Cessation::Cessation of Interim CEO and Chief Financial Officer". 30 May 2014.
28. Eratat Lifestyle Limited. SGX Announcements. "Eratat Receives SIAS Investors' Choice Award for Corporate Governance". 20 June 2013.
29. Chaoda Modern Agriculture (Holdings) Limited. Announcement & Notices. "Change of Auditors". 3 June 2003.
30. Chaoda Modern Agriculture (Holdings) Limited. Announcement & Notices. "Announcement". 1 September 2003.
31. Chaoda Modern Agriculture (Holdings) Limited. Announcement & Notices. "Announcement". 20 September 2004.
32. Chaoda Modern Agriculture (Holdings) Limited. Announcement & Notices. "Resignation of Executive Director". 30 June 2005.
33. Chaoda Modern Agriculture (Holdings) Limited. Announcement & Notices. "Appointment of Executive Directors and Resignation of Chief Financial Officer and Appointment of Vice President of Finance". 17 August 2005.
34. Chaoda Modern Agriculture (Holdings) Limited. Announcement & Notices. "Change of Company Secretary". 29 December 2006.

35. Chaoda Modern Agriculture (Holdings) Limited. Announcement & Notices. "Change of Auditors". 25 June 2007.

36. Anonymous Analytics. "Chaoda Modern Agriculture". http://www.anonanalytics.com/2013/04/initiating-coverage-chaoda-modern.html. Released: 26 September 2011.

37. Sino Techfibre Limited. Announcement. "Fire Outbreak at Office Premises, Appointment of Interim Chairperson and Interim Chief Executive Officer, Update on Investigations into Audit Issues". 21 April 2011.

38. China Animal Healthcare Limited. Announcement. "Inside Information; Update on the Progress of the Forensic Investigations and Continual Suspension of Trading". 28 December 2015.

39. Kingboard Copper Foil Holdings Limited. "Prospectus". 6 December 1999.

40. Kingboard Copper Foil Holdings Limited. SGX Announcement. "Clarification with Respect to the Article Dated 11 January 2016 Published in The Edge Singapore". 22 January 2016.

41. In the Supreme Court of Bermuda. Civil Jurisdiction. Commercial Court. 2011: No. 255. "In the Matter of Kingboard Copper Foil Holdings Limited and in the Matter of the Companies Act 1981, Section 111". [2015] SC (Bda) 76 Com (10 November 2015). 10 November 2015.

42. Teh Hooi Ling. Pulses. Savvy Investor_Wong Kok Hoi. "Don't Do What Others Do". 2 June 2009.

43. Lisa Pham. Bloomberg. "Lending in China Is So Risky That Cows Are Now Collateralized". https://www.bloomberg.com/news/articles/2016-05-25/cash-cows-fund-china-dairy-firm-that-defied-stock-market-slump. 26 May 2016.

44. Chin Hwee Tan and Thomas R. Robinson. CFA Institute. John Wiley & Sons, Inc. *Asian Financial Statement Analysis*. 2014.

8

Three Simple Valuation Techniques to Live By

Price is what you pay, value is what you get.

— Warren Buffett

After doing our due diligence and once we are convinced of its merits, it is time for our next step: to arrive at an estimation of its value, or more commonly known as a valuation. Because, at the end of the day, investing in a good company at an inflated price can lead to disaster as well.

It is important to note here that we believe that valuation of a company should only come near the end of your analysis, rather than using it as a starting point. This is because, as investors, we should be thinking like a businessperson. And we should approach our analysis in as businesslike a way as possible; understanding the business and finding a business that we are optimistic about. Only when we are confident in the business that we want to invest in do we look at the price we want to buy it at – hence the need for valuation.

And when it comes to valuation, we like to emphasise that there is no "one price". Valuations are like fingerprints, no two are the same. Why so? Because everyone thinks differently.

Valuation is about forecasting the future of the company. Therefore, investors have to make many assumptions when doing a valuation exercise. These assumptions, which are different for everyone, cause the variance in valuation between two investors. Although the commonly used formulas don't vary too much, the difference is your inputs. The Chinese have a saying, 规矩是死的, 人是活的, meaning, "Rules are dead, people are living."

As most of us can relate to property investments, let us use a residential property as an example. Assume that you have a 1,000-square foot, three-bedroom apartment which you are willing to let go for S$1.5 million, and you got to that figure based on your expectations that this place could get a net income of S$60,000 a year, an annual yield of 4%. Now, imagine that there are two bidders interested in your place. After visiting your place, Buyer A made a bid of S$1 million and Buyer B offered S$2 million. Same house, yet three different valuations. Who is right?

To make things sound even more complicated, all three are right, and yet none are right at the same time. It all comes down to each investor's own required rate of return.

- Buyer A: Has a required rate of return of at least 6%. Based on the same S$60,000 rental a year, buyer A would arrive at a valuation of S$1 million for the property.
- Buyer B: Is only looking for required rate of return of 3%. Based on the same rental, he would have an estimated valuation of S$2 million for the same property.

Think of your S$1.5 million as your intrinsic value, and Buyer A and Buyer B's offers of S$1 million and S$2 million respectively as what Mr Market might offer you – the lower one when he is sad, and the higher one when he's optimistic.

This example shows us that valuation is based on the assumptions of the investor. If investors have different assumptions, such as the rate of return required, this can lead to vastly different valuations.

Common valuation techniques for valuing a publicly listed company include:

1. price-to-book (P/B)
2. price-to-earnings (P/E)
3. discounted cash flow (DCF).

Although there are many approaches out there, most of them are evolutions or extensions of these three methods. With just these three, you should be good to go. Now let's get the ball rolling with a look at how to use price-to-book ratio as a valuation technique.

Price-to-Book Ratio

Asset valuation is a pretty straightforward method of valuing a company. We are simply valuing the company's assets and then subtracting all its liabilities. We then arrive at our estimated intrinsic value of the company. We then compare that figure with the market price of the company to derive its price-to-book ratio (P/B).

P/B can be used to value asset-heavy companies, such as companies with the likes of property, liquid investments and, best of all, cash.

One such company which we could use P/B ratio to value is Singapore-listed Haw Par Corporation Limited ("Haw Par Corporation"). Haw Par Corporation's core operating business involves manufacturing and distributing the Tiger Balm series of products. Here is how we value the company.

To provide some brief background, Haw Par Corporation has been listed in Singapore since 1969.[1] It has operations in the healthcare (Tiger Balm) and leisure (Underwater World) sectors.[2] To value the earnings from these two operating segments requires us to make some assumptions. On the other hand, Haw Par Corporation also manages a portfolio of investments in properties and publicly traded equities, where fewer assumptions are required, and this is where the P/B method shines.

After a quick look at their balance sheet, we conclude that the company has a direct and easy-to-understand balance sheet (a good thing), where many assets are carried at reasonable valuation on the books.

As at December 2015, Haw Par Corporation's shareholders' equity stood at S$2.54 billion. Some might use this figure as the book value. However, sceptics like us do not simply accept a company's numbers at face value. Some due diligence still has to be done on the underlying assets to see whether the stated values make investment sense. Remember, accounting figures might not be interpreted in the same way as how an investor looks at things.

Assets

From Haw Par Corporation's Annual Report 2015, there were a total of ten unique balance sheet items. However, from their balance sheet, out of the ten unique items, three of these items made up

97% of its total assets, valued at S$2.69 billion on its balance sheet.[3] The three items were:

- cash
- available-for-sale financial assets (AFS)
- investment properties.

We are going to show you how we analyse each of these items, and come up with an estimated intrinsic value for the company. Along the way, you might discover that for such an exercise, we do not have to be exactly right. Moreover, as long as we account for the things that matter, we should be good to go. Remember, not everything that can be counted counts, and not everything that counts can be counted.

Cash

In 2015, Haw Par Corporation had a cash position of S$316 million. Although in certain cases a company's cash position might not be what it seems, given Haw Par Corporation's long listing history and its association with one of the most reputable families in Singapore – the Wee Family – we did not see any reason to make any adjustments to their reported cash position.

We took its cash balance at face value: S$316 million.

Available-for-sale Financial Assets (AFS)

If we take a look at their 2015 Annual Report, Haw Par Corporation actually disclosed their three key investments, which totalled S$1.85 billion. It was even broken down to the companies they invested in, number of shares held in each company, the current market value and even dividend received.[4] Here were the three main investments in 2015:

1. United Overseas Bank Limited: S$1.38 billion
2. UOL Group Limited: S$271 million
3. United Industrial Corporation Limited: S$197 million.

In addition, Haw Par Corporation's financial review indicated the fair value of their other AFS, mainly Hong Kong-listed Hua Han Health Industry Holdings Limited at S$155 million.[5]

These few investments made up most of Haw Par Corporation's reported AFS of S$2.08 billion.

Although these investments are revalued based on their then current price, we would still give it a slight discount when valuing them, because in times of crisis these publicly traded shares might trade at a discount.

Assuming a 20% discount (arbitrary discount assuming a market sell down), we can value Haw Par Corporation's AFS in 2015 at S$2.08 billion × 80% = S$1.66 billion.

Investment Properties

Looking at Haw Par Corporation's notes to the financial statements on its investment properties, it is stated that they did engage external, independent and qualified valuers to determine the fair value of their properties annually. This means that the value recorded on its book is up to date.

It is possible for investors to check whether the properties are recorded using a reasonable valuation by making one of our own. Under the same financial note, it is indicated that Haw Par Corporation's net rental income for the year was S$8.46 million, with an occupancy rate of 65%.[6] Compared to the value of its investment properties, we would get a yield of 4%, which is quite reasonable. Nevertheless, for the sake of our policy of being conservative, we will apply a 10% discount.

Our estimation of its investment properties is therefore S$211 million × 10% = S$190 million.

Liabilities

Think about it: when things happen, your assets might be reduced. However, don't expect any sympathy from your creditors.

With this logic, we always take liabilities at face value. And in this case 100% of its total liabilities = S$157 million.

Finally, Adjusted Shareholders' Equity

Taking our adjusted total assets and subtracting Haw Par Corporation's total liabilities, we arrived at our estimated intrinsic value of the company of S$2 billion.

With 219 million shares, this worked out to about S$9 per share.

In simple language, based on our assumptions and estimated intrinsic value at that point in time, we believe that the company might be interesting when it trades below S$9 per share. Again, this was our estimation of the company. As we mentioned, valuations are like fingerprints; no two are identical. You can try this exercise yourself to see what value you might end up with.

Our estimated value was at a 36% discount to Haw Par Corporation's FY2015 Shareholder' Equity. Additionally, our above valuation did not even account for its profitable operating businesses.

Utility of the P/B method

Like all other valuation methods, the valuation with P/B is not a magic formula. For instance, P/B does not work well with companies involved in businesses with large amounts of intangible assets like brand name, goodwill and intellectual property. Take for example the service industry. Given that their greatest assets – their people – are not recorded on the balance sheets, using P/B for valuing most companies in the service industry might not be best choice.

As a general rule of thumb, the price-to-book ratio is effective in valuing companies with these characteristics:

- fairly valued assets, preferably with a liquid market
- asset-heavy industry
- profitable operations
- little minority interest
- little or no contingent liabilities.

Our process with Haw Par Corporation showed the utility of this valuation from an internal approach, by studying the company's assets. Keep in mind that there are also other ways to implement this technique. For instance, P/B ratio could also be externally applied in the form of peer comparables, something we will touch on in the next section on Price-to-Earnings.

Price-to-Earnings Ratio

Due to the ease of both its understanding and application, the price-to-earnings ratio (P/E) is one of the most common valuation tools in investing.

The P/E ratio indicates how much an investor is paying for $1 of a company's earnings. The higher the multiple, the more investors are paying for the company's future earnings.

Now, if a company has earnings per share of $1 and the stock is at $20, its P/E ratio is 20 times. That is how the P/E multiple works.

Generally, out-of-favour companies tend to fetch a lower multiple and popular growth companies (the next "in" thing) tend to fetch higher multiples. This means that the market expects strong growth from the company that's trading at a higher multiple (i.e. high double-digit growth or doubling in production). In contrast, companies with low P/E ratio tend to be the companies which investors have low expectations of. *Hint: It is this mismatch between expectation and actual performance that creates possible investment returns in both high-growth and low P/E ratio stocks. We think that it is always better to underpromise and outperform than overpromise and underperform.*

Another method to interpret the P/E ratio is using its inverse – the earnings yield or E/P. This gives you a quick gauge of how much return to expect out of your investment at the price you are looking at. This earnings yield can then be used for easy comparison across the board.

For example, if Singapore-listed supermarket operator Sheng Siong Group Limited ("Sheng Siong"), traded at a P/E of 20 times, you would arrive at an earnings yield of 5%. Assuming all things were constant, if we were to compare it to another company with a P/E of 30 times or 3.33% earnings yield, Sheng Siong appears to have a higher implied rate of return.

As per the P/B method, P/E valuation is only applicable to certain companies. Furthermore, as both methods are based on the past results, investors need to understand that future performance might differ from past performance. Therefore, P/E ratio might be more suitable for companies with these characteristics:

- fairly consistent earnings
- stable growth
- industries not too vulnerable to major disruption (*Hint: not tech industry*).

A P/E valuation consists of two parts, the earnings and the price, one internal and the other an external factor.

Earnings

To get a better sense of the company's "true" P/E ratio, it is important for us to make an adjustment to the company's earnings to show its "core" earnings.

These adjustments include:

- non-operating items such as government grants, interest income
- one-off income/expense
- fair value gains or losses.

As an example, we will look at Singapore-listed OSIM International Limited ("OSIM"). In 2008, the company recorded a one-time impairment of S$77 million for their investment in Brookstone, essentially wiping out that investment on its book[7] (Table 8.1). However, as it was a one-time non-cash expense, this meant that it had no impact on its cash flow. By writing it down to zero, this meant that it was the final impairment and the loss was just a one-off event and would not impact the long-term prospects of OSIM's core operations, which were still doing decently.

The company promptly returned to profitability in 2009, with net profit of S$23 million.[8] Given the situation with its impairment, it would have been quite reasonable to assume that OSIM would not continuously make losses of S$99 million year after year. With the write-down of its Brookstone investment, OSIM had actually, on paper, become a "stronger" company, without the loss-making business hanging around.

For simplicity, let us assume that OSIM could return to a net profit of S$20 million (average earnings ex-Brookstone over the five years from 2004 to 2008 were S$29 million). Next, we assume the company could fetch a P/E of 10 times, arriving at a valuation of S$200 million for the company. Fundamentally, we are aware that sales of discretionary products like massage chairs are likely to be

Table 8.1: OSIM International Limited Net Profit After Tax

OSIM FY Results (SGD million)	2004	2005	2006	2007	2008
Net Profit after Tax (excluding Brookstone)	31	37	48	12	15
Net Profit after Tax (including Brookstone)	31	47	34	3	–99

affected by the financial crisis, but we do not see the culture of massage chairs in Asian homes going away any time soon.

Between late 2008 and early 2009, OSIM traded between S$0.05 and 0.20/share.[9] Safe to say, this translated to a market capitalisation of below S$150 million. Some could contend that 2008 to 2009 was a unique time. On the other hand, we are not here for imaginary perfect-world types of situation. No one can dispute that this actually took place. And even with our conservative estimates, OSIM traded significantly lower than our earlier calculations.

Price-to-Earnings Multiple

The magic of the P/E ratio is that when it is used to compare against something else then, in financial parlance, this is known as a relative valuation. A relative valuation can be done by comparing the P/E ratio of a company with either:

1. its historical P/E range (internal); or
2. the P/E range of its competitors (external).

For an internal approach, we start by taking the company's current P/E ratio and compare it against its historical P/E ratio. A good range would be data of the past 5–10 years. Do note that these P/E ratios should be adjusted for extraordinary items, as previously mentioned.

Other things to take note of when comparing historical P/E ratios are significant events that might have happened affecting the fundamentals of the company. These changes can be categorised into two types:

1. significant internal change
2. significant external changes.

An example of a significant internal change can be illustrated by Singapore-listed Petra Foods Limited ("Petra Foods"). In 2013, Petra Foods (now Delfi Limited)[10] sold their entire cocoa ingredients business to Barry Callebaut AG.[11] Prior to the sale, their cocoa ingredient business was 68% of FY2012's revenue.[12] This meant that its business model changed drastically after the sale of its core business. Therefore, comparing the historical P/E ratio of this type of company might no longer be relevant.

When it comes to an example of a significant external change, Singapore-listed SMRT Corporation Limited ("SMRT") comes to mind. In July 2016, the Land Transport Authority of Singapore and SMRT concluded discussions on a new rail financing framework. The new framework allowed the Land Transport Authority ("LTA") to take over all operating assets from SMRT.[13] In turn, rail operators like SMRT would then become pure service providers, operating the rail network while the LTA took care of the rail assets. As this change was fuelled by factors beyond the company, it can be classified as an external change. Yet, similar to the previous example, this change would transform the business model of SMRT, making its P/E ratio comparison less relevant.

These two examples will most definitely impact the company's P/E comparison when viewed historically, because following these changes, the past is no longer that relevant to what's going to happen in the future. This will lead to the market having different expectations of the companies. Different expectations may lead to different methods of valuing the companies by the market.

On the other hand, another set of challenges arises when it comes to peer comparison. P/E ratio comparisons are generally performed between companies in the same business or industry. Typically, high-growth companies such as technology companies tend to trade at a much higher multiple compared to traditional companies like printing or engineering companies. To say that a run-of-the-mill precision engineering company with a P/E of 15 times is "cheaper" than a technology giant like Hong Kong-listed Tencent Holdings Limited with a P/E ratio of above 40 times might not be "true". But why?

Generally, the market tends to place a higher value on companies with:

- higher growth
- more consistent earnings
- operations in growth industries
- strong reputation
- dominant market share.

Other Factors Affecting Different Valuation

Even when comparing across the same industry, investors need to take note of the differences in business model, brand equity or other company-specific issues. A simple example to grasp is the differences between the Singapore commodity trading companies. Although companies like Noble Group Limited, Olam International Limited and Wilmar International Limited are all commodity firms, when we drill down into their core operations, things could not look more different.

First, companies are involved in completely different types of commodities. Another key factor is the management. Companies that are managed fantastically well can trade significantly above their peers. They may also display much higher margins, return on capital and capital allocation ability compared to other competitors.

Therefore, when comparing between companies, we need to see if they have similar business models and management skills. Interesting opportunities may arise when two fairly similar companies vary significantly in their valuation. That may warrant a deeper look.

The P/E Ratio Is Not A Fixed Rule

We need to understand that P/E ratio is not a fixed rule. A company with a P/E ratio of 5 times does not mean that the company is undervalued or a great investment. Likewise, a company with a P/E ratio of 50 times does not always mean it is overvalued, and vice-versa. In fact, a fast-growing and well-managed company with a high P/E ratio might end up being a better investment compared to a poorly managed company with no growth prospect, even if it has a low P/E ratio.

- Company at P/E of 5 times: If earnings continue to halve for the next two years in a row, you would have paid 20 times for its future earnings two years down the road. Not so cheap now, is it?
- Company at P/E of 50 times: If the earnings double for two years in a row, you were essentially paying just 12.5 times of its earnings two years in the future. Not so expensive now, is it?

We can't always accept P/E multiples at face value; at the end of the day, it's still all about the company and the business they are in.

Here is an example of how we use P/E ratio to value a consumer company listed in Hong Kong. Want Want China Holdings Limited ("Want Want") is in the dairy beverages and snack business. Although Want Want is not a common brand outside of China, many might still recognise its mascot, once they are shown the Hot-Kid or 旺仔 picture. This shows the strong branding that the company has, and Want Want has leveraged this advantage by branding the bulk of their goods with the logo of its mascot. The "Hot-Kid milk" range of dairy products and beverages made up close to 90% of this segment's revenue.[14]

Being in the consumer staples space with a strong branding by itself affords a certain degree of competitive advantage to the company. Why is this business appealing to us?

The key reasons are:

- branding
- strong distribution network
- cash flow-generative
- easy-to-understand business.

Want Want has recorded an average net profit of about US$560 million from 2010 to 2015.[15] That Want Want can continue generating net profit of about US$500 million in the future might not be too far-fetched an assumption. Right here, we are making a very general assumption that they can continue at this level of profitability, without factoring for growth.

Again, a model is only as good as the inputs. We arrived at our assumptions after considering the following:

- business – stable demand for its product
- financial track record – prudent with strong balance sheet
- cost management – good cost control with high return on equity and gross margins
- management track record – history of steering the company well
- shareholder track record (buy-backs and dividends) – strong buy-back and dividend culture
- peer comparison – one of the leading consumer companies in China.

With a P/E ratio of 20 times, we would arrive at an estimated value of US$10 billion, or HKD77 billion for the company. During January 2017, the company had a market capitalisation of about HKD62 billion.[16] Considering that we were rather conservative in our assumptions when it came to future growth, at such valuations, Want Want might warrant a deeper analysis.

However, there exists a dilemma for most investors when it comes to the P/E valuation. Unlike the P/B valuation, where things are more straightforward, the earnings portion of the P/E valuation encompasses both current and future earnings.

Future earnings are something that is never certain and this might create some uncertainty in predicting the future P/E of a company. This is because future earnings depend greatly on both the direction and growth rate of the company.

Yes, growth is also a component of value and can be a major contributor towards a company's valuation. It is all well and good to consider past performances; however, we cannot just keep our eyes on the rearview mirror. At the end of the day, investing is a forward-looking exercise.

Companies such as a pharmaceutical company nearing a new breakthrough in a new drug or companies diversifying into other areas of business will require more assumptions in predicting their future earnings. If you are right, the returns can be huge. On the other hand, if things go south, you might end up way off the mark. It doesn't even have to be something complicated. You would be surprised at the number of things that a restaurant operator could be faced with, even for a relatively simple plan of store expansion.

Tsui Wah Holdings Limited ("Tsui Wah") is the owner and operator of the famous 翠華 (Tsui Wah) brand of cha chaan teng (casual-dining) restaurants in Hong Kong, China and Macau. "Cha chaan tengs" literally means "tea restaurants". Think fast food with a mixture of Cantonese fare fused with western and Asian elements. Tsui Wah has signatures like crispy bun with sweet condensed milk, Swiss sauce chicken wings and jumbo frankfurter hot dog. You can literally taste the attraction of this business.

When Tsui Wah had its IPO in November 2012, it operated a total of 26 restaurants.[17] Post-IPO, Tsui Wah has been consistent in its goal of reaching a total of 80 stores by 2017.[18] In 2014, the company was halfway there.[19] If things went according to plan, Tsui Wah could double their revenue and, in turn, potentially double their earnings. Together with plans to centralise its operations, Tsui Wah's growth story looked pretty encouraging.

In early 2014, Tsui Wah traded at HKD5 per share, priced at close to 45 times its FY2014's Shareholders' profit of HKD156 million.[20] Yet its competitors like Hong Kong-listed Café de Coral Holdings Limited, Tao Heung Holdings Limited and Fairwood Holdings

Limited were in the range of 20–25 times. This meant that the market had high expectations for them. Already being rather efficient, with most of its existing stores operating long hours and achieving decently good profitability, it still had to grow fast enough to live up to those high expectations. At those valuations, the downside risk appeared to outweigh the potential upside.

Based on an expected restaurant count of 80 by 2017, an optimistic investor might project them to achieve future net profits of HK$300 million, or double their FY2014 profits. Assuming a P/E ratio of about 20–25 times for its future earnings, Tsui Wah could be worth around HKD6–7.5 billion by 2017. However, business is not always simple maths, not even for something as simple as store openings. Increasing revenue does not always mean higher earnings; similarly, increased store count does not always lead to increased revenue. Moreover, at a market capitalisation of HKD7 billion, it looked like future growth was very much priced into the market price.

The effect of this was best seen in 2016. Even with an increase of ten stores, up 20% from 2015, revenue was flat year on year. Revenue per store (directly operated stores) fell from HKD37 million to HKD32 million, resulting in declines in both its operating and net profit.[21]

Upon deeper investigation, you would realise that this trend was not something new. Over the past five years (2012–2016), it was pretty clear that 1% increase in revenue did not translate to a 1% increase in both operating and net profit.[22] So what gave?

At a glance, we could see that over the years, increasing operating expenses like staff costs and rental costs had hit its profitability hard. Coupled with a decrease of revenue per store, the company's bottom line was hit with a double whammy. This resulted in Tsui Wah's net profit being HK$72 million in 2016, less than half the company's FY2014 net profit.

In November 2016, Tsui Wah traded at a market capitalisation of HKD2 billion,[23] a fair distance away from the range of HKD6–7.5 billion we mentioned above. Back in 2014, it might seem that the market appeared to be overly optimistic. However, could the market be swinging to the other extreme now? That is always a question we have to keep asking ourselves.

The lesson here is not to overpay for future expectations. In most cases, when making assumptions about future earnings, it pays to err on the side of conservatism.

To summarise, the limitations of using the P/E method generally apply for companies:

- with no earnings – #Obviously
- with ultra-high growth – the current earnings have no relevance to its future
- facing structural decline in its business – earnings can go to zero or, worse, negative
- in a fast-changing industry – the prospect and earning power of the company can change rapidly, so its current earnings are of little importance.

Discounted Cash Flow

P/B and P/E ratios are two of the most commonly used metrics when valuing companies. This was mainly due to their ease of use and direct comparison. However, besides the balance sheet and the earnings of a company, its cash flow is also a critical part of its value. Therefore, one of the most effective methods of valuing these future cash flows from the company is using the discounted cash flow valuation model.

The P/B and P/E ratios are known as relative valuation methods. They only make sense if they are being compared against a reference point, and this reference point can be either the ratios of its historic records, or its peers. Without that, it would be meaningless.

On the other hand, the discounted cash flow approach, or DCF, is an absolute valuation method. The method does not need a reference point to compare to. The valuation method would help investors arrive at an estimation of the company's valuation directly, without comparing it to its peers or its past.

The definition of discounted cash flow is the present value of the entire expected cash flow from the company in the future. Simply put, the sum of the company's discounted cash flow is your estimation of the company's intrinsic value.

However, given the definitive nature of this method (compared to P/E and P/B), it also means that there are quite a number of inputs needed for this method.

Key assumptions include:

- Base operating cash flow
- Capital expenditure

- Growth rate and period
- Retention ratio
- Discount rate

$$DCF = \frac{CF_1}{(1+r)^1} + \frac{CF_2}{(1+r)^2} + \cdots + \frac{CF_n}{(1+r)^n}$$

where:

CF = Cash flow
r   = Discount rate

The formula for discounted cash flow is just the sum of all future free cash flow, discounted back to present value. The formula works like this:

$$\text{Value of company} = \frac{\left(\begin{array}{c}\text{Expected Operating Cash Flow}\\ -\text{Expected Capital Expenditure}\end{array}\right)}{\left(\text{Discount rate} - \text{Terminal Growth Rate}\right)}$$

A common variation of the DCF model is the Gordon Growth Model, or dividend discount model. In this case, instead of free cash flow being the star, the company's expected dividend is a key factor in deriving its value.

The formula for the Gordon Growth Model is:

$$\text{Value of company} = \frac{\text{Expected Dividend per Share}}{\left(\text{Discount Rate} - \text{Terminal Growth Rate}\right)}$$

Once we have mastered the simplest form of DCF, other variations are just extensions of this approach. That's all you need to know about the framework behind the DCF model. Remember, more than the formula (which doesn't change much), the key factor is the assumptions you make when it comes to the inputs.

For starters, just think about what you must consider to arrive at a reasonable estimate of a company's operating cash flow. This is important as this first step has significant effects on our final estimate. Also, keep in mind that it is important not simply to extrapolate the past into the future; doing so can often lead you to believe that a stock is worth a lot more, or a lot less than it really is, especially in a growth company.

- If a company's net income is projected to grow at 3% per year over 5 years, its growth would just be 16%.
- On the other hand, if a company's net income is projected to grow at 10% per year over 5 years, its growth would be 61%.

See the difference?

Take for example, Hong Kong-listed Tencent Holdings Limited ("Tencent Holdings"). Although dominant in China's technology space, it is still operating in a relatively new industry with so many possible applications yet to be monetised. Therefore, it is extremely difficult to predict the growth rate for Tencent Holdings, and correspondingly its valuation. From 2006 to 2015, revenue and shareholders' profit was up 3,300% and 2,800% respectively.[24] To quantify things, Tencent Holdings' revenue in 2015 was RMB103 billion. Even in 2015, the company's revenue and net profit grew by 30% and 63% respectively. Not bad for a HKD2 trillion company.[25]

However, to assume that every company can continue its phenomenal growth rate for the considerable future might be optimistic. On the other hand, a great company might also be able to live up to its expectations. That said, the difficulty in projecting such high expectations is the risk of "the higher they are, the harder they fall". Even though there is no "right" rule for how to predict the growth rate of a company, we need to be very familiar with the fundamentals of the business and industry to make our assumptions. The less we know, the more our assumptions look like guesswork. With that said, to make your life easier, you don't have to consider every single thing to make your decision; just stick to the key stuff and make a reasonable call.

However, if your assumptions were made without even considering the company's operations and future, things might end up rather uncomfortable. Imagine an investor back in 2005, looking at Singapore-listed Global Yellow Pages Limited ("Global Yellow Pages") without giving much thought to the industry's prospects.

Global Yellow Pages was traditionally in the printed directory business. Back in 2005, close to 100% of Global Yellow Pages' revenue of S$61 million came from their directory advertising in Singapore, with the majority from the sale of advertising space in its Singapore phone directories. At that time, the then management highlighted Singapore's low advertiser penetration of 11% relative to mature markets overseas.[26] To them, the future looked bright. If an investor was unaware of what was happening in the advertising industry, the picture that management was painting looked appealing. Well, that was before Google and Facebook came to the party.

Fast forward to 2015, and other than revenue being down to just S$32 million, the contribution from their sale of advertising space was just S$11 million, down by over 80%. To its credit, the company tried to diversify into a wide range of activities, from river taxi tours (Singapore River Explorer), food and beverage businesses (licensor of Wendy's Supa Sundaes brand) to property investments (freehold property in New Zealand), as well as being investors in publicly listed equity involved in mushroom farming (Singapore-listed Yamada Green Resources Limited).[27]

Global Yellow Pages' 2015 annual report even led with the tagline "Transforming through Diversification". However, our point is that if an investor projected its earnings solely based on past performance, the investor could end up rather disappointed.

Even more than with P/E and P/B techniques, the DCF approach is applicable for simple-to-understand, low-probability-of-disruption type businesses. One example, in the consumer staples field, consider Malaysia-listed Nestlé (Malaysia) Berhad, a company with decades of consistent record of profitability and free cash flow.

With increasing profitability across the board, Nestlé's record in Malaysia looked rather stellar. From 2006 to 2015, the company grew its profit after tax and operating cash flow by 124% and 110% respectively.[28] Given the business model of such a consumer staple, it is not unrealistic to expect both its profitability and capital expenditure to be relatively stable.

Let's start with these assumptions:

- Base free cash flow of RM527 million, the average of the past two years.
- The company can grow its free cash flow at 5% over the next five years.
- After five years, growth slows down to 3%.
- Discount rate of 8%.

Table 8.2: Sample DCF Calculation

FY End Dec RM (mil)	Free Cash Flow	Present Value
2016	553	512
2017	581	498
2018	610	484
2019	641	471
2020	673	458
Terminal 2021	13,856	9,430
TOTAL	**16,913**	**11,853**

Again, we emphasise that this example is purely to run you through the mechanics of how the DCF works. With an 8% discount rate, our estimation would be RM12 billion (Table 8.2).

Also, you might have noticed that we do not tend to place much emphasis on the figures being down to the exact decimal place, because in the grand scheme of things, this is only an estimation. Moreover, the thing about the DCF is that it is very vulnerable to adjustments.

For illustration purposes, if we took:

- a lower discount rate of 6%, we would arrive at an estimated value of RM20 billion
- a higher discount rate of 10%, we would arrive at an estimated value of RM8.4 billion.

In June 2016, Nestlé (Malaysia) had a market capitalisation of RM18 billion.[29] Depending on your discount rate, the company's traded value could be either over-, under- or fairly-valued compared to your estimation. See how much your assumptions will affect the final estimate. Keep in mind that the discount rate is only one of many variables!

Utility of the DCF method

You might face problems with this method if the company:

- is in a cyclical industry
- is in a disruptive industry

- has lumpy cash flow
- has a high level of minority interest
- has a low level of disclosure.

Any DCF model is only going to be as good as your inputs. As they say, "Garbage in, garbage out".

Always Remember Your Margin of Safety

If there is one thing that all value investors agree on, it is the concept of "Margin of Safety", a concept first coined by Benjamin Graham. This investment approach is applicable for almost any asset under the sun. For instance, say you invest in a secured bond priced at $100 million. If your estimation of the assets backing the bond is worth $200 million, it means that you have a margin of safety of 50%. In theory, the underlying assets need to decline by more than 50% before bondholders suffer permanent losses. Similarly, for a publicly listed company, the margin of safety principal is maintained by buying the company below our estimated value.

At this point we are reminded of a quote from the famous investor, Warren Buffett, "It is far better to buy a wonderful business at a fair price than a fair business at a wonderful price."[30] This means that it is particularly risky to invest in a mediocre business. What is worse is to invest in a poorly managed company during an industry peak. That is because, when times are great and everyone seems to be having fun, these poorly managed companies rise with the tide. It is only when the tide is down that you discover who has been swimming naked. Therefore, while we might feel that we have a wide margin of safety when investing in these companies, that "value" might prove to be just an illusion when the business cycle goes in another direction.

An observable example of such a situation is the leveraged companies found in the oil and gas industry during 2015. During the boom years, these leveraged companies saw record profits year after year as they enjoyed the expanding demand for their products and services while using relatively cheap debt financing. Since the tide came in for oil prices in 2014, many of these leveraged companies have not been having the time of their lives.

This example serves as a warning to investors: the concept of margin of safety should be used after we are fairly confident of the long-term prospect of a company. We should not be looking for investments that merely give us a significant margin of safety, irrespective of the quality of the business.

Before going into our final chapter on how all this ties in together, we think that Walter Schloss's "Factors needed to make money in the stock market"[31] is a great piece to keep in our back pockets:

Factors needed to make money in the stock market

1. Price is the most important factor to use in relation to value.
2. Try to establish the value of the company. Remember that a share of stock represents a part of a business and is not just a piece of paper.
3. Use book value as a starting point to try and establish the value of the enterprise. Be sure that debt does not equal 100% of the equity.
4. Have patience. Stocks don't go up immediately.
5. Don't buy on tips or for a quick move. Let the professionals do that, if they can. Don't sell on bad news.
6. Don't be afraid to be a loner but be sure that you are correct in your judgement. You can't be 100% certain but try to look for the weaknesses in your thinking. Buy on a scale and sell on a scale up.
7. Have the courage of your convictions once you have made a decision.
8. Have a philosophy of investment and try to follow it. The above is a way that I've found successful.
9. Don't be in too much of a hurry to sell. If the stock reaches a price you think is a fair one, then you can sell but often because a stock goes up 50%, people say sell it and button up your profit. Before selling try to re-evaluate the company again and see where the stock sells in relation to its book value. Be aware of the level of the stock market. Are yields low and PE ratios high? Is the stock market historically high? Are people very optimistic, etc?
10. When buying a stock, I find it helpful to buy near the low of the past few years. A stock may go as high as 125 and then decline to 60 and you think it's attractive. 3 years before the stock sold at 20 which shows that there is some vulnerability in it.
11. Try to buy assets at a discount rather than to buy earnings. Earning can change dramatically in a short term. Usually

assets change slowly. One has to know much more about a company if one buys earnings.

12. Listen to suggestions from people you respect. This doesn't mean you have to accept them. Remember it's your money and generally it is harder to keep money than to make it. Once you lose a lot of money, it is hard to make it back.

13. Try not to let your emotions affect your judgement. Fear and greed are probably the worst emotions to have in connection with the purchase and sale of stocks.

14. Remember the word compounding. For example, if you can make 12% a year and reinvest the money back, you will double your money in 6 years, taxes excluded. Remember the rule of 72. Your rate of return into 72 will tell you the number of years to double your money.

15. Prefer stocks over bonds. Bonds will limit your gains and inflation will reduce your purchasing power.

16. Be careful of leverage. It can go against you.

We believe that combining the knowledge of the business together with the "margin of safety" philosophy is the best approach an investor can have when approaching the stock market.

Notes

1. Haw Par Corporation Limited. About Us. "Heritage". http://www.hawpar.com/about-us/heritage.html. Accessed: 14 February 2017.
2. Haw Par Corporation Limited. "Annual Report 2015".
3. Ibid.
4. Ibid.
5. Ibid.
6. Ibid.
7. OSIM International Limited. "Annual Report 2008".
8. OSIM International Limited. "Annual Report 2009".
9. Google Finance. OSIM International Limited. https://www.google.com/finance?cid=757227292477104. Accessed: 15 February 2017.
10. Delfi Limited. General Announcement. "Change of Name of Company". 9 May 2016.
11. Petra Foods Limited. Press release. "Petra Foods successfully completes sale of Coca Ingredients Business". 1 July 2017.
12. Petra Foods Limited. "Annual Report 2012".
13. SMRT Corporation Limited. SGX Announcement. Asset Acquisitions and Disposals. "Proposed Sale of Operating Assets in Connection with the New Rail Financing Framework". 15 July 2016.

14. Want Want China Holdings Limited. "Annual Report 2015".
15. Ibid.
16. Google Finance. Want Want China Holdings Limited. https://www. google.com/finance?cid=722679. Accessed: 15 February 2017.
17. Tsui Wah Holdings Limited. Prospectus. "Global Offering".
18. Tsui Wah Holdings Limited. "Annual Report 2014 to 2016".
19. Tsui Wah Holdings Limited. "Annual Report 2014".
20. Google Finance. Tsui Wah Holdings Limited. https://www.google. com/finance?cid=472042275792381. Accessed: 16 February 2017.
21. Tsui Wah Holdings Limited. "Annual Report 2016".
22. Tsui Wah Holdings Limited. "Annual Report 2013 to 2016".
23. Google Finance. Tsui Wah Holdings Limited.
24. Tencent Holdings Limited. "Annual Report 2010 & 2015".
25. Google Finance. Tencent Holdings Limited. https://www.google. com/finance?cid=695431. Accessed: 17 February 2017.
26. Global Yellow Pages. "Annual Report 2005".
27. Global Yellow Pages. "Annual Report 2015".
28. Nestle (Malaysia) Berhad. "Annual Report 2010 and 2015".
29. Google Finance. Nestle (Malaysia) Berhad. https://www.google. com/finance?cid=286698542389796. Accessed: 17 February 2017.
30. Matthew Frankel. The Motley Fool. "3 Pieces of Warren Buffett Wisdom for an Expensive Stock Market". https://www.fool.com/ investing/2016/09/04/3-pieces-of-warren-buffett-wisdom-for-an-expensive.aspx. 4 September 2016.
31. Walter & Edwin Schloss Associates, L.P. "Factors needed to make money in the stock market". 10 March 1994.

9

How Everything Comes Together

I love it when a plan comes together
— John "Hannibal" Smith (The A-Team)

This is where all the pieces come together.

With the help of five case studies, we will bring you through our thought processes all the way from how we arrived at these companies, to understanding their operations, then all the way on to the valuation techniques employed.

Here is what we will be exploring for each company:

- business – what they do
- type of value – what type of value we are looking at
- screening – how we arrived at this company
- what's interesting – analysis of the business (financial and non-financial factors)
- major shareholders
- valuation.

Remember, our valuations are based on our own estimates, meaning that it is unique to us. As our case studies are purely for educational purposes, they should not be taken as investment advice.

When working on one of your opportunities, you may use this section to guide your investment process. With this framework in place, you would be able to customise it to fit your personal style.

Just bear in mind to always challenge the assumptions that led you to your investment decision.

From the get-go, we made known to you that our book serves as a guide on how to move from the theoretical to the practical application of a value-based approach when investing in Asia. And we plan to keep this promise.

With what we have learned up to this point, we will incorporate the knowledge obtained by applying it to five case studies, each unique in their own ways:

1. value through assets – Hongkong Land Holdings Limited
2. current earning power – Tingyi (Cayman Islands) Holdings Corporation
3. growth through cyclicality – First Resources Limited
4. special situation – Dalian Wanda Commercial Properties Company Limited
5. high growth (the Land of Fast-Growing Unicorns) – Tencent Holdings Limited.

■ **CASE STUDY**   Value Through Assets – Hongkong Land Holdings Limited

Hongkong Land Holdings Limited ("Hongkong Land") is one of the largest property companies listed on the Singapore exchange with a market capitalisation of US$16.0 billion (2016).[1] The Group owns and manages almost 800,000 sq. m. of prime office and luxury retail property in key Asian cities, primarily in Hong Kong and Singapore[2] (Table 9.1).

As part of the Jardine Matheson Group of companies (one of the largest conglomerates in Asia),[3] Hongkong Land is the property owner of many prime buildings in Hong Kong, Singapore, Indonesia, Vietnam and Thailand. In the first half of 2016, about 82% of the underlying profit of the company came from its property ownership business, including its associates and joint ventures.[4]

And with 76% of the group's gross assets in Hong Kong (with a significant concentration in the Central district), Hongkong Land is viewed as a landlord of high-quality properties in Hong Kong.[5]

Apart from being a property owner, the company is also a property developer, with projects in China, Singapore, Indonesia and the Philippines.[6]

■ CASE STUDY *(CONTINUED)*

Table 9.1: Hongkong Land Holdings Limited's Hong Kong Assets

Hongkong Land Holdings Limited
Hong Kong Assets

1	One Exchange Square
2	Two Exchange Square
3	Three Exchange Square
4	The Forum
5	Jardine House
6	Chater House
7	Alexandra House
8	Gloucester Tower
9	Edinburgh Tower (The Landmark Mandarin Oriental)
10	York House
11	Landmark Atrium
12	Prince's Building

Type of Value Discount to asset value.

Screening – How We Ended Up with This Company Who does not like property! Jokes aside, when screening for companies, the criteria we focused on included:

- tangible assets: assets must be backed by real tangible assets and not intangibles like goodwill
- substantial discount to book: looking for companies with low price to tangible book value
- industry headwinds: avoiding companies in industries facing structural declines
- track record: looking for companies with some profitability, size and reputation
- low leverage: avoiding highly leveraged companies.

Using this simple screening process, we could end up with a much more manageable basket of possible investments. To kick things off, we narrowed our universe to real-estate-based companies listed in Hong Kong and Singapore trading at way below their net tangible book value. In our case, "way below" meant a price to tangible book value of less than 0.6 times.

■ CASE STUDY *(CONTINUED)*

Next, we were also interested in companies of a certain size, and we settled for companies with a market capitalisation of over USD500 million.

Finally, we prefer to look at companies that are conservative when it comes to debt. Therefore, the company should have a total debt to capital ratio of less than 20%. Total capital generally refers to debt plus shareholders' equity. Remember, these criteria are not fixed, not at all; it all depends on your own expectation and requirement.

With these four simple metrics, and with the help of the Financial Times online Equity Screener application,[7] we were able to arrive at a list of companies to investigate within Asia (Table 9.2).

Once we have the preliminary list of short-listed companies, we can then proceed to do a short study on each company to determine whether it is worth a deeper analysis. When it came to our list above, one company stood head and shoulders above the crowd. This company is Singapore-listed Hongkong Land.

Most of the companies on our list are relatively small and do not have a strong economic moat surrounding their business. Unlike them, Hongkong Land is one of the most well-known property companies in Asia, with many valuable assets on its balance sheet. Moreover, being part of the Jardine Matheson Group of companies is also a plus in our books.

What's Interesting?   When looking at investments with value based on its assets, we prefer to approach this from a "Why is it trading at a discount?" and "What can go wrong?" approach. And Hongkong Land is no different. And we start by answering four of these issues:

1. Why is it trading below its net tangible book value?
2. Is there a catalyst?

Table 9.2: Results from the Financial Times Equity Screener

Company	Listing	Market Cap (USD billion)	Total Debt to Capital	Price-to-Book Ratio
C C Land Holdings Limited	HK	0.79	0%	0.46
Hang Lung Group Limited	HK	5.60	18%	0.58
Hongkong Land Holdings Limited	SG	16.66	12%	0.56
Hopewell Holdings Limited	HK	3.17	5%	0.53
Hysan Development Co Limited	HK	4.85	8%	0.56
Liu Chong Hing Investments Limited	HK	0.55	10%	0.39
Soundwill Holdings Limited	HK	0.52	11%	0.25
Tian Teck Land Limited	HK	0.54	1%	0.54

■ CASE STUDY *(CONTINUED)*

3. If not, can it continue to grow its book value in the future?
4. What are the risks?

Why is it Trading below its Net Tangible Book Value?   We feel that there were two key reasons why the market was pricing Hongkong Land at such levels.

- Hong Kong's property market was facing some headwinds.[8]
- Market participants looking at the company from a dividend yield perspective. In early 2017, the company had a dividend yield of 2.78%,[9] below the market average of 3.26%[10] and 3.04%[11] for the Tracker Fund of Hong Kong and SPDR Straits Times Index ETF respectively.

The Hong Kong property market saw huge price appreciation from 2009 to 2015.[12] Only in the beginning of 2016 did prices start to decline.[13] It seemed at that time that the fundamentals were not looking great for the Hong Kong economy.[14]

Even with all that being said, Hongkong Land still owns some of the most prime commercial properties in the central business district of Hong Kong, all strategically located in the Central district of the city. Due to its prime location, these properties might be more defensive in nature in terms of rental and value.

To address this concern, let us assume a "worst" scenario, in which all of Hongkong Land's Hong Kong investment properties in 1H2016 fall by 30%, meaning that the carrying value of these properties decreases from US$25 billion to US$18 billion,[15] translating into a drop of US$7 billion in value. If we account for that drop, the equity value of the company would fall from US$30 billion to about US$23 billion, or about US$10 per share.[16] During December 2016, Hongkong Land hovered about US$6.30 per share. This meant that our estimation of the company's intrinsic value, which was based on a rather pessimistic assumption of Hong Kong's property market, was still at least 50% higher than its then-current share price.

Now, to address our second concern, is the market valuing the company at such levels because of its dividend payout ratio? From the nature of its operations and assets, we cannot discount the possibility of market participants valuing the company from a dividend approach. And with Hongkong Land's dividend yield lower than both the Tracker Fund of Hong Kong and SPDR Straits Times Index ETF, this might be a valid concern.

Is there a Catalyst in the Future for the Company to be Fully Valued Again?   As a catalyst, an increase in dividend pay-out could be just what the doctor ordered.

For such an event to take place, it depends on both the capability and the willingness of the company. So how did Hongkong Land fare on this issue?

■ CASE STUDY *(CONTINUED)*

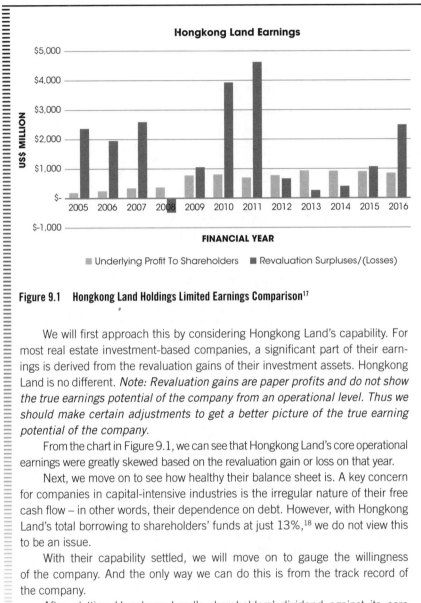

Figure 9.1   Hongkong Land Holdings Limited Earnings Comparison[17]

We will first approach this by considering Hongkong Land's capability. For most real estate investment-based companies, a significant part of their earnings is derived from the revaluation gains of their investment assets. Hongkong Land is no different. *Note: Revaluation gains are paper profits and do not show the true earnings potential of the company from an operational level. Thus we should make certain adjustments to get a better picture of the true earning potential of the company.*

From the chart in Figure 9.1, we can see that Hongkong Land's core operational earnings were greatly skewed based on the revaluation gain or loss on that year.

Next, we move on to see how healthy their balance sheet is. A key concern for companies in capital-intensive industries is the irregular nature of their free cash flow – in other words, their dependence on debt. However, with Hongkong Land's total borrowing to shareholders' funds at just 13%,[18] we do not view this to be an issue.

With their capability settled, we will move on to gauge the willingness of the company. And the only way we can do this is from the track record of the company.

After plotting Hongkong Land's shareholders' dividend against its core operational earnings (Figure 9.2), it was clear that the average pay-out ratio for the last decade was consistently at a comfortable level of about 50%.

■ CASE STUDY *(CONTINUED)*

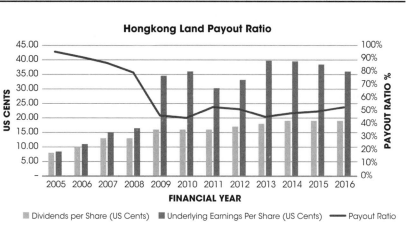

Figure 9.2   Hongkong Land Dividend Pay-out Ratio[19]

To conclude, as an outside observer, it appears that the company has the capability to increase its dividend level.

If Not, Can it Continue to Grow its Book Value in the Future?   Based on the historical track record of the company, it has been able to grow its book value very successfully. Its net asset value per share increased from just US$4.76 in 2006[20] to US$12.19 per share in 2015.[21]

That translated into a compounded annual growth rate of 11%. Furthermore, this was achieved with just a relatively conservative debt level. Looking forward, the company has also entered many growth markets such as Southeast Asia and China to diversify away from its business concentration in Hong Kong. These markets might fuel the growth of its book value going forward.

Looking Hongkong Land's investment pipeline, it does seem that Hongkong Land will be able to continue to build its asset base for many years to come.

What Are the Risks?   Over the short term, the volatile market conditions in Hong Kong together with the slowdown in Singapore's property scene might put some pressure on the company's ability to grow. As Hongkong Land is highly concentrated in these two markets, any decline in rental yield or property value in these two countries would directly impact both the revenue and book value of the company.

Over the longer term, the challenges that are facing Hong Kong as a financial hub might stagnate its economy. Hong Kong used to be the gateway to

■ CASE STUDY *(CONTINUED)*

mainland China. However, as China is opening itself up to the world, the need for businesses to use Hong Kong as a transit point might be reduced greatly in the future. The opening of a free-trade zone in Shanghai and the liberalisation of its currency and financial markets might reduce the importance of Hong Kong. If that happens, the growth for the company within Hong Kong would become very limited.

The shareholder and management structure of the company is also a concern. Even though slim, there always exists a possibility that the major shareholders interest might put minority shareholders at a disadvantage in some decisions. Although such instances are not common in the past, it is still a risk we have to think about.

Major Shareholders (3 March 2016)[22]

• Jardine Strategic Holdings Limited: 50.01%

Valuation   When it comes to valuations, we have to make certain fundamental assumptions, and we will go with two for each case study. In the case of Hongkong Land, our key assumptions are:

• Hong Kong and Singapore remain as key financial centres in the near future
• The bulk of Hongkong Land's properties do not vanish overnight

Due to the nature of Hongkong Land's assets and operation make-up, the valuation technique we selected was rather straightforward – the Price-to-Book methodology. This was primarily because the bulk of Hongkong Land's assets were investment properties that are revalued every year. Therefore, the properties are quite reflective of the current market expectations. Furthermore, the company had minimal debts and liabilities.

In summary, even if we were to consider our "worst" case scenario, whereby its portfolio of investment properties in Hong Kong was hit by a 30% decline, Hongkong Land was estimated to be worth about US$10 per share, over 50% higher than its November 2016 market price of US$6.30.[23] For reference, Hongkong Land's Price-to-Book ratio over a 10-year period from 2007–2016 is shown in Table 9.3.

Conclusion   Although the catalyst from Hongkong Land is uncertain, its long track record of growing its book value gives us more confidence in the company's future developments. In simple words, even if the market did not re-rate the company, the management would still work towards building up its net tangible book value, allowing shareholders to enjoy the growth. Well, on the bright side, at current levels, one can still look towards a dividend yield of 3%.

■ CASE STUDY *(CONTINUED)*

Table 9.3: Under Hongkong Land Case Study Section

FY	Price-to Book Ratio		
	Min	Average	Max
2007	0.62	0.74	0.85
2008	0.34	0.64	0.84
2009	0.28	0.51	0.75
2010	0.51	0.64	0.84
2011	0.40	0.59	0.72
2012	0.42	0.53	0.64
2013	0.50	0.60	0.71
2014	0.50	0.57	0.61
2015	0.54	0.62	0.72
2016	0.42	0.48	0.54
10-Year Average	**0.45**	**0.59**	**0.72**

■ **CASE STUDY**   Current Earning Power – Tingyi (Cayman Islands) Holdings Corporation

In 2014, PepsiCo, Inc. signed a deal to supply beverages to Walt Disney Co's first China resort – Shanghai Disney Resort. This was the first time in 25 years that PepsiCo sold beverages through Disneyland.[24] Why did Disneyland choose PepsiCo over Coca-Cola?

With over 50% of China's ready-to-drink ("RTD") tea market in 2015,[25] Tingyi (Cayman Islands) Holdings Corporation ("Tingyi Holdings") might be the reason. Founded by the Taiwanese Wei brothers, Hong Kong-listed Tingyi Holdings is a giant in China's instant noodles and RTD tea markets. Almost all of Tingyi's sales are within the PRC. In short, Tingyi Holdings is an investment in the Chinese consumer food and beverage sector, especially in the instant noodle and RTD tea markets. For Tingyi Holdings, it was represented by its "Master Kong" – 康师傅 brand.[26] In 2011, Tingyi Holdings and PepsiCo entered into an agreement for a strategic alliance, bringing the companies to the top of the carbonated soft drinks ("CSD") market, and further strengthening their beverage position in China.[27,28]

Missed your chance on Coca-Cola back in the late 1990s? Ironically, this opportunity might still be available through Tingyi Holdings and its partnership with PepsiCo.

■ CASE STUDY *(CONTINUED)*

Type of Value   Current earning power and growth potential.

Screening – How We Ended Up with This Company   We found this company through what we called a "top-down" approach. A top-down analysis can be done by starting at the big picture of the economy. In this example, we started from looking at the growing consumerism in China, expecting consumer spending to grow in China. We then narrow our search to easy-to-understand consumer staples companies in China, given the more stable demand of its products. Here is a summary of how we narrow it down to Tingyi Holdings.

- China consumer story – Long-term growth of consumerism in China
- easier-to-understand consumer staples – stable demand business
- F&B sector – defensive
- strong cash flow and low leverage – showing strength of the company
- close to 52-week low share price – one good area to look for undervalued companies.

What's Interesting?   In Tingyi Holdings' case, we will be focusing on these four points of interest:

1. proxy for the China Consumer Story
2. 52-week low share price
3. barriers of entry – distribution
4. the partner of choice.

Proxy for the China Consumer Story   As one of the leaders in China's food and beverage industry, Tingyi Holdings is a proxy for the China consumer story. Given its huge size and market share, it might be considered as a mature business. Yet there might still be growth, albeit slower than fast-growing technology companies. The company's chairman, Wei Ing-Chou, mentioned when the company was founded that the Chinese on average ate five packages of noodles per year. In 2011, that number was 30. At the same time, the price of each package of noodle has increased. In the next 20 years, he predicts that it will double.[29] And for the potential of beverage operations in the Chinese market, we leave you with an extract of a 2012 press release, with PepsiCo Chairman and Chief Executive Officer Indra Nooyi highlighting that "China will soon surpass the United States to become the largest Beverage market in the world. As a result of this new alliance with Tingyi, PepsiCo is extremely well positioned for long-term growth in China".[30]

Instant noodles are not new technology untested in the market. Many mature economies have seen the rise of the popularity of instant noodles in the past. Therefore, urbanisation and modern retail channels should benefit Tingyi even more.

■ CASE STUDY *(CONTINUED)*

52-Week Low Share Price   The last time Tingyi Holdings saw a market capitalisation of about HKD40 billion (USD5 billion) was way back in 2006.[31] In 2015, its revenue was 290% higher; its shareholders' profit was 72% higher and its shareholders' equity was up by over 200%.[32] And 2015 was considered a bad year for the company.

Hong Kong-listed consumer staples like Want Want China Holdings Limited, Tingyi Holdings and Hengan International Group Co. Limited were three of the four most shorted stocks on the Hong Kong benchmark index back in July 2016.[33] The story behind this was that consumers are reportedly showing a preference for healthier food. In just six months from January to June 2016, Tingyi Holdings' market capitalisation fell by almost a third, to a price level not seen since 2006. To place things in context, its share price was down more than 70% from its peak in 2011.[34]

Possible reasons why the company's share price tanked:

- previously traded at a rich valuation
- transition phase with the first non-family Chief Executive Officer appointed in 2015[35]
- operational issues in its core operations.

However, these issues were not structurally damaging. Tingyi was still:

- cash-generative – the company was still very cash-generative. Furthermore, the company was operating with a negative cash conversion cycle. This means that they are getting paid by their customers before they had to pay their suppliers; a nice business model
- the market leader in China's instant noodles and RTD tea market (2016) – 52% of instant noodles (sales value) and 43% of RTD milk tea (sales value).[36]

Additionally:

- Tingyi Holdings has a long and proven track record.
- The integration with PepsiCo China was slowly settling – lower integration accounting charges (reduction in termination benefits).[37]
- Most importantly, already has the infrastructure and network in place – a huge asset for the company.

Barriers to Entry – Distribution   Competition Demystified by Bruce Greenwald is a great book on moats.[38] In the book, the rule of thumb in identifying whether barriers to entry exist in an industry involves looking for the existence of these two points:

1. stability of market share among a handful of competitors, with a dominant firm
2. profitability of the companies.

We already know that Tingyi Holdings is the market leader in China's instant noodles and RTD tea markets. Moreover, in the instant noodles and RTD tea market, the market share among the top three to four players is relatively stable.

■ CASE STUDY *(CONTINUED)*

The top four players in both the instant noodles and RTD tea market in China have consistently made up over 80% of the market share, a sign of high barriers to entry.[39] And as the biggest bigger player in both markets, Tingyi was the elephant in this room. Together with its closest competitor, Uni-President China Holdings Limited, these two companies had a duopoly-like hold when it came to instant noodles and RTD tea operations. To further strengthen its position, Tingyi, with its newly integrated PepsiCo operations, is now dominant in three of its key operations.

Other than its products (some might say a drink is a drink is a drink), the key advantage Tingyi Holdings had was its massive distribution capability. Back in 2011, Tingyi Holdings' Chairman Wei Ing-Chou even mentioned that the company thrived on distribution.[40] In the mass-market consumer product industry, owning the market looks to be more important because:

- Barriers to replicating consumer staple products are not that high.
- It is far more difficult to develop a strong nationwide distribution and production network.

As market leader, Tingyi Holdings could leverage on their scale and research and development efforts to launch products that are popular in the market, and use the company's distribution reach to their advantage. In addition, the PepsiCo alliance added a whole new dimension to things. More PepsiCo products could lead to more shelf space. And with Tingyi Holdings' extensive distribution network, distribution of more products should not be an issue. A virtuous cycle.

Economies of scale depend on the ability to spread out fixed costs and with the manufacturing process. Therefore, Tingyi has a tangible competitive edge in their much-heralded distribution network:

- Advertising and promotion: Dollar for dollar, if Tingyi spent the same percentage of revenue, they would outspend their competitors and have a wider audience to address.
- Distribution: Water is heavy to transport and expensive to deliver; the more customers in a given region, the more economical it is for the company per unit of goods.

Tingyi's strategic alliances also brought advantages in the field of research and development ("R&D"). With PepsiCo alliance, a global perspective was brought into the room. With PepsiCo's new Shanghai R&D centre, the largest outside North America catering to the entire Asian region, Tingyi can tap into PepsiCo's expertise to boost its product offering.[41]

The Partner of Choice   Sanyo Foods Co., Ltd., Asahi Breweries Limited and Itochu Corporation are three of the largest global food and beverage companies. What do they have in common? Before it was cool, these three Japanese firms

■ **CASE STUDY** *(CONTINUED)*

followed the same strategy to ride on the China consumer story – they all invested in Tingyi.[42] We know Berkshire Hathaway as the company people come knocking on the door of when they want to divest. In Tingyi Holdings' case, they looked to be the go-to company for the distribution of consumer goods in China. So why did PepsiCo decide to partner with Tingyi Holdings?

It might be due to Tingyi Holdings' 598 sales offices, 71 warehouses, 29,985 wholesalers and 115,435 direct retailers in China (2016).[43] This was also huge enough to attract other players like Disneyland and Starbucks to join the partnership. With PepsiCo, a huge beverage player themselves, this deal demonstrated the strength of Tingyi Holdings. Many multinational companies invested and failed to make meaningful profits in China. This was the case for PepsiCo as well. Instead of continuing to invest money into China, PepsiCo essentially decided, *if you can't beat them, join them.*

Disneyland's landmark arrangement to get beverages from Tingyi-PepsiCo was just the tip of the iceberg. In 2015, PepsiCo became the exclusive food and beverage sponsor of the NBA in North America – upending the long-standing arrangement the NBA had with Coca-Cola.[44] Basketball is a big thing in China and guess who became PepsiCo's beverage partner in China. In 2015, Tingyi Holdings became the NBA's partner in China through the Master Kong brand, a slam dunk for Tingyi Holdings.[45]

Shareholders (31 December 2015)[46]

- Ting Hsin (Cayman Islands) Holding Corp.: 33.40%
- Sanyo Foods Co., Ltd: 33.61%

Valuation   We will look at the valuations of Tingyi Holdings through three differ-ent yet simple methods, with not much in the way of projections used. The idea is: if simple calculations can do the job, why should we complicate things?

Our key assumptions are:

- People continue to eat instant noodles
- Decent recovery in profitability for the beverage arm

Normalised Earnings   We can use a normalised earnings method to value Tingyi Holdings. Some of the assumptions are:

- Instant noodles net profit = US$300 million
  - revenue of US$4 billion
  - instant noodles operating margin = 10% (five-year average: 10%)[47]
  - operating profit = US$400 million
  - financing cost = US$0 (three-year average = ~US$0 million)
  - tax rate = 25% (statutory rate in the PRC).[48]

■ **CASE STUDY** *(CONTINUED)*

- Beverage net profit = US$50 million
  - revenue of US$6 billion
  - beverage operating margin = 3% (five-year average: 4%)
  - operating profit = US$180 million
  - financing cost = US$50 million (three-year average = US$36 million)
  - tax rate = 25% (statutory rate in the PRC)
  - as Tingyi owned 47.51% of Tingyi-Asahi Beverage Holding Co., Ltd[49] (investment vehicle of the Group that holds the Group's beverage business in mid-2016),[50] Tingyi Holdings is only entitled to its proportional share of earnings from the beverage business.

- Other assumptions:
  - instant foods breakeven
  - no other income
  - no contribution from associates.

  We would then arrive at a shareholders' profit of about US$350 million.

  At market capitalisation of US$5 billion, Tingyi was valued at 14 times our estimated earnings in mid-2016.

Tingyi-Asahi Beverage Holding Co., Ltd ("TAB") Valuation   As part of the strategic alliance, PepsiCo has a call option to increase their indirect stake in TAB from 5% to 20%. We will look at this through the lens of PepsiCo. The exercise price is based on a US$15 billion valuation of TAB if this option was exercised in 2013. This valuation would increase 15% annually until 2015, translating to a valuation of US$20 billion for 100% of TAB.[51]

  From how we looked at it, this valuation seems to be on the rich side.[52] Given the reduced profitability in its beverage operations in recent years, we could take a wild stab and apply a 70% haircut to Tingyi Holdings' diluted stake of 40% in TAB. This added up to about USD2-3 billion.

  With just 10 times P/E the company's cash cow of its instant noodles arm, a value of US$3 billion was estimated. In total, Tingyi Holdings' instant noodles and beverage arm could possibly be estimated at US$5-6 billion. In June 2016, Tingyi had a market capitalisation of US$5 billion.

Share Repurchase   In 2015, Tingyi Holdings repurchased 1.2 million of their shares at an average price of HKD13.84, the first such exercise in at least the past five years. This was when the company had a market capitalisation of over HKD70 billion (US$9–10 billion). In June 2016, Tingyi had a market capitalisation of US$5 billion.

Conclusion   In our three estimations, we did not factor in much growth for the company. This was to demonstrate the versatility of the margin of safety approach.

  Additionally, the key point behind using three separate indicators was an internal check to find out if any of our estimates was too out of line.

■ **CASE STUDY   Growth in Cyclicality – First Resources Limited**

Established in 1992 and listed on the Singapore Exchange since 2007, First Resources Limited ("First Resources"), with planted area of 207,575 hectares,[53] was among the leaders in the palm oil industry. But wait, what exactly is palm oil?

Palm-based products are literally everywhere. A walk around your nearby supermarket would surprise you how much palm oil is used. From Singapore's Gardenia bread and Japan's Nissin instant noodles to Mars Incorporated's M&Ms, Mondelez International's Oreo cookies and even Unilever N.V.'s Skippy peanut butter, all have some form of palm oil in their products. In 2012, four vegetable oils – palm, rapeseed, sunflower and soybean – made up 76% of the world's vegetable oil production, with palm oil being the most efficient vegetable oil. One hectare of oil palm plantation can produce up to ten times more oil than other leading oilseed crops![54]

Oil palm cultivation is not rocket science, and due to its requirement for manual labour, oil palm cultivation has not changed drastically over the past few decades. However, better agronomy practices have improved productivity over the past decade. Palm oil cultivation is a front-end-loaded investment with significant capital required at the start. On average, a well-managed commercial estate could break even in about 7–8 years.

Oil palm tree is a perennial crop with an economic lifespan of 25 years.[55] It starts yielding fruit about three years after planting.

The four main stages of an oil palm tree are:[56]

- immature: 0–3 years
- young: 4–7 years
- prime: 8–17 years
- tall: ≥ 18 years.

In 1991, world production of palm oil was 11.5 million metric tonnes ("tonnes").[57] In 2012, palm oil production more than quadrupled to 55.3 million tonnes, with Indonesia and Malaysia contributing towards 86% of the global production.[58] *Fun-fact: The sweet spot for planting oil palms is ten degrees latitude to the north and south of the equator. Latitude-wise, it's from the tip of East Malaysia to the bottom of Java, Indonesia.[59] Thus, it is no surprise that these two countries have consistently been the leaders of the palm oil industry.*

In 2011, it was estimated that approximately 77% of crude palm oil ("CPO") and about 28% of crude palm kernel oil derivatives worldwide were used for edible products.[60] With over seven billion people today (2016),[61] palm oil plays a huge role in mitigating global food concerns.

Type of Value   Cyclical play with growth potential.

■ CASE STUDY *(CONTINUED)*

Screening – How We Ended Up with This Company

- Food demand globally: The growing global population.
- Depressed underlying commodity price: CPO prices on a decline since 2012.[62]
- CPO upstream players: Companies with largest exposure to CPO movements.
- Bursa Malaysia and Singapore Exchange listed companies: Most of the largest palm oil companies are listed on these two bourses.

With so many Asian-listed CPO-related companies, how and why did we end up with just one? For this case study, we thought it would be useful to run through our thought process. To start with, we limited our scope to players with plantings above 100,000 hectares. Why so?

To spread out fixed costs, commodity businesses need economies of scale. Based on our estimation, a company with mature planted area of 100,000 hectares could potentially deliver about US$200–300 million (assuming CPO yield of 4 tonnes/hectare at US$650/tonne) in revenue, a rather substantial amount. In 2015, Malaysia-listed Sime Darby Berhad and Singapore-listed Golden Agri-Resources Limited led the pack, with planted area of 605,046 hectares[63] and 485,606 hectares[64] respectively.

Next, we narrowed our focus onto companies with the bulk of their operations involving producing CPO, especially those with significant contributions from upstream operations – namely, players with significant contributions from other agriculture operations like Singapore-listed Wilmar International Limited and Golden Agri-Resources Limited, and companies with significant downstream contributions like Malaysia-listed IOI Corporation Berhad. And lastly, conglomerates like Malaysia-listed Sime Darby Berhad and Kuala Lumpur Kepong Berhad were also left out.

After screening, we ended up with just a few companies, like Bumitama Agri Limited and First Resources, companies with good operational track records. We dare say these few companies are more manageable compared to our initial list of 10–15 companies.

What's Interesting?   In First Resources' case, these four points stood out for us:

1. Operational and financial efficiency
2. Management and structure
3. Commodity prices
4. Scalable growth runway

Operational and Financial Efficiency   Other than having economies of scale, commodity operators must be efficient. Simply put, companies with high yield and a low-cost base are qualities of a well-managed upstream operation.

■ CASE STUDY *(CONTINUED)*

For productivity, let us start from talking about the fresh fruit bunches ("FFB") yield. FFB is the term used for the harvested fruits of an oil palm plantation. FFB yield refers to the fruits produced on a per hectare basis, measured in tonnes per hectare. For landlords, a measure of productivity is the occupancy rate, the higher the better. This concept also applies to FFB yield. In our opinion, a five-year record is a decent timespan to get an idea of how good a company is at planning, planting and harvesting its plantation. Given that these plants are in their ecological sweet spot, their yields shouldn't stray too far from the average.

Additionally, we must also consider the age profile of the estates. For instance, an estate with trees in their prime yielding 20 tonnes/hectare per year is decent. On the other hand, an estate in its prime only delivering 15 tonnes/hectare may not be ideal. The thing about palm oil cultivation is that its yields are rather consistent and, notwithstanding bad weather conditions, good practices tend to lead to sustainable results. But on the other hand, a mistake like poor planting could lead to years of regret; once the tree is in the ground, you have to wait for another 25 years.

From First Resources' FFB yields in Table 9.4, it looked to be a company with "good practices and sustainable results". From our analysis, much of its drop in production post-2012 was attributable to unfavourable weather conditions, new mature areas and acquisitions of external poorly managed plantations.

The second thing we look at when analysing a palm oil producer is its cost structure. In this business, it definitely pays to be a low-cost producer. Generally, the larger the planted area and the higher the productivity, the better you are able to spread out your fixed costs. At its core, productivity in the palm oil plantation industry is measured in terms of its FFB and CPO yield. For instance, 10,000 hectares with FFB yield of 20 tonnes/hectare could yield about 200,000 tonnes of FFB in a year. If the same 10,000 hectares yielded only 10 tonnes/hectare, you might only end up with 100,000 tonnes of FFB. Yet, from a fixed-cost point of view, these 100,000 tonnes of FFB cost you much more, given that your cost of operating the estate is about the same in both cases. We focus on FFB because if a company takes good care of their upstream, the rest should fall into place.

In 2015, First Resources reported a unit cash cost of CPO nucleus production of US$204/tonne on an ex-mill basis.[65] At the lowest point in the past five years (2012–2017), monthly CPO prices were in the range of US$450–500/tonne.[66]

Table 9.4: First Resources Limited's FFB Yield

FY End	2011	2012	2013	2014	2015
FFB Yield (tonnes/ha)	22.2	23.0	18.7	18.7	19.0

■ CASE STUDY *(CONTINUED)*

Even if we took the entire operating expense, we estimate operating cost to be below US$450/tonne. *Note: Always remember production cost per tonne is based on the tonnage.*

Management and Structure   When we analyse the management, we like to see "management walking the talk", meaning that they consistently deliver on their targets. For upstream palm oil operators, one way to look at this is from their plantings schedule. We can view it from the perspective of their planted area targets and age profile.

In their 2012 Annual Report, First Resources aimed to expand through new plantings of 15,000 to 20,000 hectares per year, with a target of 200,000 hectares of oil palm within the next five years[67] (around 2017–2018).

At the rate First Resources is going (Table 9.5), they look to be able to achieve 200,000 hectares of planted area from just their nucleus plantings. From their track record, First Resource's planting game looked strong. In 2016, First Resources reported a weighted average age of nine years, and a balanced age profile in all four stages (Immature: 29%, Young: 27%, Prime: 23% and Old: 21%)[68] showed good planning by the management.

Next, we also need to pay attention to the company's structure, the more straightforward the better. We compared the company structure of First Resources to two other Singapore-listed oil palm companies. Looking at their non-controlling interest to total equity in 2015, Bumitama Agri Limited, First Resources and Indofood Agri Resources Limited reported 8.6%,[69] 4.8%[70] and 40.7%[71] respectively. In Indofood Agri Resources Limited's case, this meant that 40.7% of the Group's assets do not belong to its equityholders.

Among the three, First Resources looked to have the most straightforward structure. In Indofood Agri Resources Limited's case, they had a significant portion of non-controlling interest as they were required to consolidate non-wholly-owned entities like their 72.6% stake in their publicly listed subsidiary Indonesia-listed PT Salim Ivomas Pratama Tbk. As the financial statements of a company with high non-controlling interest might be challenging for investors to understand, we prefer companies with a straightforward structure, because, as minority shareholders, it is always good to keep things simple.

Table 9.5: First Resources Limited's Planted Area

FY End	2011	2012	2013	2014	2015
Total	132,251	146,403	170,596	194,567	207,575
Nucleus – Total	113,143	125,805	148,727	165,936	178,338
Nucleus – Mature	74,704	85,888	104,493	114,377	128,042
Nucleus – Immature	38,439	39,917	44,234	51,559	50,296

■ CASE STUDY *(CONTINUED)*

Commodity Prices   For a commodity producer, there are two main ways of increasing its revenue:

- controllable factor – increase in production
- uncontrollable factor – increase in the underlying commodity prices.

As we explained in the previous section, First Resources was actively expanding its production. Therefore, we will devote this section to the uncontrollable side of commodity linked companies. No matter how one spins this tale, companies involved in the commodities business are always exposed to the price effects of the underlying commodity.

Here was how the average monthly CPO price looked from 1996 to 2016:[72]

- 1996–2000 = USD439/tonne
- 2001–2005 = USD362/tonne
- 2006–2010 = USD701/tonne
- 2011–2015 = USD817/tonne.

Considering just the period from 2010 to 2016 alone, monthly CPO prices fluctuated between US$483 and 1,249/tonne.[73] Although no investors can accurately predict CPO prices consistently, we still do need to understand the supply and demand relationship for CPO prices. But why?

Think of the underlying commodity price as a multiplier for a commodity producer. Just for illustration, assume you need $1 to produce 1 tonne of CPO. Taking all things as constant, if 1 tonne of CPO can fetch $2, your profit would be $1, giving you a profit margin of 50%. On the other hand, if the price of CPO is $3 per tonne, you would arrive at a profit of $2 or a profit margin of 66%!

Although we are unable to accurately catch the bottom, there are price levels we felt comfortable with. Back during late 2014 to early 2015, CPO prices caught our attention when prices fluctuated around US$500/tonne. However, our consideration was based on other more reasonable factors that pointed towards prices bottoming:

- New plantings in the industry appeared to be slowing down
- Higher-cost players were under pressure at these price levels
- Recent consolidation among key industry players:
  - Sime Darby Berhad's acquisition of New Britain Palm Oil Limited[74]
  - Felda Global Ventures Berhad acquisition of Asian Plantations Limited[75]
  - Privatisation of Tradewinds Plantation Berhad[76]
  - IOI Corporation Berhad's acquisition of Unico-Desa Plantations Berhad.[77]

At the end of the day, we should not just depend on commodity prices to make our decision. The company we invest in still has to have value financially. However, the best time to start investing in a cyclical industry like commodity is during a time of weakness. In Howards Marks' *The Most Important Thing*

■ CASE STUDY *(CONTINUED)*

Illuminated, he highlighted *The Poor Man's Guide to Market Assessment.*[78] In this short test, Howard Marks established a simple exercise that might help us to take the market sentiment of the current markets. And if you find that most of your ticks are in the left-hand column, you might want to be more conservative. Table 9.6 shows a short excerpt of the exercise.

At the end of the day, it does not mean that if we can figure out where we stand in a cycle, we will know exactly what will happen next. But it does help not to get caught up in the midst of any irrational exuberance or a market bubble when it is taking place.

Scalable Growth Runway   After discussing about the uncontrollable, let's end this section with the controllable factors. In the palm oil business, there are generally two ways to increase production:

- increasing planted area
- increasing yields from oil palms approaching prime age.

And we like players which excel in both areas.

First, planters can grow by increasing their planted area. No land means no crops, which translates to no money. As good (location and price) plantation land appears to be getting scarce in the market, we are looking for companies with sizeable unplanted land. What do we mean by the ability to increase their planted area? Here are two scenarios:

- Plantation A: planted area of 100 hectares, with 200 hectares unplanted
- Plantation B: planted area of 200 hectares, with 100 hectares unplanted.

Even with identical land of 300 hectares, Plantation A could potentially increase its earnings by 200% compared to Plantation B's 50%.

In 2015, First Resources produced 687,248 tonnes of CPO. With the company's total nucleus planted area of 178,338 hectares (inclusive of 50,296 hectares of immature nucleus planted area),[79] First Resources looked to have both

Table 9.6: Howard Marks' The Most Important Thing Illuminated's Checklist

Market Sentiment	Bullish	Bearish
Economy	Vibrant	Sluggish
Outlook	Positive	Negative
Lenders	Eager	Reticent
Capital Markets	Loose	Tight
Capital	Plentiful	Scarce
Terms	Easy	Restrictive
Interest Rates	Low	High

■ CASE STUDY *(CONTINUED)*

the resources and the expertise to achieve a CPO production of 1 million tonnes between 2017 and 2018.

Next, our focus is on the plantation's average age profile. This follows the concept of being vested before the upcycle of production after its tree matures. As the prime age for an oil palm is from 7 to 18, we prefer estates closer to the age of 10 rather than 20, to allow us to enjoy the upswing in production. With over 56% of plantings in the young and immature stage,[80] First Resources has one of the youngest age profiles in the region, positioning it well for strong production growth over the next few years as its trees mature.

Major Shareholders (14 March 2016)[81]   Eight Capital Inc.: 63.18%

Valuation   From 2010 to 2016, monthly average CPO prices fluctuated between US$483 and 1,249/tonne. If anything, this demonstrated the difficulty in forecasting CPO prices. As we said, predicting CPO prices is not part of our repertoire, and we will not try to do that. However, when it comes to such companies, commodity prices cannot be completely avoided. For this example, we will assume CPO to be in the range of US$600–700/tonne.

Our key assumptions are:

* CPO continues to be in demand
* Planted area doesn't vanish overnight

Now let us go back in time to 2013, with 148,727 hectares of nucleus plantings (30% immature) and an average age profile of eight years.[82] This meant that First Resources could:

* increase planted area significantly
* expect increase in yields when plantings mature.

These two factors have provided us with a margin of safety in our calculation. To put it simply, increase in planted area and yields lead to higher production. This could mitigate potential drops in CPO prices. Furthermore, growth can also provide us with a margin of safety. Fast forward to 2016, and First Resources seems to be very much on track with its target of 200,000 hectares of oil palm, corresponding to 1 million tonnes of CPO.

Let us assume the following:

* CPO price of US$600–700/tonne
* CPO production cost (with overheads) of US$300–400/tonne.

This might result in an operating profit in a believable range of US$300–400/tonne. With 1 million tonne CPO, this adds up to USD300–400 million. After deducting interest expense of USD20 million (FY2015 interest expense USD22 million) and a tax rate of 25% (corporate tax rate for companies in Singapore and Indonesia is 17% and 25% respectively),[83] it might be possible to

■ CASE STUDY *(CONTINUED)*

expect net profit to be in the range of US$200–300 million. Now if we assume a price-to-earnings ratio of 12 times, this means that the company could be valued somewhere between US$2.4–3.6 billion. And back in June 2015 and June 2016,[84] the market was pricing the company near the low end of our estimation.

Keep in mind that we were not even considering possible profits from its downstream operations and other operations. You could also think of this as an extension of the margin of safety principle. Moreover, we are not even considering the upside to CPO prices.

Conclusion   At the end of the day, companies in the commodities business are still exposed to the effects of the underlying commodity, and other factors beyond one's control. And this might be a key reason behind why many are not keen on investments in commodity related companies. Due to that, we must remember the concept of having a margin of safety.

■ CASE STUDY   Special Situation – Dalian Wanda Commercial Properties Co., Limited

Dalian Wanda Commercial Properties Company Limited ("Dalian Wanda Commercial Properties Company") is part of the Dalian Wanda group of companies, one of the largest conglomerates in China. Dalian Wanda Commercial Properties Company is the property arm of the group and it operates more than 142 shopping complexes named "Wanda Plaza" and also more than 79 luxury hotels around China in 2016.[85]

Type of Value   Substantial gap between its market price and the buyout offer after the offer was announced.

Screening – How We Ended Up with This Company   By reading the news. We kid you not.

We came across Hong Kong-listed Dalian Wanda Commercial Properties Company simply by reading the news or, more accurately, when the news of its privatisation offer surfaced in public domain. In June 2016, this buyout saga was all over the newspapers.

What's Interesting?   This is a case study on a special situation type of investment that only lasted for two months. Normally, such a short investment duration hints at a speculative venture. However, if Mr Market feels very generous, even a one-day holding period matters not. As long as the reasoning and analysis makes sense, we can tip our hats to Mr Market and gladly take it. In fact, a shorter time horizon for this type of investment works to our benefit.

■ CASE STUDY *(CONTINUED)*

Investments based on special situations typically involve some form of major corporate actions taking place in a company. Examples of corporate actions may include, but are not limited to: mergers and acquisitions, privatisation, rights issue, private placement, spin-off, carve-outs or the pay-out of a special dividend. Other than corporate actions, possible scenarios could include positive events like the company being one of the front runners in the bid for a major project or negative events like lawsuits against the company.

In essence, any major event happening to a company that can significantly alter its value can be considered a special situation. If you discover that the market might be mispricing the company with respect to the probability of the event happening, you might be able to benefit from such opportunities.

This opportunity came about when Dalian Wanda Commercial Properties Company announced that the company received a buyout offer from its major shareholder, Dalian Wanda Group.

The cash offer, which came on 30 May 2016, was set at HK$52.80 per share, valuing the property company at a premium of approximately 10.9% over the audited net asset value per share in the company.[86] This offer came less than two years after Dalian Wanda Commercial Properties Company debuted on the Hong Kong Stock Exchange at HK$48 per share.[87] The share price traded about the range of HK$38.00 per share for the past few months before the offer was made public. After the offer was announced, the share price of the company shot up to around HK$47.00 per share and held at that price point.[88]

HK$47.00 per share was still about 11% lower than the offer price of HK$52.80 per share.

The huge gap between its share price and its offer price was attributed towards certain reports that some major shareholders, in particular, Blackrock Inc., would not approve the deal as Blackrock's entry point into the company was at a much higher price.[89]

However, the conclusion from our analysis was that these reports did not fully grasp the essence of the matter. Blackrock Inc. is not the beneficial owner, but the company is merely acting as a brokerage nominee for its clients. Certain media viewed Blackrock Inc. as one of the large single shareholders of the company when in fact, Blackrock merely acted as a custodian for many small investors with beneficial interest in Dalian Wanda Commercial Properties Company. Therefore we gathered that Blackrock Inc. would not have the voting power to prevent the deal from going through.

Moreover, looking at the shareholder structure of Dalian Wanda Commercial Properties Company, apart from Dalian Wanda Group's stake in the company, the remaining ownership was concentrated among ten shareholders. The H shares only account for about 14% of the outstanding stock.[90] Of the listed

■ CASE STUDY *(CONTINUED)*

shares, about half are owned by 11 minority shareholders, who mostly entered at IPO prices.[91]

Here lies the puzzle. If we were to place ourselves in Dalian Wanda Group's shoes, it seems highly unlikely that we would announce our offer without first consulting the views of the remaining major shareholders. With such a small number of major shareholders, we believed preliminary discussions would have already been ongoing before Dalian Wanda Group came out with the final offer. In any case, even after it was reported that China Life Insurance Company Limited – one of the largest shareholders of Dalian Wanda Commercial Properties Company's H shares – provided a letter of intent favouring the privatisation plan on 25 July 2016,[92] market prices were still below HK$48 the very next day.[93]

Thus, although the market appeared to be convinced that the privatisation would have some issues, we viewed the situation from another perspective. Due to the reporting on the shareholder status of Blackrock Inc. and the small number of major shareholders, we felt that the probability of the buyout was quite high. For us, the kicker was the major shareholders in Dalian Wanda Commercial Properties Company. If we took a closer look at the company's "Interest and Short Positions of substantial shareholders in shares and underlying shares", it was stated that Citigroup Inc. and BlackRock, Inc. were in fact not listed as beneficial owners.[94]

Major Shareholder

Domestic Shares (30 May 2016)[95]

- Dalian Wanda Group Co., Ltd: 43.71%
- Wang Jianlin: 7.37%.

H Shares (31 December 2015)[96]

- China Life Insurance Company Limited: 7.42%
- Kuwait Investment Authority: 7.42%
- Citigroup Inc.: 6.58%
- BlackRock, Inc.: 5.99%

Valuation   With the information at hand, we could then work out our risk and reward on this investment. As mentioned before, if we invested and the deal went through, we stood a chance of gaining about 11%. If the buyout was unsuccessful, the share price of the company might fall. Since the overall market

■ CASE STUDY *(CONTINUED)*

was already recovering during that period, we assumed that the share price of the company might also fall around 10–15% if the deal did not go through.

Our key assumptions are:

- No other regulatory concerns
- Odds of deal going though > Odds of deal not going through

So, the risk and reward for this investment were evenly split. Our confidence that the chance of the buyout was way more than 50% gave us the incentive to make an investment in the company. This is because there looked to be a much higher chance of us gaining 12% than losing around 10% to 15%.

Conclusion   By August 2016, Dalian Wanda Commercial Properties Company's H-share shareholders eventually voted for the company to be bought out and we walked away with a healthy profit.

If you have been following our analysis, we have to make quite a few assumptions for these types of special situation plays.

Here are the assumptions we made:

1. It is highly unlikely that the Dalian Wanda Group would make such an offer without preliminary discussions with major shareholders.
2. In the event of an unsuccessful offer, the share price will only fall by 10% to 15%.
3. The probability of a buyout is more than 50%.

Although it panned out for us this time round, we are clearly aware that nothing is a sure thing. At the end of the day, assumptions are still assumptions. There is always the possibility that things will not pan out as we expected. Thus, we need to be conscious of our portfolio sizing for special situations.

Another key aspect of such an investment is that we must be disciplined in the time frame of the investment. We invest because we expect a certain event to occur. If Dalian Wanda Commercial Properties Company was not taken private by the offer and the share price fell, we should exit the investment regardless of the losses. If we held on to the investment in the hope of recovering some money in the future, it would be against our investment process and that would have drastic negative implications on our investments in the long run.

If we keep holding on to the investments that did not pan out, hoping to recover some losses, then eventually our whole portfolio will be filled with investments that we are unhappy about, rather than investments that we are optimistic about.

■ CASE STUDY   High Growth (The Land of Fast-Growing Unicorns) – Tencent Holdings Limited

Tencent Holdings Limited ("Tencent Holdings") is one of the largest internet companies in China.[97] Together with Baidu Inc and Alibaba Group, these three companies are commonly known as BAT in China.[98]

Tencent Holdings is the owner of famous applications with a massive user base in China, such as QQ and WeChat. QQ is the main gaming social media network in China and WeChat is the main internet messaging application in the country, like Whatsapp or Facebook Messenger. In 2015, the company reported close to 850 million active accounts in QQ and 700 million active accounts in WeChat.[99]

Tencent Holdings has four main streams of revenue:

- online games
- social networks
- online advertising
- ecommerce transactions.

Tencent Holdings is still managed by its founder, and also its current Chief Executive Officer, Mr Ma Huateng. Mr Ma is also one of the largest shareholders of the company, with a 9.1% stake[100] in the HK$1.9 trillion company (October 2016).[101]

Type of Value   Huge growth potential.

Screening – How We Ended Up with This Company

- Technology – the next revolution
- Multi-bagger potential
- Profitable technology company in China
- Not overleveraged.

We narrowed our screen to filter for fast-growing companies based in China by restricting our search universe to the two Chinese exchanges and the Hong Kong exchange.

Some criteria on our list are companies which have seen strong growth over the past decade in:

- revenue
- operating profit and operating margin
- earnings per share
- free cash flow.

It is very important to look at all four factors. First, the revenue line tells us that the company is growing its business. Next, the operating profit and operating margin indicates whether the company can grow its business without

■ CASE STUDY *(CONTINUED)*

hurting its margins. With both factors assured, the earnings per share reveals whether the company is growing without diluting shareholders. And finally, the growth in free cash flow allows us to determine whether the company is capable of increasing their free cash inflow.

After going through these four factors, we are left with the final hurdle – leverage. Our last check is on the debt level of the company. This is done to ensure that the company is not growing by using excessive leverage. Once that is out of the way, we should be left with a list of companies that are worth our time to do a deeper analysis on.

What's Interesting? For Tencent Holdings, we will be focusing on these three factors:

1. High growth potential
2. Already free cash flow-generative
3. High future optionality

High Growth Potential We have all heard stories of investors invested in companies which gave them ultra-high returns. Investors who have been invested in well-known companies such as Apple Inc, Microsoft Corporation, 3M Company and Procter & Gamble Company since the early days would have seen their returns in multiple folds of their capital.

Interestingly, we are also able to find such companies in Asia too. The share price of Shanghai-listed Kweichow Moutai Company Limited has also increased more than 5,600% August 2001 to February 2017.[102]

All these companies have one thing in common. They have demonstrated strong growth for years, even decades! So, if we want to find such companies to invest in, we have to focus on one key concept – growth potential, the potential for fast growth.

Already Free Cash Flow Generative What makes Tencent Holdings stand out from other companies with huge growth potential is that the company is already very much profitable, even at this point of their growth.

From our preliminary screening, Hong Kong-listed Tencent Holdings – one of the largest internet companies in China – stood out because the company demonstrated very strong growth and is even growing its free cash flow at a significant rate. On top of that, it hardly has any debt on its balance sheet. The company also has a long history as a listed company, with its growth prospects looking better by the day.

Tencent Holdings earns its revenue through two major avenues, Value-added Services ("VAS") and online advertising. Its services such as QQ or

■ CASE STUDY *(CONTINUED)*

WeChat have some free features for users, but they also have many value-added services that users can buy to enhance the whole social network experience.

VAS contributed towards 78% and 85% of the company's revenue and gross profit respectively in 2015. Tencent Holdings also generates income from allowing users or companies to place an advertisement on their platform. In the same year, online advertising contributed 17% and 14% of revenue and gross profit respectively.[103]

Tencent Holdings also saw amazing growth in the past decade. Its revenue and net profit have increased from just RMB3 billion and RMB1 billion in 2006[104] to RMB103 billion and RMB29 billion in 2015.[105] That represents a compounded growth of 43.4% and 40.1% in revenue and net profit over the past decade respectively. No matter how you interpret it, we have to say that we are impressed.

Since its initial public offering in 2004, the company has returned more than 25,700% return to shareholders based on the increase of its share price up to March 2017.[106] Moreover, the business had also substantially grown its free cash flow over the past decade.

Huge Future Optionality Even though the company has seen such tremendous growth, its prospects are still very bright. With such a large gaming community within its social media network, Tencent Holdings is the partner of choice of many international gaming companies with plans of entering the Chinese market. The company's plan is simple, yet very effective:

- Attract users to partner platforms.
- Increase products and services.
- This in turn attracts more users to partner platforms – a virtuous cycle.

One such partner is none other than Electronic Arts Inc. – one of the largest gaming producers in the world. Electronic Arts Inc. have a partnership with Tencent Holdings to distribute their games in China, which have been translated and tailored for Chinese consumers.[107,108] Other than games, Tencent has also made headway into the live and on-demand video arena, with the National Basketball Association ("NBA") extending their partnership with Tencent Holdings as NBA's exclusive official digital partner in China for five years.[109]

In addition, Tencent Holdings is already adding other services and content onto its two social networks. A range of services the company provides include:[110]

- community portal
- emails
- RTX – enterprise messenger
- security software mobile
- Tencent mobile application store

■ **CASE STUDY** *(CONTINUED)*

- mobile browser
- media player
- online payment
- music portal
- video streaming
- sports streaming
- mobile video
- digital publishing
- WeChat digital stores.

Other than these services that it is developing to add to its existing ecosystems, Tencent Holdings is also one of the biggest venture capital investors in China.[111] Most notably, Tencent Holdings is an investor in Didi Chuxing,[112] the main ride-hailing company in China, and JD.com,[113] the second-largest e-commerce retailer in China. In 2016, Tencent made one of its largest investments with an acquisition of up to 84% of Supercell Oy. This transaction valued Supercell OY at USD10.2 billion.[114]

In short, we concluded that Tencent Holdings is far from running out of growth opportunities. In fact, the contrary is true; the company's avenues of growth are seemingly endless!

In summary, if you are looking to invest in the likes of Facebook, Inc., Netflix, Inc., Paypal Holdings Inc, Electronic Arts Inc., Activision Blizzard, Inc. or Alphabet Inc (Google) etc., why not just try Tencent Holdings?

Key Risks The huge selection of growth areas in the company can by itself become a risk. The company needs to be selective on where it focuses its resources in fueling its future growth. If the company starts to overstretch its resources, it might damage the business instead.

Other than diworsification (a phrase coined by Peter Lynch),[115] another key risk of the company stood out. Given that the company operates in a sensitive industry in China and that it is one of the largest companies in the industry, there is a risk of more regulations in the future if the government attempts to limit Tencent Holdings' influence in China.

There are precedents in the United States of America concerning regulatory intervention. In the past, Microsoft Corporation was almost broken up by regulators in the United States after being accused of monopolistic practices.

Given that Tencent Holdings operates mainly in China, has a huge influence on the Chinese population and China has very strict censorship requirements, increased regulations are certainly a risk for the company.

Major Shareholders (31 December 2015)[116]

- Naspers Limited: 33.51%
- Ma Huateng: 9.1%

■ **CASE STUDY** *(CONTINUED)*

Valuation – The Elephant in The Room   Yet, there is an elephant in the room when we are analysing the company. In late 2016, Tencent Holdings traded at around 50 times earnings, and only offered a dividend yield of 0.2%.[117] No matter how you look at it, the valuation of the company seemed rather steep – not your traditional kind of a value stock.

Our key assumptions are:

• Continued acceptance of new technology
• Continued ability to grow and monetise ecosystem

This characteristic tends to occur in many fast-growth companies. Interestingly, it might not even be that big an issue. That is because with its fast growth, there is a possibility that Tencent Holdings can grow into its valuation, and then some. Being a value investor does not just mean that you only look at companies that trade at a P/E ratio of less than 10 times. Growth is also a form of margin of safety. Even Benjamin Graham appeared to think so. In Benjamin Graham and David Dodd's *The Intelligent Investor*,[118] they wrote: "Thus the growth-stock approach may supply as dependable a margin of safety as is found in the ordinary investment provided the calculation of the future is conservatively made, and provided it shows a satisfactory margin in relation to the price paid."

In Tencent Holdings' case, a P/E ratio of 50 times was not its peak P/E ratio. The company saw its P/E ratio peak during 2007, even before the great financial crisis. During that period, its P/E reached more than 100 times! And even if an investor invested right at the peak, the total return from the investment between 2007 and late 2016 would still be around 1,600%.[119] This is an example of where growth functions as a form of margin of safety.

That was fuelled by the fact that its revenue and net income have increased from just RMB4 billion and RMB2 billion in 2007 to RMB103 billion and RMB29 billion in 2015 respectively. With its 2015 earnings per share, its price-to-earnings for the investor based on its 2007 cost was only about 6 times. Tencent Holdings is one example of how fast-growth companies can grow into their steep valuation.

Conclusion   Fast-growing companies typically trade at higher-than-market-average valuation that depends on the company delivering on its expectations. Although it might seem obvious, we want to emphasise that because the future is never certain, future earnings are also never certain, even more so when it comes to companies with high growth expectations placed upon them.

If the growth did not pan out as expected, such companies might experience drastic falls in valuation. That is why it is important to have a diversified portfolio, as we as investors can never know which of the fast-growing companies we invested in will become the next big thing.

Notes

1. Hongkong Land Holdings Limited. Google Finance. https://www .google.com/finance?q=SGX%3AH78&ei=2Mi2WJiJJI-6ugSAxq_ oBw. Accessed: 3 March 2017.
2. Hongkong Land Holdings Limited. 2016 Half-Yearly Results. "Presentation". 29 July 2016.
3. Hongkong Land Holdings Limited. About Us. "Corporate Overview". http://www.hkland.com/en/about/corporate-overview.html. Accessed: 4 March 2017.
4. Hongkong Land Holdings Limited. "Presentation".
5. Ibid.
6. Ibid.
7. *Financial Times.* Equities. "Equity Screener". https://markets .ft.com/data/equities/results. Accessed: 4 March 2017.
8. Mukul Munish. *South China Morning Post.* "Dangers of a bubble in Hong Kong's property market, authors of UBS Global Real Estate Bubble Index Report warn". http://www.scmp.com/specialreports/ property/topics/weekend-property/article/2026000/dangers-bubble-hong-kongs-property. Published: 7 October 2016.
9. Hongkong Land Holdings Limited. Google Finance.
10. The Tracker Fund of Hong Kong. "Fund Details and Performance". http://www.trahk.com.hk/eng/fundinvperf.asp. 2 March 2017.
11. SPDR Straits Times Index ETF. "Fund Overview". http://www.spdrs .com.sg/etf/fund/spdr-straits-times-index-etf-ES3.html. 3 March 2017.
12. Rating and Valuation Department, The Government of Hong Kong Special Administrative Region, http://www.rvd.gov.hk/doc/en/ statistics/his_data_7.xls, February 2017.
13. Centa-City Index. Centadata. http://www1.centadata.com/cci/ cci_e.htm. Accessed: 7 April 2017.
14. Frederik Balfour. Bloomberg. "Hong Kong Housing Prices to Fall a Further 10%, Nomura Says". https://www.bloomberg.com/news/ articles/2016-08-30/hong-kong-housing-prices-to-fall-a-further-10-nomura-says. 30 August 2016.
15. Hongkong Land Holdings Limited. 2016 Half-Yearly Results. "Presentation".
16. Hongkong Land Holdings Limited. News Release. "Half-Yearly Results for the six months ended 30th June 2016". 28 July 2016.
17. Hongkong Land Limited. "Annual Reports 2006–2016".
18. Hongkong Land Holdings Limited. "Half-Yearly Results for the six months ended 30th June 2016".

19. Hongkong Land Holdings Limited. "Annual Report 2006–2016".
20. Hongkong Land Holdings Limited. "Annual Report 2006".
21. Hongkong Land Holdings Limited. "Annual Report 2015".
22. Hongkong Land Holdings Limited. "Annual Report 2006–2016".
23. Hongkong Land Holdings Limited. Google Finance.
24. Adam Jourdan. Reuters. "PepsiCo re-enters 'Magic Kingdom' with Shanghai Disneyland deal". http://www.reuters.com/article/us-pepsico-idUSBREA1Q13020140227. 27 February 2014.
25. Tingyi (Cayman Islands) Holding Corp. "Presentation on 2015 Annual Results". 22 March 2016.
26. Tingyi (Cayman Islands) Holding Corp. "2015 Annual Report".
27. Jourdan. "PepsiCo re-enters 'Magic Kingdom' with Shanghai Disneyland deal".
28. Tingyi (Cayman Islands) Holding Corp. "Strategic Alliance with PepsiCo Inc. Discloseable Acquisition, Discloseable Disposal and Connected Transaction, Possible Major Disposal, Possible Major Acquisition, Possible Major Disposal, and Connected Transaction, Possible Non-Exempt Continuing Connected Transactions, and Resumption of Trading". 4 November 2011.
29. Russell Flannery. Forbes. "Noodles and Teas". https://www.forbes.com/global/2011/0606/taiwan-billionaires-11-wei-ing-chou-tingyi-noodles-teas.html. 25 May 2011.
30. PepsiCo, Inc. Press Release. "Tingyi Holdings and PepsiCo Finalize Strategic Alliance in China". http://www.pepsico.com/live/pressrelease/Tingyi-Holding-and-PepsiCo-Finalize-Strategic-Alliance-in-China03312012. 31 March 2012.
31. Tingyi (Cayman Islands) Holding Corp. Google Finance. https://www.google.com/finance?cid=673324. Accessed: 6 March 2017.
32. Tingyi (Cayman Islands) Holding Corp. "2010 & 2015 Annual Reports".
33. Kana Nishizawa. Bloomberg. "Hong Kong Bears Pile Record Short Bets on China Consumer Stocks". https://www.bloomberg.com/news/articles/2016-07-21/hong-kong-bears-pile-record-short-bets-on-china-consumer-stocks. 22 July 2016.
34. Tingyi (Cayman Islands) Holding Corp. Google Finance.
35. Tingyi (Cayman Islands) Holding Corp. "2014 Annual Report".
36. Tingyi (Cayman Islands) Holding Corp. "Presentation on 2016 First Quarterly Results". 26 May 2016.
37. Tingyi (Cayman Islands) Holding Corp. "2014 & 2015 Annual Report".
38. Bruce Greenwald and Judd Kahn. *Competition Demystified*. Published by the Penguin Group (USA) Inc. Paperback edition published 2007.

39. Tingyi (Cayman Islands) Holding Corp. "Presentation on 2016 First Quarterly Results".

40. Flannery. "Noodles and Teas".

41. PepsiCo, Inc. Press Release. "PepsiCo Opens Food and Beverage R&D Center in Shanghai to Drive Innovation and Growth Across Asia". http://www.pepsico.com/live/pressrelease/PepsiCo-Opens-Food-and-Beverage-RD-Center-in-Shanghai-to-Drive-Innovation-and-Gr11132012. 13 November 2012.

42. Asahi Group Holdings, Ltd. Announcement. "Tingyi-Asahi Beverages Holdings Co., Ltd has entered into a strategic alliance with PepsiCo, Inc.". 4 November 2011.

43. Tingyi (Cayman Islands) Holding Corp. "Presentation on 2016 First Quarterly Results".

44. Beth Kowitt. *Fortune.* "PepsiCo nabs NBA sponsorship rights from Coca-Cola". http://fortune.com/2015/04/13/pepsico-nba-sponsorship/. 13 April 2015.

45. PepsiCo, Inc. Press Release. "PepsiCo And NBA Announce Landmark Marketing Partnership; PepsiCo Partner Tingyi's Master Kong Becomes League Beverage Partner in China". http://www.pepsico.com/live/pressrelease/pepsico-and-nba-announce-landmark-marketing-partnership-pepsico-partner-tingyis-04132015. 13 April 2015.

46. Tingyi (Cayman Islands) Holding Corp. "2015 Annual Report".

47. Tingyi (Cayman Islands) Holding Corp. "Presentation on 2012, 2013, 2014 & 2015 Annual Results". 18 March 2013; 24 March 2014; 23 March 2015; 22 March 2016.

48. Tingyi (Cayman Islands) Holding Corp. "Presentation on 2015 Annual Results".

49. Ibid.

50. Tingyi (Cayman Islands) Holding Corp. "2015 Annual Report".

51. Ibid.

52. Tingyi (Cayman Islands) Holding Corp. "Presentation on 2015 Annual Results".

53. First Resources Limited. "Annual Report 2015".

54. Sime Darby Plantations. Sime Darby Berhad. "Facts and Figures". Information as at April 2014.

55. Malaysia Palm Oil Board. "Malaysia Palm Oil Industry". http://www.palmoilworld.org/about_malaysian-industry.html.   Accessed: 8 March 2017.

56. First Resources Limited. Results Presentation. "Full Year and Fourth Quarter 2015". 25 February 2016.

57. Bumitama Agri Limited. "Initial Public Offering Prospectus". 3 April 2012.

58. Felda Global Ventures Holdings Berhad. "Corporate Profile". May 2014.
59. Malaysia Palm Oil Board. "Malaysia Palm Oil Industry".
60. Sime Darby Plantations. "Facts and Figures".
61. Population Reference Bureau. "2016 World Population Data Sheet".
62. Indexmundi. Commodity Prices. Palm oil. "Palm oil Monthly Price – US Dollars per Metric Ton". http://www.indexmundi.com/commodities/?commodity=palm-oil&months=360. Accessed: 9 March 2017.
63. Sime Darby Berhad. "Annual Report 2015".
64. Golden Agri-Resources Limited. "Annual Report 2015".
65. First Resources Limited. "Annual Report 2015".
66. Indexmundi. Commodity Prices. Palm oil.
67. First Resources Limited. "Annual Report 2012".
68. First Resources Limited. "Full Year and Fourth Quarter 2015".
69. Bumitama Agri Limited. "Annual Report 2015".
70. First Resources Limited. "Annual Report 2015".
71. Indofood Agri Resources Limited. "Annual Report 2015".
72. Indexmundi. Commodity Prices. Palm oil.
73. Ibid.
74. Sime Darby Berhad. Press Release. "Sime Darby Plantation Completes NBPOL Acquisition". 2 March 2015.
75. Felda Global Ventures Holdings Berhad. Announcement. "Compulsory Acquisition of Shares in Asian Plantations Limited". 31 October 2014.
76. Tradewinds Plantation Berhad. Maybank Investment Bank Berhad. Announcement. Take-overs & Mergers (Chapter 11 of Listing Requirements). "Unconditional Take-over Offer by the Joint Offerors through Maybank Investment Bank Berhad to Acquire". 25 April 2013.
77. IOI Corporation Bhd. "Annual Report 2014".
78. Howard Marks. Columbia University Press. *The Most Important Thing Illuminated.* Copyright 2011.
79. First Resources Limited. "Annual Report 2015".
80. First Resources Limited. Results Presentation. "Full Year and Fourth Quarter 2015". 25 February 2016.
81. First Resources Limited. "Annual Report 2015".
82. First Resources Limited. Results Presentation. "Full Year and Fourth Quarter 2013". 25 February 2014.
83. First Resources Limited. "Annual Report 2015".
84. First Resources Limited. Google Finance. https://www.google.com/finance?cid=627507017117064. Accessed: 9 March 2017.
85. Dalian Wanda Commercial Properties Co., Limited. "Interim Report 2016".

86. Dalian Wanda Commercial Properties Co., Limited. Joint Announcement. "Voluntary Conditional General Offer by China International Capital Corporation Hong Kong Securities Limited on Behalf of the Joint Offerors to Acquire All of the Issued H Shares in Dalian Wanda Commercial Properties Co., Ltd. and Proposed Withdrawal of Listing of H Shares and Resumption of Trading". 30 May 2016.

87. Dalian Wanda Commercial Properties Co., Limited. "Annual Report 2014".

88. Dalian Wanda Commercial Properties Co., Limited. Google Finance. https://www.google.com/finance?q=HKG%3A3699&ei=TXy1WNni G8mF0ASxsIrQDw. Accessed: 10 March 2017.

89. Prudence Ho. Bloomberg. "Wanda Property Deal Faces Hurdles as APG Balks Over Price". https://www.bloomberg.com/news/ articles/2016-06-29/wanda-property-deal-faces-hurdles-as-investor-balks-over-price. 29 June 2016.

90. Dalian Wanda Commercial Properties Co., Limited. "Interim Report 2016".

91. Dalian Wanda Commercial Properties Co., Limited. "Annual Report 2014".

92. Dalian Wanda Commercial Properties Co., Limited. Joint Announcement. "Voluntary Conditional General Offer by China International Capital Corporation Hong Kong Securities Limited on Behalf of the Joint Offerors to Acquire All of the Issued H Shares in Dalian Wanda Commercial Properties Co., Ltd. and Proposed Withdrawal of Listing of H Shares and Resumption of Trading". 25 July 2016.

93. Dalian Wanda Commercial Properties Co., Limited. Google Finance.

94. Dalian Wanda Commercial Properties Co., Limited. "Annual Report 2015".

95. Dalian Wanda Commercial Properties Co., Limited. "Interim Report 2016".

96. Dalian Wanda Commercial Properties Co., Limited. "Annual Report 2015".

97. Lulu Yilun Chen. Bloomberg. "Tencent Now China's Top Company in Private Economy Triumph". https://www.bloomberg.com/ news/articles/2016-09-05/tencent-becomes-china-s-top-company-in-private-economy-triumph. 5 September 2016.

98. Bien Perez. *South China Morning Post.* "BAT – Baidu, Alibaba and Tencent – lead charge in China mergers and show no sign of slowing down". http://www.scmp.com/business/companies/ article/1934083/bat-baidu-alibaba-and-tencent-lead-charge-china-mergers-and-show. Updated: 8 April 2016.

99. Tencent Holdings Limited. "Annual Report 2015".

100. Chen. "Tencent Now China's Top Company in Private Economy Triumph".

101. Tencent Holdings Limited. Google Finance. https://www.google .com/finance?cid=695431. Accessed: 10 March 2017.

102. Yahoo Finance. https://goo.gl/mrKrc8, February 2017.

103. Chen. "Tencent Now China's Top Company in Private Economy Triumph".

104. Tencent Holdings Limited. "Annual Report 2006".

105. Chen. "Tencent Now China's Top Company in Private Economy Triumph".

106. Yahoo Finance. https://goo.gl/PIKK5N. Accessed 20 March 2017.

107. Tencent Holdings Limited. "Corporate Overview 3Q2016". Accessed: 12 March 2017.

108. Bien Perez. *South China Morning Post.* "Tencent to partner with more developers to fuel its mobile games expansion". http://www.scmp.com/business/china-business/article/1561387/tencent-partner-more-developers-fuel-its-mobile-games. Updated: 21 April 2015.

109. Tencent Holdings Limited. Financial Releases. Other Releases. "NBA and Tencent Announce Groundbreaking Partnership to Make Tencent the Exclusive Official Digital Partner in China". 30 January 2015.

110. Tencent Holdings Limited. "Table 1: Tencent Service Offerings". Accessed: 12 March 2017.

111. Crunchbase Inc. "Tencent Holdings". https://www.crunchbase. com/organization/tencent#/entity. Accessed: 12 March 2017.

112. Chris Neiger. The Motley Fool. "Who Owns Didi Chuxing?". https:// www.fool.com/investing/2016/06/23/who-owns-didi-chuxing.aspx. 23 June 2016.

113. JD.com, Inc. Form 20-F. "Annual Report Pursuant to Section 13 or 15(d) of the Securities Exchange Act of 1934 For the Fiscal Year ended December 31, 2015".

114. Tencent Holdings Limited. Financial Releases. Other Releases. "Tencent to Acquire Majority Stake in Supercell from SoftBank". 21 June 2016.

115. Investopedia. "Diworsification". http://www.investopedia.com/ terms/d/diworsification.asp. Accessed: 12 March 2017.

116. Chen. "Tencent Now China's Top Company in Private Economy Triumph".

117. Tencent Holdings Limited. "Annual Report 2015".

118. Benjamin Graham & David Dodd. First Collins Business Essentials. *The Intelligent Investor.* Edition 2006.

119. Yahoo Finance. Tencent Holdings Limited. https://goo.gl/PIKK5N. Accessed: 20 March 2017.

Conclusion

Value investing is a lifelong journey. Value investing is not a get-rich-quick scheme.

We like to think of value investing as more of a get-rich-slowly (but surely) philosophy. It is a topic that we have spent over a decade understanding and practising, and will probably spend the rest of our lives mastering. This might explain why value investing is not for everyone, but rather for those with great patience and a thirst for knowledge. As Benjamin Franklin said, "Take time for all things: great haste makes great waste."

Up to this point, you might have the impression that value investing is just about the money. This is not a feel-good book that tells you monetary returns are not the focus of investing. They are!

We personally know of many investors that have practised the concept of value investing and have obtained financial freedom in their lifetime. We really hope the material shared in this book would help you move closer towards your own financial goals.

However, value investing has brought us more than just financial benefits. It might be a cliché, but our journey down this path of value investing has taught us to be better people. Among many other things, value investing has taught us the value of patience, the benefits of doing your homework, the importance of learning from your experience and understanding people – if you listen attentively, the opportunity might just be lying right at your feet. To us, we treat our investment journeys like a game – but with money involved, we treat it as a serious game, one that we enjoy. Why else would we spend our Friday nights reading annual reports?

If the book has been beneficial to you, we hope that you will share the idea of value investing and this book with the people around you. Value investing is not a zero-sum game. The more people who understand the concept of value investing, the easier it would be for the market to recognise the value in the market. In that way, the market would reward us for spotting these valuable companies, benefiting all investors.

Over the course of our book, we looked at the major trends in Asia. We discovered what makes the Asian market unique, and how we should adapt to it. We pieced together the jigsaw behind annual reports and saw how all the seemingly unrelated pieces came together to tell us a story. We have shared the wisdom of some of the greatest value investors in Asia with you. We have explored the three key methods of finding value in the market – through asset value, current earning value and growth potential. What's more, to show that we are not kidding you, our book also contains many real-life current and historical case studies that will help you better navigate these waters.

It is now up to you to experiment with the different styles of investing as described in the book. Take some time to figure out which style of investing suits you best. You can start by forming a circle of competence of the markets and industries that you are most comfortable investing in, and branch out from there. Go out there, do not be afraid to share your ideas with like-minded investors. Personally, we have found sharing ideas with like-minded investors to be one of the best steps a value investor can take.

And finally, you need to have the courage of your knowledge and experience. If you have formed an opinion from the facts and if you know that your judgement is sound, act on it – even though others may hesitate or differ. You are neither right nor wrong because the crowd disagrees with you. You are right because your data and reasoning are right.

We have prepared more resources for you on this next stage of your investing journey. Your bonus chapters are available at https://www.valueinvestasia.com/valueinvestingbook/.

(Scan the QR code to access the website)

You can also continue to follow us, through our Facebook or Twitter, as we explore the Asian stock markets.

Congratulations for taking the lead in taking control of your own financial future. And thank you for joining us in our journey of spreading the idea of value investing in Asia.

We will see you at the top.

Contact Details

Email: info@valueinvestasia.com
Facebook: facebook.com/valueinvestasia
Twitter: twitter.com/valueinvestasia

INTERVIEWS
An Interview with Wong Kok Hoi of APS Asset Management

"Don't do what others do"

— Wong Kok Hoi, CFA

In May 2017, we met with Mr Wong Kok Hoi for an exclusive interview at his office in Singapore. Founded in 1995 and headquartered in Singapore, APS Asset Management ("APS") started with assets under management (AUM) of just US$15 million. As at April 2017, its AUM has grown to US$2.7 billion. APS has also expanded into a company with 65 staff over six offices worldwide.

Mr Wong, the founder and Chief Investment Officer of APS, has over 36 years of investment experience, including being the Chief Investment Officer at Cititrust Japan, Senior Portfolio Manager at Citibank Hong Kong and Senior Investment Officer of Government of Singapore Investment Corporation. Mr Wong was also the recipient of the Mombusho Scholarship in Japan and graduated with a Bachelor of Commerce from Hitotsubashi University. After that, Mr Wong went on to complete the Investment Appraisal and Management Program at Harvard University.

From the start, APS started with an ambitious objective – to manage Asian assets for predominantly institutional investors, rather than the regular boutique investment firms' path in the 1980s of managing family and friends' money. Even after 22 years, the core values and vision of APS have not changed, APS still specialises in the Asian markets, employing investigative research and independent thinking in their investment process. Today, nearly 95% of their assets under management come from institutional investors such as public and private pension funds, endowments and foundations, and the rest are from family offices, financial institutions, sovereign wealth funds and corporates.

Started as Far East ex-Japan long-only manager, APS subsequently ventured into other strategies. As at 2017, APS offered six strategies.

Long-Only Strategies

- APS China A Share
- APS Far East Alpha
- APS Japan Alpha
- APS Vietnam Alpha

Long-Short Strategies

- APS Asia Pacific Long Short
- APS Greater China Long Short

APS's China A share fund, a pure China A-shares strategy, is the firm's single largest fund, with assets under management of US$2 billion.

In just the past two years (2015–2016), APS was awarded the following:

- Eurekahedge Asian Hedge Fund Awards 2016 – Winner of "Best Singapore-based Hedge Fund: APS Greater China Long Short Fund"
- AI Hedge Fund 2016 Awards sponsored by BarclayHedge – Winner of "Most Consistent Asian L/S Fund: APS Asia Pacific Long Short Fund" and the Winner of the "Best Long/Short Asset Manager – Singapore"
- 2016 Preqin Global Hedge Fund Report – Winner of Top Performing Hedge Fund in 2015: APS Greater China Long Short Fund
- HFM Asia Hedge Fund Performance Awards 2015 – Winner of the "Long/Short Equity Overall" Category (APS Asia Pacific Long Short Fund)
- Singapore SME 1000 Award, 28th Annual – Winner of Net Profit Excellence Award (Finance), Winner of the Sales/Turnover Excellence Award (Finance) and Winner of the Promising SME Award (Crossing $20 million turnover).

We spent about two hours with Mr Wong, and the following was what we learned from our exclusive interview with him.

What Makes APS Unique?

Mr Wong sees APS as a pure alpha manager, driven mostly by the goal to generate alpha. Alpha is the term used in the financial industry to indicate excess returns above the market index. As a fund, APS does not restrict itself to investments of any size, geographical (within Asia) or sectors. In short, APS goes to where the alphas are.

APS was founded with three goals in mind, and to this day, Mr Wong and his team still: (1) do investigative bottom-up research, (2) specialise in Asian investments, and (3) serve global institutional asset owners.

Investment Philosophy and Strategy

APS uses a "Four Alpha-Hats" Investment Approach. This is first done by classifying stocks according to their alpha attributes. Next, APS conducts research on these companies with the help of four different "hats".

Mr Wong quipped that in school, we learn from finance professors that alphas are alphas. But as market practitioners, Mr Wong observed that alphas produced by different types of companies behave very differently. With that knowledge, Mr Wong and his team classifies alphas into four buckets – structural, dynamic, economic and opportunistic.

- Structural alpha: Stocks that possess structural strengths and core competencies resulting in likely outperformance over the long term. These include companies with a long-term durable moat, companies riding on long-term structural trends, or companies with core competencies of strengths not easily eroded away in the next 5–10 years. APS's investment horizon typically is longer than 3 years for this type of alpha.
- Dynamic alpha: Stocks that are in the cyclical industries such as semi-conductor companies, property companies or airline companies. Although these companies have the potential of a strong alpha in an upcycle, on the flip side, a downcycle would produce strongly negative alpha. Mr Wong commented that the key here is understanding when to get out and not to overstay. APS's investment horizon is about two years for dynamic alpha stocks.

- Economic alpha: This is where the traditional value stock fits in. In this group, the companies might have low or no growth rate. Typically, they might trade at a very low valuation in the single digit P/E multiples range. But because they are selling at a fraction of their underlying intrinsic value, these companies may still produce alpha for APS to capture. APS's investment horizon is 1–3 years.
- Opportunistic alpha: Stocks experiencing special events such as restructuring, product repositioning, mergers and acquisitions. APS's investment horizon is relatively short here at 3–12 months.

The four hats approach is essentially how APS conducts research and constructs its portfolios.

- Benjamin Graham hat: Mr Wong commented that back in 1965, there were only about 100 CFA holders worldwide. By 1985, there were probably close to 8,500. Today, there are over 100,000 CFA holders worldwide. This means that the type of security analysis done at APS is also done at many other firms, translating to a markedly reduced value-add. Hence, one cannot just rely only on the traditional, more commonly known as the "Benjamin Graham", type of security analysis to produce alphas. In summary, it is a necessary but not sufficient condition to produce alphas.
- Businessman hat: When investing, one must think like a businessman. At APS, Mr Wong and his team find that looking at a business or company from the perspective of a businessman forces them to take a deep dive and think long term. This is because as a businessman, when you buy a company, you might be stuck with it for 5, 10 or even 20 years. This is unlike a listed stock, where you can just sell it the very next day if you change your mind. So, the things a businessman looks at might be quite different, and this is very valuable in APS's investment process. For instance, a businessman would want to invest in a business with sustainable core competencies, run by competent and smart managers – exactly what an investor should look for as well.
- Sherlock Holmes hat: Like the detective, APS puts on their Sherlock Holmes hat to investigate companies, the reason

being that the investment terrain in Asia can be tricky and uneven, with corporate practices varying from country to country. For instance, Mr Wong joked that there is no point in asking management if they are honest or smart. More often than not, management tends to tell you what you want to hear. Instead, it might be more useful to check with third parties like former employees, competitors and customers. Competitors very often will give you a shockingly honest assessment of their peers, and can be a more illuminating source of information compared to just reading sell-side reports or industry research reports. This hat also includes a study of possible red flags with the checklist containing instances like frequent changes in the company's C-Suite level officers, directors, auditors, etc. As a parting note, Mr Wong noted that this does get better with experience, especially when it comes to understanding management.

- APS hat: Relative to the conventional tracking error approach, APS believes if they can construct a portfolio with the four buckets of alphas, it would result in an optimal alpha portfolio. APS tends to build their portfolio with 50–70% of their portfolio invested in structural alphas, 20% in dynamic alphas, 15% in economic alphas and minimal exposure to opportunistic alpha.

On APS's Investment Process

APS typically approaches an investment as follows:

- Generate original ideas: APS looks for long-term structural trends, contrarian ideas, new industries and companies, and company-specific leads.
- Understand source of alpha: APS then groups these ideas into the four alpha groups – Structural, dynamic, economic and opportunistic.
- Inside-out Research and Valuation: Thorough research is done by understanding the business model, conducting site visits, engaging in staff interviews, looking at the management's reputation and track record, and finally valuing these companies.
- Build alpha diversified portfolio: Once the ideal investments are found, APS proceeds to invest in these stocks with the help of the APS hat.

- Monitoring and review: Lastly, APS constantly monitors the companies in its portfolio, looking for changes in company or industry fundamentals.

Mr Wong then went on to share with us examples of some investment opportunities APS had considered from the approach of a structural, dynamic and economic alpha, respectively.

Structural Alpha

For an example on structural alpha, Mr Wong introduced us to Venustech Group Inc. ("Venustech"), the largest cybersecurity company in China. APS initiated a position in the company about 4 years ago. From Mr Wong's perspective, there were a number of reasons supporting APS's positive view of Venustech as an investment, one of which is his belief that cybersecurity will be a strong structural theme in the next 5 to 10 years. The cybersecurity industry is a fast-growing industry globally, and with the economy moving towards a digital economy, it seems inevitable that cybersecurity defences have to be increased even further, especially so in China. This is because over the past few decades, China, compared to western countries, has considerably underinvested in this area. With this as a backdrop, Mr Wong expects the capital expenditure in China's cyber industry to grow by 20% a year, for years to come. And Venustech – the largest cybersecurity firm in China – looks poised to take advantage of these favourable tailwinds. On a company-specific basis, Venustech spent close to 20% of their revenue on research and development in the past year, a significant amount. Furthermore, not only is Venustech growing organically, the company also has a track record of growing through the acquisition of smaller companies with new technologies.

Dynamic Alpha

The term "dynamic" by itself suggests something unstable, or in flux. How this plays out is for an investor is to buy at the trough, or close to the bottom of the cycle. The key challenge is being able to spot the trough. According to Mr Wong, these are some factors that help his team to identify such opportunities:

- most companies in the industry might be loss-making for 2, 3 or more years
- share prices for companies in this sector have dropped significantly, by more than 70%

- these companies tend to have price to net asset value (P/NAV) of less than 0.4 times
- sell-side analysts might have dropped coverage on some of these companies
- as earnings shrink, these companies tend to trade at a high P/E ratio.

Hence, one must not be afraid in the absence of a P/E ratio, or even P/E ratios in the triple digit range. Mr Wong states this is when investors should make a move. In the peak years, when earnings are strong, the P/E ratio tends to be low. When earnings peak, that is when many cyclical companies will have low P/E multiples. In short, investing in dynamic alpha is a counter-intuitional exercise with respect to PER.

A recent example was Singapore's oil and gas industry. In general, the oil and gas industry is very cyclical. For many years, this industry performed rather well, with decent dividend pay-outs. However, just prior to the crude oil collapse, Mr Wong and his team concluded from the signs that things did not look good for the industry. These signs included supply and demand considerations, capital expenditure patterns of these companies, their overleveraged balance sheet positions as well as rosy assumptions on the underlying commodity. True enough, once crude oil came crashing down, most of them got into trouble.

As a parting note on companies that fall under APS's categorisation of dynamic alpha, Mr Wong cautioned us to constantly remind ourselves that these are companies in cyclical industries, and not to get sold on the allure of a new paradigm when they do well.

Economical Alpha

The key thing about economic alphas is that, growth-wise, we should not expect too much from these companies. What we need to do is to make sure that these companies have low capital expenditure requirements and pay good dividends. This way, they would be able to give us a fair yield on our investment. And if they are trading at a discount, that is where the alpha can be found.

One such company that APS invested in is Hong Kong-listed Shenzhen International Holdings Limited ("Shenzhen International"). Shenzhen International consists of three major businesses – toll roads, logistics business and a 49% stake in Shenzhen Airlines. At the point of investment, Shenzhen International was trading at less than one-third of APS's estimation of its intrinsic value.

Alpha Combinations

With the key alphas covered, Mr Wong highlighted that sometimes a stock might have the features of more than one, two or even three alpha groups. In one of his previous interviews, Mr Wong mentioned that Macau casino industry was a candidate for a short position. A short is a position taken by an investor when he is betting on the decline of the stock price of a company. In this particular case, the Macau casino industry contained elements of various alpha features.

First, Mr Wong believed the structural growth story in Macau is over. This is because the present administration led by Xi Jinping does not encourage the Chinese to go Macau solely for gambling. But more importantly, all the gaming concessions in Macau have a limited concession period. Currently, there are six main concessions in the island, two of which will expire in 2020, with the other four expiring in 2022. Currently, no one has any idea on how these concessions will be renewed, and there is a significant risk if some of these concessionaires are not able to renew their concessions.

Next, Mr Wong detailed the dynamic element of this investment thesis. Typically, Chinese tourists would go to Macau when they are doing well economically. And as one would expect, when the economy started slowing down, the Macau gaming industry followed its lead. After Xi Jinping took office, the industry went into tailspin, demonstrating to us the cyclicality of the gaming business.

Finally, to touch on the economic aspect, the market capitalisation for most Macau gaming operators doubled in the last 18 months (early 2016 to mid-2017). And this is with the knowledge of increasing capacity. For this and the above reasons, the share prices of some of these casino operators do not appear justifiable from APS's point of view.

On Company Visits

APS is a strong believer in company visits, as it allows one to pick the minds of management. Mr Wong mentioned that when you start with a report of a company, you will form an opinion of the company. However, that is just one perspective into the window of the company. As the saying goes, seeing is believing, thus Mr Wong believes in going on-site to do his due diligence, guided by the idea that "You won't form conclusions on what you see, but it makes you ask questions." And this will give you yet another input into your analysis of the company.

Some years ago, Mr Wong encountered a company which, despite high top-line growth, had consistently low return on equity. Mr Wong could not understand the reason. That was until he made a company visit. Upon arriving, Mr Wong noted that the garden of the company was beautiful, it was nicely manicured. This implied that the company spent a lot of money on unproductive things. True enough, during a tour of the factory, there were idle machines and workers. This stuff cannot be seen from the annual reports alone.

In contrast, a Taiwan-listed company which Mr Wong had a chance to visit some years ago had a machine running right next to the reception area. Pretending to be naïve, Mr Wong questioned the general manager on this and the response was a simple, "Why not?" With a management deploying capital as wisely as this, it might have been a factor contributing towards high profitability, with good return on equity year after year, even through recession periods.

One final example on the importance of company visits is illustrated by a food catering business that APS was looking at some years ago. This was the largest caterer in China, supplying millions of lunch boxes a day to government departments, factories, etc. Earnings growth was 50% p.a. for five years in a row; however, P/E multiples were in the teens. Mr Wong joked that this company was looking like the cheapest growth stock in the universe! Moreover, this company was the official sponsor for Beijing Olympics. With all this, Mr Wong and his team could not understand why the market was valuing it so cheaply. APS also noted that there were blue-chip fund managers on the company's shareholder list. Right before their visit, Mr Wong recalled that it was discovered that this company had an unusually high level of capital expenditure for a food catering operator – its five-year cumulative capital expenditure was four times its five-year cumulative profits. This led to Mr Wong and his team questioning the company's need to spend so much. To that, management responded that this was for distribution centres and kitchenware. But Mr Wong was not sold – this was nowhere close to "French cooking" – and wondered to himself about the utility of spending hundreds of millions in kitchenware and distribution centres. A second red flag that stood out was the company's frequent reliance on bank loans and shareholder funds for additional capital.

At this point, Mr Wong and his team felt that something was probably not right. But they did not want to form a judgement too early, so the team decided to take a look at the company's "French kitchen equipment". Upon setting foot in the facility, APS analysts found out that for a food caterer for millions of lunch boxes, the place was not clean – unacceptable standards for an operator in the food industry. This was when APS got nervous. Additionally, the kitchen and distribution centres did not seem to justify the investment they had made. Not surprisingly, within a year, company went bankrupt.

Asia's Investment Outlook

In Mr Wong's opinion, there are a few macro trends investors should take note of.

First, the emergence of China as both an economic and military power. Already the second largest economy in the world, China cannot be taken lightly. Take commodity prices for example – in 2016, commodity prices shot up on China's increased spending in infrastructure projects. In the coal industry, when it was reported that China closed down some of its coal mines, coal prices went through the roof, with many coal mining stocks enjoying strong rallies.

Second, the emergence of middle class consumers in Asia. This has significant impact on industries all over Asia, and tourism is one of them. Today, the Chinese are the number one spender on tourism globally, and Mr Wong expects this gap to widen.

Finally, Mr Wong also noted that we could expect a low interest rate and low-growth environment over next five years.

Industries Beyond APS's Circle of Competence

An industry that Mr Wong tends to avoid is the banking sector, for the simple reason that Mr Wong and his team believe that it is difficult to analyse banks.

Take for instance the non-performing loan ("NPL") ratio. Mr Wong highlights that it is very tough for even an experienced analyst or a fund manager to accurately ascertain the bank's "true" NPL ratio. Even in serious cases, take for instance the global financial crisis – even the regulators were informed at the eleventh hour. So how is it possible for an external investor to accurately analyse a bank's financials? Mr Wong felt that investing in banks would require a huge leap of faith on the part of the investor. With that said, he makes an exception for investing in banking stocks—after a financial crisis or after a deep recession.

On Reviewing of Positions

Mr Wong commented that APS conducts a review of its investments all the time, simply because fundamentals change continually. For instance, one cannot set a fixed date of, say, every Monday or the first day of the month to review our portfolios. Events happen in real time and so should our reviews.

If somehow you learn that the fundamentals of your investments have changed, you should review them right away. However, if there are no fundamental changes to your company, there is no need to review your positions at all. Mr Wong recalled an investment into one of the telecommunication companies in Thailand some years ago. Within a week of their investment, a new government announcement allowing new entrants into the industry prompted them to sell off their position right away.

On Spotting Red Flags

APS's investment universe also extends to cover even Australian equities. Mr Wong talked about an Australian electronics retailer – Harvey Norman Holdings Limited ("Harvey Norman"). Harvey Norman was selected by APS as a short candidate.

First, the dynamic alpha presented itself in the slowdown of Australia's property market with its impact trickling down to the entire retail industry. Second, it was reported that Amazon had plans to enter the Australian market soon. And Mr Wong keenly noted that Amazon is a disruptor that sells electronics, furniture, bedding and fittings at low prices.

Finally, APS put on their Sherlock Holmes hat and uncovered several accounting irregularities, subsequently producing a negative report on the company two years ago, calling the company out. Harvey Norman was later investigated by Australian regulators, shareholders' associations and shareholder proxy groups for similar accounting irregularities, proving that APS's initial investigation about the company was spot on.

On Market Exuberance

Mr Wong recounted an old story – while on a business trip in Switzerland, a taxi driver started to brag to him about his Japanese stocks. That was when Mr Wong decided that things had gone too far. Shortly after, he unloaded most of his Japanese stocks. Just weeks later, in December 1989, the market crashed.

Mr Wong mentioned that there are many signs when the market appears to be overvalued. A litmus test is when you start hearing teachers, housewives, cab drivers, etc. talk about stocks. This is a time when one must keep one's sanity and not be greedy.

On Transparency and Disclosures

Mr Wong believes regulators in the region should step up their efforts in protecting investors. He mentioned that from time to time there will be "naughty boys" in the market ready to abuse innocent investors.

Besides having clear and stringent rules, regulations supervision and enforcement are absolutely vital to the long-term healthy development of capital markets.

Advice to Investors

We asked Mr Wong for some words of wisdom to share with you. Here is his advice:

1. Do not invest in things you do not understand.
2. Do not invest with the crowd; do not seek comfort from group think.
3. When something is too good to be true, it is often not true.
4. Do not trade – many people think that they are smart enough to time the market, but the empirical evidence shows conclusively that market timing is a money-losing activity.
5. Invest for the long term.

An Interview with Tan Chong Koay of Pheim Asset Management

Success in fund management is based on hard work, research and an ability to read the major trends

— Dr Tan Chong Koay

In February 2017, we were fortunate to be able to meet with Dr Tan Chong Koay at his Singapore office. Born in Jeniang, Kedah, Dr Tan is the founder and CEO of Pheim Asset Management ("Pheim"), and the author of the best-selling *Rising Above Financial Storms*. In 2010, Pheim had assets under management of over US$1.8 billion.

Following the completion of his MBA from Western Illinois University (USA) in 1974, Dr Tan returned to Malaysia. Starting out as an investment executive in South East Asia Development Corporation, which wholly owned Asia Unit Trusts Bhd, the first such entity in Malaysia, Dr Tan was convinced that fund management would be with him for the rest of his life. In the next phase of Dr Tan's professional investment career, he was a fund manager with Arab-Malaysian Merchant Bank, which was then the largest merchant bank in Malaysia. In 1987 (the year of the infamous "Black Monday" crash), he was rated Top Manager for Retirement and Pension Funds in Malaysia. In the early 1980s, Dr Tan did his PhD paper on fixed income funds. In 1987, he created, developed and launched Arab-Malaysian Gilts, the first unit trust fund in Malaysia to invest in Malaysian government and bank-backed securities, which earned him the name of "Pioneer of Fixed Income Unit Trust" in Malaysia.

Dr Tan founded Pheim Asset Management Sdn Bhd ("Pheim Malaysia") in 1994 and Pheim Asset Management (Asia) Pte Ltd ("Pheim Singapore") in 1995.

In January 1994, Pheim Malaysia started operations, just when the Malaysian market hit its all-time high. Since inception, Pheim Malaysia has been profitable every single year for 23 consecutive years. Notable investors in Pheim's Malaysian Emerging Companies

Growth Fund have included the Government of Singapore Investment Corporation ("GIC"), financial institutions and other high net worth individuals. When Pheim Singapore started in 1995, the company was also given the ASEAN mandate by GIC. In 1997, Pheim Malaysia, with its good track record, secured the coveted appointment as an external fund manager for domestic equity for the largest pension fund in Malaysia. There is probably no other external fund manager that has managed this pension fund for 20 years.

To demonstrate the magnitude of Pheim's track record, Pheim SICAV SIF – ASEAN Emerging Companies ("Pheim ASEAN Fund") Fund was the only fund in history to be ranked No 1 by Morningstar for the 1- to 15-year periods in US dollar terms, for the Morningstar ASEAN Category. On the fund's 20th anniversary on 3 February 2015, Lipper Thomson Reuters informed Pheim that the Pheim ASEAN Fund had taken the top position for all the 1- to 20-year periods among all Equity Asean funds of the Lipper Global classification under the International Offshore Universe in terms of total returns in US$. Over the 20-year period, the fund recorded a return of 497.37%, outperforming the FTSE AW Asean Index by 452.81%, and also its closest competitor by 402.85%.

Dr Tan received the following notable awards and accolades for his contribution to the industry and society:

- "The Warren Buffett of Asia" by World Wealth Creation Conference 2017 for being one of the best performing fund managers and for truly enhancing value-investing.
- One of the 80 Global Chinese Eminent Business Leaders – Beijing-based *The China Daily* (2014)
- Best of the Best Awards, CEO of the Year for Malaysia – *Asia Asset Management* magazine (2008 and 2010)
- Outstanding Entrepreneurship Award – Asia Pacific Entrepreneurship Awards (2010 and 2016)
- China Top 10 Financial Intelligent Persons Award – China Culture Development Institute, PRC (2010)
- Most Respected Chinese Entrepreneurship Award in Asia Pacific – China Economic Trading Promotion Agency, PRC (2012).

Dr Tan also served as a committee Member of the Investment Management Association of Singapore (2004–2009), and as a

Member of the Investment Advisory Committee for the Lee Kuan Yew Fund (11 years) and the Lee Kuan Yew Fund for Bilingualism Ltd (3 years) until 1 March 2015.

What Makes Pheim Unique?

Pheim has a consistent track record of significant outperformance in Asia. In 2003, Watson Wyatt Investment Consulting, Singapore, in conformity with the Level 1 verification of compliance in accordance with the AIMR Performance Presentation Standards (AIMR-PPS), verified that Pheim Singapore outperformed the respective benchmark every year for every composite for nine consecutive years (1995–2003) since inception. Additionally, as verified by Watson Wyatt Investment Consulting, Malaysia, Pheim Malaysia's Malaysian Composite (for the combined Malaysia mandated accounts) outperformed the KLCI benchmark every year for ten consecutive years (1994–2003) since inception. In the Award-Winning Funds Supplement (July 2004) issue of *Smart Investor*, Singapore, it was mentioned that "No one asset manager has ever ranked No 1 for so many periods in the history of this category (Offshore ASEAN) by Standard & Poor's". Pheim was also the only Malaysian boutique company that handled the sovereign wealth funds of three separate government entities, of Norway, Malaysia and Singapore. It is also notable to mention that Pheim was believed to be the first manager appointed by the Norwegian government. Over two decades, Dr Tan believes that today's Pheim is stronger, and more experienced as a company.

Additionally, Pheim is an investment house that is not market cap sensitive. In the fund management universe, most funds are restricted to large cap companies. However, the biggest growth is often seen in small and mid-cap companies. Pheim is exciting in the sense that it is one of the few houses that cover companies over the entire spectrum of small, medium and large market capitalisation. Traditionally, Pheim is strong in companies in the small and mid-cap space. This is where you might be able to uncover multi-baggers. When some of these small and medium market capitalisation companies get hit, their valuations become so cheap. Within two years of the Asian Financial Crisis, Pheim made more than 15 times their investment in PT Tempo Scan, 10 times from Dialog and 7.5 times from Unisem.

On the flip side, if things go the other way, an investor might get hurt much more than with a large cap. And Dr Tan has a single advice to get out of such situations: literally get out; as an investor, you must be willing to divest your investments when your thesis does not pan out. Generally, over the years, this diversification contributed towards Pheim's resilient performance.

Next, with Pheim and Dr Tan specialising in Asia for decades, another advantage the team has is their on-the-ground knowledge and experience. Knowing the place and country well is a great plus. However, networking alone is not enough; Dr Tan emphasises that an investor needs to combine this with a good philosophy. Networking gives you information, but doesn't tell you when to get out.

In terms of employee growth, Pheim is also a company with a knowledge-based culture. When it comes to investment opportunities, Dr Tan encourages a cohesive learning environment. He enables everyone, new or old, to engage in discussions, to come together; this results in the people at Pheim gaining experience exponentially. Life is not just about making money; what matters is whether one can add value.

Pheim and the funds it manages have chalked up various achievements and won numerous awards. Among the more notable ones are:

1. Pheim ASEAN Fund:
   - best-performing fund by Lipper Thomson Reuters for all the 1- to 20-year periods among all Equity ASEAN funds of the Lipper Global classification under the International Offshore Universe in terms of total returns in USD on its 20th Anniversary on 3 February 2015; the total return in USD for the 20-year period ending 3 February 2015 was +497.37% vs FTSE ASEAN Index's return of +44.565 vs its top rival's return of +94.52% (2015)
   - outperformed all its benchmark indices for all 1-year to 19-year periods ending February and March 2014 in terms of total returns in US$; it also outperformed all its peers in the Morningstar ASEAN Equity category for the same periods (2014)
   - ranked No 1 in terms of total returns in USD by Morningstar, for *all* 1- to 15-year periods ending December 2010 for the Morningstar ASEAN Equity Category (2010).
2. Dana Makmur Pheim (Balanced Islamic Fund):
   - won a total of 14 awards from The Edge-Thomson Reuters Lipper since inception:
     - Best Fund among *Malaysia Islamic Funds* for the third consecutive year under Mixed Asset MYR Balanced – Malaysia

Category for the 3-year and 5-year periods ending December 2016, and for the second consecutive year for the 10-year period ending December 2016 (2017)
- Best Fund among *Malaysia Provident Funds* under Mixed Asset MYR Balanced – Malaysia Category for 3-year and 5-year periods ending December 2016 (2017)
- other awards, i.e. Best Mixed Asset MYR Balanced Islamic Fund for the 10-year period ending 2012, 5-year period ending 2007 and 1-year period ending 2004 and 2003
- won a total of seven awards from Thomson Reuters Lipper – Global Islamic classification:
  - Best Fund under Mixed Asset MYR Balanced – Malaysia Category for the 3-year, 5-year and 10-year periods ending December 2015 (2016)
  - Best Fund under Mixed Asset MYR Balanced – Malaysia Category for the 1-year, 2-year and 3-year periods ending December 2014 (2015)
  - Best Fund under Mixed Asset MYR Balanced – Malaysia Category for the 1-year period ending December 2013 (2014).

Dr. Tan managed EPF Domestic Malaysia mandate for 20 years ending March, 2017 with an unprecedented outperformance of more than 300%. Pheim's long-term track record speaks for itself. The team at Pheim works very hard to achieve the best results. And awards are simply tangible evidence of the results achieved from the all the hard work put in. The string of awards received by Pheim over the years are a testament to the fact that Pheim consistently delivers the best results over the long term.

Investment Philosophy and Strategy

Dr. Tan's key unique and proven Investment Philosophy is simple, **"Never fully invest at all times."**

A fund should be fully invested near the bottom of the market and trimmed near the peak. But it should never be fully invested at all times, as Asian markets tend to be volatile.

When the market is down, Dr Tan's general rule of thumb is to invest up to 90% of the fund. In 1998, Pheim was invested as high as up to 98% after the Asian Financial Crisis period.

A key difference between Pheim and other funds is its willingness to hold cash. Because, when a fund sells, this fund might underperform the market as the market continues to moves up. When the market is seen to be overvalued, Pheim's cash allocation was as high as 65% cash back in 1987. Throughout Pheim's history, there were also times when one or two funds had cash positions as high as 85%.

Dr Tan mentioned that it is unlikely Pheim will hold such a high level of cash in their funds today, because not only has the company grown larger; over the years the team has also accumulated a wealth of experience, and has a better grasp on uncovering undervalued stocks. If there is ever a divestment, Pheim targets to utilise between 50 and 60% of its proceeds.

Investment Process

Typical investment thesis includes companies with:

- focused and experienced management (CEO with 10–20 years' experience)
- high earning growth potential
- attractive profit margins
- strong balance sheet
- low leverage
- strong in their field
- reasonable valuation
- low broker coverage.

Dr Tan referred to two case studies from his book.

1. Geahin Engineering Berhad: Geahin Engineering specialised in making steel frames for skyscrapers. Before investing in the company's IPO in 1995, Pheim requested a factory visit. When Dr Tan and his team arrived at the factory, they were surprised to find that it looked old; but the workers were very busy. The management explained that, due to their additional projects, they were going to move to a larger factory soon. The company was in a niche business and was expected to make higher profits in the coming year. After the company visit, the team noticed that Geahin Engineering had low gearing, was very focused and had good growth potential.

Pheim Malaysia participated in the IPO and bought additional shares up to just under 5% of the company's issued capital at an average cost of RM4.37 per share. After net profit increased from RM5.4 million (1994) to RM8.9 million (1995), growth slowed to 12% in 1996 at RM9.94 million. Pheim gradually sold the shares from early 1996 to mid-1996 at prices ranging from RM7.30 to RM23.94.

2. Unisem (M) Berhad: Due to its efficient operation Unisem is a semiconductor company with strong cash flow and profit margin. In 1998, Dr Tan visited Unisem's factory in Ipoh, Perak. Dr Tan noted that Unisem's factory was impressive, noting that it housed some of the most advanced equipment and had one of the best assembly and testing machinery layouts in the ASEAN region. Unisem also received external recognition (MS ISO 9002) for the quality of its operations in its first year. After meeting with Unisem's Chief Operating Officer, Dr Tan was in no doubt that the company was in very capable hands.

   Unisem faced competition primarily from the regional operators. Japanese and American companies were not in direct competition as they were more involved in frontline activities, whereas Unisem and its Asian counterparts were in the backline operations (wafer fabrication, assembly and testing). Its closest competitor, MPI, was involved in the manufacturing of lead frames (extremely competitive industry where Japanese manufacturers have the upper hand), hence Unisem had a higher profit margin.

   At that time, MPI was also suffering from a hedging misstep. Anticipating that the ringgit would strengthen, MPI hedged its mainly US dollar-pegged revenue while leaving its US dollar costs unhedged. Unisem's other competitor was Thailand's Hana Microelectronics, which had not resumed full operations after a fire damaged its plant. In Unisem's case, the company had been very conservative in forecasting its prospective earnings, and in 1998, Dr Tan and his team felt that the global drop in semiconductor sales was only a temporary setback and semiconductor sales would pick up in 1998. And with PCs accounting for about 55% of semiconductor sales, the rising demand for cheaper PCs, OEMs were likely to increase their outsourcing further to reduce costs.

Unisem also met Pheim's criteria of having strong cash flow with no US dollar loans and low gearing. At that time, Unisem was in a net cash position and the construction of Phase II of its factory was internally funded. Unisem received payments in US dollars and benefited from the weak ringgit against the US dollar, hence the company was in a strong position. Eventually Pheim invested in Unisem, taking the view that Unisem was well-run and financially sound and the IPO was reasonably priced at RM5.10 per share. Pheim believed that Unisem was one of the few companies in Malaysia that had established size, stability and earning power. Pheim eventually divested the last batch of its holdings in Unisem near RM44, at its peak, in February 2000.

3. Other instances included:
   • PT Tempo Scan Pacific Tbk
   • Dialog Group Berhad
   • PT Astra Agro Lestari Tbk
   • Inari Amertron Bhd.

Investment Universe

Dr Tan looks for companies that have positive contributions towards society as he believes that responsible investing will result in sustainable excellence. Accordingly, Pheim embraces environmental, social and governance best practices in their endeavour to achieve positive outcomes.

Dr Tan views commodity companies as exciting, because they run in cycles. However, you have to know how to track them. When these companies get played to extreme highs, you have to know when to get out.

To do this, one needs to have a good feel of the business cycle to understand which part of the cycle one is in. One of Pheim's recent successes was attributed to their funds not being weighted in the oil and gas industry.

Additionally, Dr Tan avoids companies involved in casino operations.

On Market Timing

The team starts with the compilation of 20–25 years' worth of market data. Next the team proceeds to study the market's price-to-earnings ratio, the highs and lows of each year, analysing the market's position compared to its historical showing. Intuitively, one should sell when the market P/E is at the peak. Dr Tan notes that one of the key contributors to his investment success is his ability and willingness to sell when the market appears to be toppish.

The above is a quantitative way of looking at things. However, investment is not just a science, investment is also an art which requires your experience and feel for the market. By constantly interacting with CEOs and business, Dr Tan generally has a good "feel" of where the market is.

Investors can also look at this from a top-down perspective. If the economy looks toppish, and almost every company you read about or visit mentions that they cannot make more money, it is a sign of things to come. Dr Tan believes that all of us share almost the same thoughts on valuation. The key is being able to find out before others. When you hear about it, it is already too late.

This next piece of advice is highly applicable to us. A clear sign of danger is when you start to see people going wild, especially when people start to go along the lines of, "if I ask you to buy shares, if you follow me you will make money". This is indeed a simple, yet effective rule of thumb to always keep in mind that the market could be currently overvalued.

On What Makes Asia Unique

Dr Tan thinks that Asia is unique in the sense that, as a region, Asia is among the fastest-growing economies in the world. The Asia ex-Japan region has a population bigger than any other region on this planet. This offers opportunity.

With diverse cultures, the spirit of entrepreneurship, as well as Asian's emphasis on education, Asia is a very dynamic place to be in. The ASEAN region has several distinctive dynamics that will drive economic growth such as the youthful population, rapid urbanisation, low labour costs, massive infrastructure needs and an emerging digital world. Additionally, ASEAN is also a region rich with resources, being the largest producer of palm oil, natural rubber, coconut, pineapple, fisheries and nickel.

There are many opportunities in Asia. The key lies in picking the right one. You have to pick the right people and the right company to invest.

Overall there is still growth in Asia. An example is Indonesia. From an investment perspective, Indonesia is a big fishing ground that is still largely unexplored. Coincidently, fisheries might be an interesting industry to look at. However, there aren't many publicly listed fisheries.

The Difference between Investing in the United States and Asia

Asian markets are much more volatile than markets in the United States.

- From 1980 to 2016, US had only two huge drops (1987 and 2008).
- In comparison, Asia was affected in the following years: 1987, 1993, 1997, 2000, 2001, 2003, 2008, and 2015.

Sometimes in Asia, sentiments can rapidly move in either direction. Dr Tan stresses that in Asia, very often when the market goes down, it goes all the way down, affecting both big and small companies. If big caps are so cheap, we do not have to look at companies with small market caps.

However, the frequency of large cap companies falling 90% does not come every day. Unless these large companies meet with a very severe situation, it is very unlikely for these companies to disappear. This happens more frequently to small cap companies. Hence, Pheim is still very interested in small and mid-cap market capitalisation range.

Lastly, with the huge swings present in Asian markets, an investor must be willing to divest and wait out at times. An investor needs to be able and willing to sell shares when the market is overvalued. In short, one has to be able to react fast. An investor has to be flexible in investing; it does not mean that if your target is 50% you stick to it without thinking. If there are better opportunities or higher risk present, an investor has to assess the situation as it is, and make a decision.

On Company Visits

When conducting company visits, Dr Tan's focus is on the ability and character of the Chief Executive Officer and the key management team. It helps if the Chief Executive Officer has more than 20 years' worth of experience in his industry.

Dr Tan highlights that by the time you meet with the Chief Executive Officer, you should have already done your homework.

At this stage, you should have an idea of the state of the company's operations, financials and valuation. The key objective of this company visit is to gauge the character and capability of the company's key management. Dr Tan prefers Chief Executive Officers that are hard-working and focused.

In Dr Tan's opinion, a sign of a capable Chief Executive Officer is that, upon setting foot in the office, the Chief Executive Officer is likely to tell you most of the important history and future development of the business within 20 minutes, knowing the ins and outs of the company like the back of his hand.

On Corporate Governance in Asia

Entrepreneurs can make mistakes as they take risks. When they take risks, sometimes they lose and sometimes they win.

In an ideal world, you would want to invest in a company with the guy at the top that's honest, sensible, hard-working and practical. However, such a person does not come by easily. But it does not stop you from trying to find such a person.

In reality, there are trade-offs. If you only invest when everything is perfect, there is a sizeable chance that you might underperform. In Dr Tan's opinion, the priority is the person's ability to deliver. When it comes to the topic of corporate governance, the key is knowing how to handle it. Experience will bring you through.

On Exchange-Traded Funds ("ETF")

As a fund manager, Dr Tan believes that if one doesn't strive to outperform the benchmark, there is no point being a fund manager; Pheim's funds have consistently outperformed the index over the long term.

Dr Tan is of the opinion that the ETF is not a "smart" product. This is because instead of reducing volatility, ETFs as a whole tend to result in more volatility. This stems primarily from the nature of ETFs being low-cost, making it both cheap and easy for investors to get in and get out of these vehicles, resulting in short-termism.

Another reason contributing towards volatility is when these ETFs are forced either to buy shares when investors invest in the fund, or to sell shares when investors redeem to get out of the fund. Due to the size of some of these ETFs, these movements are not minor.

What investors can do is to take advantage of the situation by investing in such companies at a discount in the event of such sell-downs.

Advice to Investors

Dr Tan has the following advice for investors:

- Write and remember the mistakes you make. And as a reader, you should not just accept what you read at face value, you have to analyse or get advice and decide for yourself.
- Most people know how to buy but they don't know how to sell; you have to be willing to sell when the market is toppish.
- We all share the same thoughts on valuation, you just have to go out, be disciplined and put things into practice.
- Investment is not about your academic results, investment is about your focus, hard work, and how you handle the major market trends.
- You have to be able to withstand volatility. If not, the stock market is not a place for you.
- Investment managers should not do what they like. Instead they should do what is right for their investors.
- Sometimes, doing nothing avoids losses. When Dr Tan started Pheim at a market high, he hardly invested and avoided losses.
- An investor must combine fundamental analysis, and the ability to read how the market or people are going to behave.
- Do not get discouraged by mistakes made even though the company's management lied to you. At times, investors run into bad patches.
- Talk to intelligent investors who have a long-term track record and are better than you.
- The past and the present are important but it is the future that matters.
- A business that embraces environmental, social and governance (ESG) best practices is a good business and will eventually achieve positive outcomes.
- Buy a stock that many want to buy later.
- The key to investment success is to find a formula to overweight winners most of the time.
- Never hesitate to sell a share when you think it is grossly overvalued.

- If you follow a proven investment philosophy, your chances of winning improve.
- Trying to buy a share at the lowest and then selling it at the highest is unrealistic.
- In a volatile environment, the investment philosophy "Never be fully invested at all times" should perform better than "Fully invested at all times" in the long run.

We hope you will benefit from Dr Tan's wisdom as much as we did.

An Interview with Wong Seak Eng, Kevin Tok and Eric Kong of Aggregate Asset Management

Value investing is simple to understand, but very hard to implement
— Aggregate Asset Management

In early 2015, we were able to get the opportunity to meet with the team behind Aggregate Asset Management. Aggregate Asset Management is a fund management company based in Singapore. The firm started its flagship fund – the Aggregate Value Fund – in December 2012.

Aggregate Asset Management was co-founded in 2012 by three passionate value investors, Wong Seak Eng, Kevin Tok and Eric Kong. Before co-founding Aggregate Asset Management, Wong Seak Eng had a wide range of experience in the audit, corporate finance and fund management industry. Kevin Tok had strong experience in the sales and marketing of financial services as he worked in insurance companies such as AIA Group and Manulife. Eric Kong worked with financial firms like Citibank and United Overseas Bank and was also a partner with a boutique investment firm before co-founding Aggregate Asset Management.

Aggregate Asset Management prides itself as being the only fund management company in Singapore that does not require its clients to pay a fixed management fee. Instead, the company prefers to charge a performance fee on returns, ensuring that its interests are aligned with its investors.

Aggregate Asset Management aims to achieve a net return of 10% a year over the long term for their clients. And by "long term", the company means a period of five years or more. By the end of 2016, the Aggregate Value Fund generated a return of about 10.55% per annum over the four-year period. We sat down with the team to find out just how they do it.

Investment Philosophy and Strategy

Aggregate Asset Management's philosophy is value – the fund invests in undervalued securities listed in Asia by employing a bottom-up approach to security selection through fundamental analysis.

First, Aggregate Asset Management believes that to succeed in investing, they cannot be doing what everyone else is doing, they have to be contrarian. This means they do not just follow the ideas of large funds or popular blue chips. They focus on generating ideas through internal stock screenings and public news flow.

Unlike many funds, Aggregate Asset Management does not make investment decisions based on economic or industry trends, choosing instead to focus on specific companies. The team likes to search for companies that have fallen out of favour with the market, and also those which are experiencing temporary declines in their business.

In summary, Aggregate Asset Management likes companies with strong balance sheets that are trading at steep discounts to their net assets.

Investment Process

Aggregate Value Fund is a long-only value fund investing in Asia companies. By using quantitative screenings, the team is able to filter out the best and subsequently study them in depth.

The team starts by screening for companies with:

- strong balance sheet
- low price-to-book ratio
- net-net working capital, more commonly known as "cigar-butt investments"
- high risk-to-reward payoff, or a high margin of safety.

Typically, they might end up with a shortlist of about 3,000 stocks. From that list, they would then generate an internal scoring system for their watch list. They might invest a small amount in the companies that pass their scoring system, generally at less than 1% of the portfolio. Aggregate Asset would only increase that position over time, when they are more comfortable with the company. The firm diversifies widely to avoid concentration risk on one particular stock. The team tends to allocate not more than 5% in any given investment.

Next, the team highlighted that their analysis involves a company's current and past financial statements, company announcements and any available public information. After analysing these documents, the team is then able to come up with a valuation for an indication of the attractiveness of a stock, or its "margin of safety". The "margin of safety" is the difference between a stock's market price and its intrinsic value.

Eric then made a very interesting point. They see themselves more as wholesalers of stocks instead of concentrated stock pickers. The team does not actively meet management of companies to find new investments. Rather, they tend to rely mostly on public information available, such as financial statements or the news. This means that Aggregate Asset's portfolio is made up of a wide variety of stocks, all in small allocations. In this way, the fund would not be impacted too much if one of their holdings did not go as expected. The advantages of this approach are that the chances of blow-ups and serious permanent impairment are low.

However, this does mean that as a retail investor, without a large asset base or the time to cover such a variety of companies, one would find it challenging to replicate their strategy.

Investment Universe

The fund comprises investments in Hong Kong, Malaysia, Singapore, South Korea, China and Thailand. The companies under consideration have to meet Aggregate Asset Management in-house screening and internal scoring process prior to investment. As mentioned, the team is attracted to companies that have fallen off the radar or those that have suffered a temporary decline in their fortunes.

Aggregate Asset Management has its own circle of competence, companies that the team is comfortable with. Thus, the team sticks to this circle and avoids investments in companies outside this circle. A subset of this circle also includes certain ethical considerations. Companies outside of this circle include companies in "sin" industries, for example companies involved in alcohol, gaming and tobacco operations. They would also avoid information technology companies, new initial public offerings or businesses that are just starting up. In this manner, the team can minimise unforced errors, simply by being more conservative in their selections.

Additionally, the team highlighted that they do not invest in Initial Public Offerings (IPO) as they want to be able to assess a company's track record prior to investment.

When to Sell a Stock

According to the team, the fund tends to hold on to a stock for at least five years as undervalued stocks need time for their value to be realised. The team does not set target prices for their investments. Instead, they review each investment on a case-by-case basis.

They tend to sell out only if the business is failing, in the process of being privatised or if better opportunities are found.

Detecting Red Flags

As a function of their investment approach (focusing on companies trading at very cheap valuation), it is inevitable that they would end up with mostly small and medium cap companies. With such a scenario, we wanted to find out from the team how they detect red flags and value traps in the companies they come across.

There is no shortcut. Aggregate Asset Management goes about mitigating such risks by doing their homework. The team follows a company for some time before investing. The reason for this is to give the team sufficient time to gauge both the actions of management and the performance of the company.

On What Makes Asia Unique

Aggregate Asset Management is a fund manager that invests purely in the Asian stock markets. We were therefore curious about the biggest difference the team found between markets in Asia and developed markets like the United States.

An interesting point they brought up is how companies in the US market can be less reliant on valuation. There are more examples of great companies that continue to perform well for shareholders even when they are trading at sky-high valuations. That is not the case in Asia. In Asia, investors need to be more cognisant of the price they pay for an investment. Buying an investment at too high a price can be a terrible mistake.

Investors' Advice

Before leaving, the team dropped these nuggets of wisdom:

- Do not jump straight into buying your first investment.
- Spend more time learning the basics, on how to read a financial statement, on how to question the merit of a business, and how to value a company.
- Do not dream about finding huge gains from your investments. Instead, focus on how to minimise your losses, your return will follow.
- Never stop learning, never stop reading.

We hope you will benefit from their advice as much as we did.

An Interview with Yeo Seng Chong of Yeoman Capital Management

If we get the "3-Rights" right, time is our friend

—Yeo Seng Chong

In March 2015, we went down to the office of Yeoman Capital Management to meet with its Executive Chairman and Founder, Mr Yeo Seng Chong.

Yeoman Capital Management is a Registered Fund Management Company (RFMC) in Singapore. Mr Yeo is a pioneer in the fund management industry in Singapore, having founded the company together with his wife, Mdm Lim, in 1999. Since 2005, the company has been running the flagship Yeoman 3-Rights Value Asia Fund, an Asia-Ex-Japan fund, since January 2005.

Mr Yeo had a wide range of experience before starting his fund in 1999. He had professional experience in both the public and private sector with listed firms like Centrepoint Properties Limited, Metro Holdings Limited and Singapore Technologies Industrial Corp (now part of SembCorp Industries Limited).

Mr Yeo frequently shares his investment wisdom through news and digital media such as *The Business Times, The Sunday Times* and *The Manual of Ideas*. We spent the afternoon with Mr Yeo to better understand his approach.

Investment Philosophy and Strategy

According to Yeoman Capital, since 1999, the collective funds have returned 12.74% per annum (net of all fees) to its investors for the 19 years and 2 months period up to Q4 2016. That far exceeded the performance of its benchmark, MSCI Far East Ex. Japan (MSEL CFFX), which returned 3.84% per annum over the same time window (implying an excess return of 8.90% p.a.). Yeoman Capital has achieved all this through its strong long-term investment process, focusing in the small-cap universe. At the end of 2016, the weighted average market capitalisation of all its holdings is S$240 million.

Yeoman Capital has been able to achieve this level of performance due to its investment strategy, with the basic premise of viewing stocks as operating businesses. Mr Yeo has a simple method of articulating his investment style. He coined his style of investing as the "3-Rights" approach. He focused on finding investments that meet his criteria of the:

- right business
- right price
- right people.

Finding the "right business" means that companies should show a reasonably strong balance sheet, stable cash flows and a considerable operating and listing history. Additionally, the right business should not be overleveraged and should have a reasonable capital efficiency in terms of its return on equity. Preferably, Yeoman Capital looks for companies with strong cash flow generation with a history of rewarding shareholders with dividend distributions.

Yeoman Capital is very disciplined in finding an investment at the "right price". That means that the company has to provide a large "margin of safety" for Yeoman Capital in terms of valuation before it can be considered.

Lastly, having the "right people" is extremely important. Yeoman Capital looks for companies with a management team who are very experienced in their field. The management must have demonstrated good corporate governance, have a history of being fair to minority shareholders and demonstrate transparency in its financials before the fund considers investing in them.

Investment Process

So how does Mr Yeo start screening for companies?

Mr Yeo shared with us that the firm uses a quantitative screening method. The team starts by scanning for companies with metrics such as:

- low price to tangible book value, preferably having a ratio of 0.6 or lower
- pays a dividend

- strong balance sheet, preferably in net cash
- good return on equity history
- no major losses in its operating history
- has a history of positive free cash flow
- has a long listing history
- no history of large dilution to shareholders.

Once they have found a shortlist of companies to investigate further, Mr Yeo starts looking into more qualitative measures. This includes looking at the ability of the management. He prefers companies with a strong leader, someone with a long-term vision of the company. Mr Yeo avoids companies with directors who have questionable backgrounds.

As regards what type of companies or industries Mr Yeo avoids, he replied that it is simply the opposite of what he screened for in a company. Companies with high capital expenditure, low return on equity and who do not pay a dividend do not make the cut into his shortlist. One industry that is notorious for possessing some of these traits is the airline industry.

Due to the large number of stocks in his portfolio (ranging from 60–80 securities), Mr Yeo tends to avoid interacting too much with the managements. He likes to let the data speak for itself; interacting too much with the management might result in more noise. However, if possible, the team will still schedule a company visit.

Mr Yeo is very careful when it comes to asset sizing. He normally allocates a portfolio weight of between 0.5% and 1.5% to each stock selected. From then on, he will only add to the position after monitoring its performance and management performance for a few reporting periods.

When to Sell a Stock

The average holding period for Yeoman Capital is around five years. So when does he sell a company?

For Mr Yeo, there might be a few reasons. For one, he would definitely sell out an investment if he comes to the realisation that a mistake was made. Possible mistakes include investing in a fraudulent company or finding that the thesis of the investment did not pan out. He would also consider selling when a company reaches its full value or when a better opportunity comes along. Mr Yeo commented that "Everybody wants to get a prestigious name such as Apple or

Google in their portfolio and they will pay any price, any valuation to get their wish, but a good business at a high price or high valuation does not always mean a good investment, in my opinion."

Therefore, he has thought out this 3-Rights strategy, which has served him well so far.

On What Makes Asia Unique

One key reason why Mr Yeo does not hold on to his investment for a very long term (i.e. forever), as preached by legendary investor Warren Buffett, is due to the business environment in Asia. Asia by itself is a very diverse market, it is not just one big market. Cultures are very different when we compare country to country. For instance, in heavily populated places such as India and China, not only is there a difference in culture between regions, even the language used might not be the same! Therefore, it is much harder for companies in Asia to duplicate their business model and scale up, as many companies in places like the United States of America do.

Because of this, Mr Yeo felt that selling out of a fully valued company and investing back into another undervalued stock is the right way to address the situation here.

Advice for New Investors

Before leaving his office, we asked Mr Yeo for his advice to investors. He gave the question some thought and responded that it is very important for investors to do their own research instead of relying on others.

Doing our own research allows us to gain a better understanding of the company. Not only that, this process will also enable us to improve our investing skill and it will give us more confidence if we are to invest in the company. In parting, Mr Yeo added, "Don't rely too much on projections, projections tell more about the projector than the future".

For further information, readers may look up the company's website at www.yeomancap.com.

An Interview with David Kuo of Motley Fool Singapore

Know what you buy and why you buy them

— Dr David Kuo

In October 2014, in a crowded and noisy Chinese restaurant, we sat down with the Chief Executive Officer of The Motley Fool Singapore, Dr David Kuo. The Motley Fool Singapore is a registered investment advisor with the Monetary Authority of Singapore (MAS). The company provides free investing education articles and paid stock recommendations to subscribing members through its website, http://www.fool.sg.

The Motley Fool is an international investment advisor, started from the United States by co-founders Tom and David Gardner. Today, The Motley Fool has offices in the US, Canada, United Kingdom, Germany, Australia and Singapore.

Dr Kuo has been with The Motley Fool UK for more than 16 years before coming back to Singapore to kick-start the first Asian office for The Motley Fool. Dr Kuo also appears regularly in the media, speaking about his views on the market and investing. He is well-known to have a unique way of describing investing, filled with unforgettable metaphors and funny stories.

He started late in becoming an investor. He only started active investing after he completed his PhD in Chemistry. Even after that, Dr Kuo admitted that he made many mistakes along the way before finding the investment style that suits him best; being an income investor. We talked to Dr Kuo about his investment style and what he thinks of investing in Asia.

Dr Kuo often describes himself as an income investor. This means that he is focused on dividend-paying companies. He looks for companies with strong cash flow generation and tends to avoid commodity-like businesses.

We asked Dr Kuo to describe more about his investment process and how he generates investment ideas. According to him, as he is a strict *dividend investor*, he tends to look for stocks with high dividend and then analyse if the dividend is sustainable. If the same company is something with a low price-to-book ratio, all the better. He commonly values his investment based on the dividend discount model or using ratios like the price-to-earnings or price-to-book. That is why in Asia, he is particularly interested in the Real Estate Investment Trust (REIT) market, given their higher yield and recurring revenue model.

We asked for his view about what would he consider to be his most- or least-preferred type of investments. Dr Kuo stated that he does not believe in finding the *best* investment in the market. This is because it is impossible for an investor to know which investment will end up giving them the best return. This is why he emphasises diversification. It is important for any investor to have a diversified portfolio so that they will not be caught out by huge losses just because one sector or company is not doing well. Having said that, Dr Kuo tries to avoid commodity-like business, as he feels that these businesses do not have pricing power in their products and might easily be affected by macro factors.

As Dr Kuo has generally invested in the European market in the past, we wanted to know what he thinks is the key difference between Asian companies and companies from the western markets. Dr Kuo replied that he does not feel that there is a huge difference between the two. However, in Asia, there are still many companies that have majority shareholders with an extremely large stake. This means that these major shareholders might be too big, implying that there is little need for them to prioritise the interests of minority shareholders. Investors in Asia need to be aware of this. For Dr Kuo, he avoids such companies altogether.

We wondered if he felt that it is a challenge for Asian firms to expand outside of their home countries due to the rich cultural diversity in Asia. However, Dr Kuo does not see it this way. Instead, he felt that expanding regionally or even internationally is not a barrier to Asian firms. Most companies that have successfully globalised, he observed, require a very strong local base before they can attempt to expand outside their home countries. One example is the banks in Singapore. Although all three Singapore-based banks can be considered as regional banks, they are extremely dominant in Singapore, which gave them the resources and confidence to venture overseas.

Given his experienced investing in multiple markets, we sought his opinion on what he thinks are the key misconceptions about investing in Asia. With a cheeky smile, he replied that people still see the Asian market as a big casino. Moreover, he felt that many investors still tend to believe that there is a secret formula that can make us a great investor straight away. Dr Kuo believes that it is very important for investors to understand that there are no magic formulas. The market will reward you if you are disciplined enough in your process and have a long-term horizon to your investment.

In our research, we came across many companies listed in Asia that are almost perpetually trading at a huge discount in terms of their book value. We sought Dr Kuo's advice on why he feels this is happening. Dr Kuo described these companies as value traps. He reminded us that not all "cheap" companies are great investments. Many of them are traps for investors and we should avoid them. He said common reasons for their perpetual discounts can vary, but typically some of these companies might have issues including very poor liquidity, no growth or cases where the main shareholders have such a large stake in the company that minority investors would be completely at their mercy.

We learned a great deal during our two-hour chat with him. Before we parted, we asked if he has some advice for investors who just starting out. David thought about that question for a while and gave us four investing tips we can all live by:

1. Know why you buy and what you buy.
2. Start an investing diary to keep track of your thoughts and reasons for investing in a company. Refer to it regularly to see how your thought process changes.
3. Be patient with investing. Study, understand and hold your investment for the long term. Do not rush into an investment.
4. Always invest with your spare cash. Do not invest with leverage or cash that you might need in the next few months.

Index